# Peakland Air
## The No

Pat Cunningham DFM

The reality of Aviation:
shiny aircraft, frequent coffee;
and Flight Safety paramount

'As you promised, magnificent scenery; so what crashed here?'

Wies White

'Pat, you're Above-Average rated, you love flying, you consistently fly more than any other instructor here – so how come you're not better at it?'

Squadron Leader Brian Jones, Refresher Flying School, RAF Manby

Landmark Publishing

Published by

Ashbourne Hall, Cokayne Ave
Ashbourne, Derbyshire DE6 1EJ England
Tel: (01335) 347349 Fax: (01335) 347303
e-mail: landmark@clara.net
web site: www.landmarkpublishing.co.uk

ISBN 13: 978-1-84306-330-8

ISBN 10: 1-84306-330-1

British Library Cataloguing in Publication Data: a catalogue record for this book is available from the British Library.

Printed by Bath Press Ltd., Bath

**Front Cover:** De Havilland Rapide G-ALBC, courtesy of Mr Ron Duggins

**Back cover top:** Cessna G-BFRP, courtesy of Area Ranger Gordon Miller

**Back cover bottom; left:** Data plate from Meteor WA791 or VZ518, Sliddens Moss, courtesy of Mr Alan Jones

**Right:** Simple Altimeter, Hampden X3154, Rushup Edge, courtesy of Mr Frank Worsley

**Page 1:** The author, and a DC9: the reality of Aviation; shiny aeroplanes, regular coffee, and flight safety paramount. Lower right inset, courtesy of Katherine Burnett.

# CONTENTS

# CONTENTS: CRASH SITES BY GEOGRAPHICAL LOCATION

In addition to those acknowledged to the rear of this Northern book of the Peakland series, I owe an especial debt to the following:

The pioneering air-crash researchers, interviewers, and joint authors of the *Dark Peak Aircraft Wreck* series (1979 and 1982) who paved the way. To Ron Collier, who returned to the family business after National Service but whose love of aviation led him to devote twenty-five years to the Volunteer Reserve (Air Training Corps): he raised two ATC squadrons (No.1196 Romiley & Marple, and No.468 Hattersley), and found time to qualify as a private pilot. To Roni Wilkinson, a successful author of aviation stories for boys in the 1960s; who, as Graphics and Features Manager, Artist, and Studio Manager, of the *Barnsley Chronicle*, produced the *Dark Peak* series in serial form; subsequently becoming Design Manager, Pen & Sword Books Ltd. Additionally, to Mrs Susan Collier who, in July 2006, was able to supplement the details Mr Wilkinson furnished of his association with her husband.

Alan Clark and Mark Sheldon, crash-site enthusiasts with whom I reciprocally shared early fieldwork results, and particularly to Mark who vetted the crash-site element in the initial draft of all three books.

John Woodside, for his expertise in the areas of Air Traffic Control, airfield procedures, aircraft operating, and aircraft handling. Retired from a career in Air Traffic Control but in 2006 still a professional pilot – and of over thirty years' standing – his insightfully analytical input has been of great value.

Veteran crash-site researchers John Ownsworth, and Alan Jones (an aviation artist, in addition), both of whom were extremely supportive throughout and especially helpful in furnishing extra-archival details of several northern and central sites. This also applies to David W. Earl, author of the *Hell on High Ground* series; equally to Arnold Willerton, of Hyde, a researcher since boyhood.

Malcolm Barrass, whose superlative website, *Air of Authority* (www.rafweb.org), is only a pale reflection of his encyclopaedic knowledge of Aviation and RAF historical organisation. Throughout the writing and researching of the Peakland series his experience as a college lecturer in technology, as a pilot, and as an officer with a lifelong commitment to Youth and the Air Training Corps, has been a never-failing source of archival facts and dependable personal opinion.

Despite the inestimable assistance I have received any errors remaining, and all opinions expressed, are my own.

Pat Cunningham DFM, November 2006

# Schematic map of crash sites in *'Peakland Air Crashes: The North'*

(Halifax JP182, Lake District)

Anson NL185

**HUDDERSFIELD**

P-51 Mustang 44-72181

**Castleshaw Moor**
Barracuda MD963
Garnecock

Wellington Z1327

**Farnley Tyas**
Oxford AB662

**Emley Moor**
Whitley

**Shepley**
Tiger Moth

**M62**

**Diggle**
Hurricane (spurious?)
Hampden

B-17 43-37667
Lancaster (spurious?)

**MARSDEN**

**A62**
Junkers Ju 88 B3+DC
Sabre 19234

**HOLMFIRTH**
Halifax (spurious?)
Master W8506

**Gawber**
German bomber
Gladiator K6133

Junkers Ju 88
Spitfire

**Holme Moss**

**A635**
Liberator 42-94841

**Hoylandswaine**

**Moorside**
**Saddleworth Moor**
Heyford K4874
Heinkel He 111

Mosquito PF395
Swordfish P4223

**Dodworth**

Meteors WA791, VZ518
Battle
German bomber

**Chew Reservoir**
Lysander V9403

Meteor (spurious)

**OLDHAM**
**Dovestone Reservoir**

Tiger Moth T6464

Trainer, EFTS

**PENISTONE**

PB4Y-1 Liberator 63934   Dakota G-AHCY

**A625 (T)**
1914-8 aircraft
Heinkel He 111

**Deepcar**
Tiger Moth

Hudson AM531

Hudson (spurious?)
Spitfire
Chipmunk WB579
Hurricane
Lancaster PA411
P-38 Lightning 42-67207

Wellington R1011

**STOCKSBRIDGE**
German bomber
Wellington MF627

**Wentworth**
Hart K4423

**Rawmarsh**
Hind
Vampire XE854

German bomber   Trainer, FTS
**Gressbrough**
German bomber?

**ROTHERHAM**

Zodiac G-YOXI

**Stalybridge**
Hurricanes P2851, 765, 854

V1 Flying Bomb
Oxford LX518

Trainer, FTS
Consul TF-RPM   Anson N9912

Wellington DV810

DH90 Dragonfly

**Blenheim T1884**   Avian G-EBVZ

**Torside**
Blenheim L1476

Botha W5103

Stirling LL628

Hunter G-BTYL

Anson DJ680   DH9A

V1 Flying Bomb

**HYDE**
**Mottram**
Beaver 52-6145
**Bleaklow**
Lancaster KB993   Wellington WS5719
Defiant N3378

B-29 44-61999 'Over Exposed'

**Howden Moors**

Junkers Ju 88

Skytrain 42-108982

Master W8474
DH9 F2751

**GLOSSOP**
Swordfish
**A57**
Defiant N1766
Meteor RA487

**Ladybower Reservoir**
German bomber

Blenheim K7172

Liberator 42-52003
Sabres XD707 XD730
Jet Ranger G-ODIL   Rapide G-ALBC

Magister N5418

Halifax HR727

**Kinder Reservoir**
**HAYFIELD**
Hampden AE381   Harvard FT415

Hudson (spurious?)
Anson N9853   Wellington WS5719

Wellington X3348

**EDALE**
Cessna
G-BFRP   Tutor K3308

Hawk G-AISF   Anson NL185

Heyford K6875

Wellington X3154

Oxford NM683

Spitfire P7883

Thunderbolt 41-6227

Oxford HN594
Blenheim Z5870

Leopard Moth AV986

Hampden X3154

**Rushup Edge**

**CHAPEL-EN-LE-FRITH**

Junkers Ju 88,
of KF106 ?

**Wath upon Dearne**
Lysander P9119   Spitfire K9941
**Huxton Roberts**

**M18**

**SHEFFIELD**
V1 Flying Bomb
Beighton

V1 Flying Bomb
Ringinglow (?)

**M1**

The primary aim of the *Peakland Air Crashes* series is to supply walkers with the provenance of the aircraft wreckage they chance upon in the area, 'Peakland' being the resurrected term for a Pennine swathe embracing the White and Dark Peaks of Derbyshire and the adjacent parts of Staffordshire, Cheshire and South Yorkshire. Essentially, Peakland embraces that part of ancient Mercia (including modern Sheffield, Rotherham, and Barnsley) into which the Danish influence was slow to intrude, being hampered in the north by the high ground once inhabited by the eponymous *Pecsaeton* ['peek-seeton'] people, and in the south by the lowland forests.

A secondary aim of the series is to enable the walker to confidently plan visits to other wreck-sites; to which end *Peakland Air Crashes*, written from the professional flier's point of view, focuses upon where the crash happened, why it happened, and the appearance of the site in 2006.

Yet although the series deals with air crashes, it should be borne in mind that the vast majority of flights are carried out in perfect safety. As was the case with the author's first flight, in 1947, a seven-and-sixpenny (35.5 pence!), twenty-minute joy-ride in a Dragon Rapide at the embryo Heathrow. The lady pilot took off with her eight passengers, climbed to altitude, overflew swathes of dolls'-sized houses, returned to align herself with the tents paralleling the Bath Road, and landed. A very sedate performance. And for the author, the precursor of nearly twenty thousand hours of flying during forty years of RAF and civil aviation, as crew and as pilot, and in both peaceful and operational settings. Widening the aspect, it epitomised, in fact, the gratifyingly prosaic pattern for virtually all flights undertaken since the dawn of heavier-than-air flight.

Viewed against such a backcloth it can be seen that the 306 crash sites, and the 312 individual aircraft, to be encountered in this Peakland series are very much at variance with that pattern. Indeed, many of the aircraft concerned had been dispatched in company with other machines which, although encountering essentially identical flight conditions, subsequently returned to safe landings. Certainly each of the Peakland crashes serves to illumine the celebrated remarks of Captain A.G. Lamplugh.:

'*I am convinced*', he wrote, concluding his 1931 paper on civil air accidents, '*that aviation in itself is not inherently dangerous…but I do personally feel that the air, to an even greater extent than the sea, is terribly unforgiving of any carelessness, incapacity or neglect.*' He explained that by '*unforgiving*' he meant that '*carelessness, neglect or overconfidence are paid for more quickly and more dearly than in other forms of transport*'.

His conviction notwithstanding, the Peakland was often to prove surprisingly forgiving to aviators, largely because for every crag edging the several massifs there are many miles of relatively flat moorland. Yet the notion of any Peakland Mystery Zone should be discounted from the outset, for many areas of Britain, both highland and low, have garnered their crops of aircraft, some equally as bountiful; and there is nothing mysterious about any of these crashes.

Nor is it surprising that the majority of them occurred during the years encompassing the Second World War. For that was a period in which hurriedly-trained aircrews were sent off with pitifully little experience, in virtually all weathers, by night and day, to European destinations three and four hours distant; and then left to find their way back to often blacked-out airfields, navigating largely without radio aids, and therefore relying on meteorological data that, at best, had been an estimate, and by any token was by then hours out of date. And so, as in a fatal *leitmotif*, courts of inquiry would report, 'pilot descended below cloud when uncertain of his position', and commanders would first fulminate, and then despair, as the tenets of good airmanship were seen to be so frequently cast aside.

For RAF regulations abounded with admonitions against descending blind: 'Cloud must never be entered in the neighbourhood of and below the level of high ground'. And the RAF's *Air Navigation* manual, with the original 1941 emboldening of the text reproduced here, further stressed, 'Above all do not descend below cloud unless absolutely sure there is no high ground nearby'. But then most operational crews whose aircraft crashed in a cloud-shrouded Peakland were convinced that they were letting down over their Lincolnshire bases, where the four-hundred foot Wolds presented the only obstruction. In similar fashion, many others, on innocuous-seeming training exercises, were serenely flying tracks as far as fifty miles from where they imagined themselves to be.

And if it is hard to credit that trained, or even trainee, aircrew could stray so far off track, it has to be remembered that they had few of the modern aids which now more nearly make air navigation a precise science. All too often, with radio silence imposed to obviate hostile intrusion, the only navigational aid was dead reckoning – deduced reckoning – which depends upon up-to-date winds for its accuracy. So that for two and three hours on end a navigator might have to rely on nothing but a forecast wind that had been suspect from its conception.

For it has to be appreciated that an aircraft's flight is constantly affected by the wind. Given details of the wind, then a course for a destination can be calculated, and a time determined for reaching it. Let that wind alter, however, whether in speed or direction, and both the course and the lapse time will be affected.

Further, should an aircraft stray just one degree from its compass course, then having travelled sixty miles it will be a full mile to one side of its planned track. So that a typical Second World War aircraft flying at two hundred miles an hour, but inadvertently steering one degree off heading, would be over twelve miles astray after returning from certain European targets. Then again, very few pilots, or indeed automatic pilots in the 1940s, would have been capable of flying so accurately for that length of time, a heading error of some four degrees being much more likely. This alone would put the machine nearly fifty miles off track.

In practice, by the time the navigator's watch showed them to be overhead their base, many returning crews had been totally unable to re-establish their position. Clearly luck – given due recognition even in the RAF's *Air Navigation* manual, which styled it 'that undefinable element' – had some part to play, for just a glimpse of the ground might have allowed any crew member to update the navigator's plot.

But failing that, if the best navigational information obtainable held that the aircraft was over its base, then the machine could be descended in the hope of breaking cloud while still at a safe level above the local high ground. Only what if, approaching that safe level, no break in the cloud was forthcoming?

In that case the captain had four alternatives: to fly out to sea, and then descend towards the coast; to fly to another airfield which might be clear of cloud; to gingerly descend below the safe level in the hope that, on finally breaking cloud, the airfield would be close at hand; or to circle at a safe height, hoping for a weather clearance until the fuel was low, and then bale out. Except that the last would mean abandoning a perfectly good aeroplane.

In this context the psychological drives acting upon the crews must be considered; and not only the mindset of a nation at war. For although most wartime fliers who came down in the Peakland area had less than five hundred hours' flying experience and few as much as one thousand, yet all were volunteers, and being both young and dashing were, therefore, decidedly 'press-on', in the parlance of the day.

All these are very relevant factors when related to flight safety. And each merely sketched in. But far too sketchy nonetheless, without mention of the aircraft altimeter, and without at least a skeletal description of contemporary altimeter practice.

For the altimeter is nothing but a barometer which indicates height against the datum to which it is set. Accordingly, a crew at one of the near-sea-level Lincolnshire or Yorkshire airfields would set their altimeter to read zero when the aeroplane was on the runway. And, in contrast to modern practice, this was how the altimeter was left throughout the sortie. But wherever the machine flew, the altimeter would show only the height above that datum. So if the aircraft climbed to 2,100 feet overhead, it would truly have that much clear air below it. But let it move over Kinder Scout, at its 2,088-feet-above-sea-level elevation, and although the crew would still see 2,100 feet on their altimeter the aircraft would be skimming the rocks by only twelve feet.

And every crew member was well cognisant of that. Therefore, if the decision was made to descend blind through cloud, then as the throttles were eased back and the nose lowered, it would be as if a relative silence had fallen, as every eye strained uneasily downwards through the cloud-filled night.

But of course, for the great majority, the calculated risk paid off, and on breaking cloud the grudgingly-lit lights of the flare path flickered into sight. The Peakland Air Crashes series deals only with the unlucky few – the very few – for whom it did not pay off.

## THE CRASH SITES

As late as 2006 a fair number of the aircraft crash sites featured in this Northern book of the series were still marked by debris. Many of these, however, lay on high trackless moorland where water channels and rock-strewn heather often made the debris difficult to distinguish even at the range of a foot or two. In contrast, on relatively low-lying, often cultivated, ground, there was frequently nothing to see. In all cases, however, the provision of a dependable grid reference aims to afford the walker a frustration-free visit. To accomplish this every location was verified by repeated site visits, initially determined by a Global Positioning System (GPS), and then re-plotted against the Ordnance Survey map.

The GPS-equipped walker will have heeded well the maker's warnings regarding this wizardly aid's limitations; and have reflected, perhaps, into what close kinship they bring the walker and the aviator. For, historically, at least, the aviator has always flown in the full knowledge that none of the instruments upon which the exercise of his craft depends ever tells him the unvarnished truth: that his airspeed indicator lies about his speed, his altimeter about his height, and his compass about his direction. So that his competence has always been measured by his sensible use of the tools at his disposal.

Just the same, although the walker is furnished with a proven reference, some sites may still require a patient cast-about in order to locate them on the ground. However, in this series the visitor is assured that each incident really did happen at the reference shown, or in the immediate area indicated, whether surface debris remains or not. To further assist location, the photographs portray the general area of the site, with just a few showing the debris – mostly re-interred – by which the site was positively identified.

Yet any walker may legitimately ask why such piles of aircraft wreckage still litter our countryside; for the Ministry of Defence, if they so wished, could clear the sites within a matter of hours. But then in the course of time souvenir hunters seem set to do the job for them.

Given that crash sites do exist, however, then what is likely to be found varies. For the most part there will be a sparse heap of metal fragments, globs of molten aluminium, a bare patch amidst flourishing heather, and powder-blue corrosion beneath the peat. Often the metal will have been gathered into a circle of rocks, although this is often indicative of an impact point elsewhere. Similarly, salvage teams habitually tumbled the wreckage into a convenient gully and burnt or buried it in order to obviate its distracting any future search-and-rescue undertaking.

On occasion there may be an unofficial – albeit Service-related – memorial, and not infrequently, a Remembrance Day cross, with scarlet poppies to give a touch of colour. But for all the wide conception that the sites are officially viewed as war graves, there is no indication yet that Authority will one day furnish suitable markers.

Not that all these crash sites garnered by the Peakland are graves of any sort, if the insensate aircraft themselves are discounted; for several airmen survived unexpected encounters with its flat moorland, while others were permitted to live after their aircraft had been flown directly into its cliffs. Then again a few aircraft crashed after being abandoned, their crews having very properly saved themselves by taking to their parachutes.

Regarding the visiting of crash sites in general, the walker should be aware that Service sites are held to be under the protection of the Ministry of Defence. Of more practical moment is that, despite the regrettably-aggressively named 'Right to Roam' legislation of September 2004, many sites are on private land; from which it follows that the normal courtesies should be scrupulously observed. And this is of particular importance when sites are on working farms. This notwithstanding, it became gratifyingly clear in the course of research that every landholder courteously approached, whether owner or tenant, was not only accommodating, despite the intrusion, but keenly interested in the circumstances surrounding the accident associated with their property.

On the subject of the appropriation of aircraft debris found on site, there is little enough worth saying. In the past, enthusiasts have removed many parts, ostensibly to positively identify the aircraft, and of these parts, some have been lodged in museums and private collections. Many others, however, have been scavenged as souvenirs, and very often discarded on the return journey from the site; after all, few sitting rooms are enhanced by lumps of corroded metal. But as the RAF commanders found in their day, crews continued to descend blind, no matter how many appeals were made, or strictures issued; similarly some people will scavenge. Pragmatically viewing the problem then, all that can be done is to determine a location for each crash site before the last vestige disappears; reason enough in itself, perhaps, for this series.

## THE CRASH-SITE NARRATIVES

Each entry is introduced by the aircraft type, its registration, and a descriptive locality of the crash site. This is followed by the precise ten-figure map reference – or in a few, unavoidable, cases merely by 'area of' – and the height of the site above sea level. Next comes the unit or organisation, together with the date of the crash. All available details of the crew, or occupants, are then given, and on the first appearance of any type, a photograph, most often Crown Copyright, of the aircraft.

The narratives are derived, in the main, from the Air Ministry Form 1180s which summarise RAF crash investigations; from the War Department Form 14s for American aircraft; from Air Accidents Investigation Branch Bulletins for civil aircraft; and from witness accounts taken at first hand.

Over the years various enthusiasts have made lists of crash sites, with some entries proving either doubtful or downright spurious. As this series aims to set a benchmark, the most persistent of these are included not only to save the walker wasting time in fruitless visits but also to record the suspect entry for a posterity in which it might be validated.

Each narrative concludes with a description of the site in 2006.

The author, throughout, has unashamedly adopted the dedicated aviator's view that anything to do with Flight Safety demands critical evaluation; for criticism – and most especially, self-criticism – underpins aviation just as surely as does the heartfelt relevance of 'There, but for the Grace of God ...'

## Avro Anson Mk.1 N9853, Edale Moor, Kinder Scout

SK 10123 87866 618m
No.16 (Polish) Service Flying Training School, RAF Newton (east
of Nottingham), No.21 Group, Flying Training Command
11 December 1944

Occupants: six: two crew, four passengers, Polish Air Force under RAF Command; all survived:
Flight Lieutenant Aleksander Chelstowski, pilot
Flight Sergeant Stefan Pasinski, wireless operator
Flight Lieutenant Melcinski, flying instructor, passengering
Flight Lieutenant Witold Siuda, flying instructor, passengering
Flying Officer Jan Klimczak, electrical-engineering officer, passengering
The name of a sixth Pole, another flying instructor, has not been established

Although designed as a maritime reconnaissance aircraft, the Anson was to serve as a crew trainer for much of its long and successful life. While generally well liked there is no doubt that it had its drawbacks, even as a crew trainer. It had virtually no performance on one engine, it was noisy, draughty, and cold, and if the rubber 'in-flight relief' tube had been kinked by a previous user it could be rather 'orrid to boot. Nor was the task of manually operating the undercarriage on the earlier versions any sinecure, for it had to be cranked some 160 times. In its favour, however, the Anson was sturdy and dependable and with its 158 mph (138 knots) cruising speed it proved equally valuable as a communications aircraft.

So it was that, when Flight Lieutenant Aleksander Chelstowski and wireless operator Flight Sergeant Stefan Pasinski, both members of the Polish Air Force under RAF Command, got airborne from Newton on 11 December 1944, in Anson N9853, it was to carry out a communications task. Their detail was to take three Newton-based Polish flying instructors to RAF Millom, to the south-west of Broughton-in-Furness, Cumbria; additionally, Newton's electrical-engineering officer, Flying Officer Jan Klimczak, had himself authorised to travel up in order to carry out a staff inventory check.

The meteorological section had advised of snow-bearing cloud massing along the route above the hills, but just twelve minutes after getting airborne Flight Lieutenant Chelstowski totally lost sight of the ground. Accordingly, faced with weather deteriorating more quickly than expected, he decided to descend from his cruising height and fly beneath the cloud, evidently with the idea of maintaining contact flight; as a pilot claiming nearly 800 hours' total flying time, and 137 on Ansons, he would hardly have become uncertain of his position that early in the flight.

It transpired, however, that the cloud was actually draped upon the surface; only before Flight Lieutenant Chelstowski could appreciate this, satisfied though he might have been that his altimeter showed what he considered an adequate clearance, he had flown his aircraft into the snowy, deeply-rutted moorland top of the Kinder Scout plateau at an altitude of 2,030 feet above sea level. Moreover, despite the general flatness of the terrain it was not a soft impact, so that the aircraft rolled onto its back and broke up.

Gradually collecting themselves the shaken, but only slightly injured, passengers, Flight Lieutenants Melcinski and Siuda, were able to extricate their bewildered pilot by way of the shattered windscreen. However, they found that Flying Officer Klimczak, who had been in the right-hand seat beside the pilot, was trapped fast in the wreckage, and having hurt both arms and a leg, was periodically lapsing into unconsciousness. They found too that wireless operator Pasinski had suffered some seemingly severe trauma to his body. Just the same, the best they could do for the two more seriously injured men was to wrap them in parachutes for warmth.

Had they known it they were virtually on track, but as the weather conditions ruled out search aircraft being able to contact them in any reasonable time, Flight Lieutenant Melcinski elected to go for help. In a state of shock, as he will have been, it must have been a daunting undertaking, as a survey of the crash-site terrain shows, even in fine weather. As it was, he blundered in a south-easterly direction, found and followed a watercourse, descended Grindsbrook Clough, and duly raised the alarm in Edale.

He did well, for by early afternoon rescuers began to arrive at the scene, when it was found that the wireless operator had damaged his liver but that the pilot was more dazed than injured. Flying Officer Klimczak, however, once he had been cut free, was found to have broken all three of his damaged limbs – being in the cruise, the passengers had, understandably, been released from their lapstraps. But undoubtedly the fact that Flying Officer Klimczak was barely conscious eased his passage down to Edale. Indeed it was to be many days before he fully recovered consciousness, and he would only return to duty after nearly two years of surgery and recuperation; notwithstanding which he served on for another two years before finally taking a disability discharge from the RAF.

Even before the court of inquiry had begun its deliberations Flight Lieutenant Chelstowski's commanding officer had rounded upon him, declaring that, in his opinion, his subordinate should no longer fly as a pilot. And with rather less clouded judgement the members of the court of inquiry were quite unequivocal in their condemnation of Flight Lieutenant Chelstowski's conduct of the flight. They found that in conditions of poor visibility he had descended his perfectly serviceable aircraft from a safe height and destroyed it, injuring some of his passengers and crew in the process. Further, they discovered such lapses in the pre-planning of the flight that the Air Officer Commanding (AOC) ruled that 'pre-flight preparations were haphazard and inadequate and deserving of severe censure'. The ultimate outcome was that Flight Lieutenant Chelstowski continued to fly, but with the daunting endorsement of 'Gross Negligence' entered into his flying log book.

In passing, it is noted that the AOC held that, being uncertain of his position, the pilot, 'should have been flying at least 1,000 feet above the highest ground on route as he could not see the ground'. Which shows that in that era the aircraft would have been considered safe had it maintained 3,088 feet on the altimeter, Kinder's summit being 2,088 feet above sea level. In comparison, the 'safety height' from the early fifties onwards would have demanded a minimum altimeter reading of 3,800 feet, affording a far larger margin to accommodate navigational errors, but also to compensate for errors associated with the pressure altimeter: its acceptable limits of accuracy, the mis-setting of its subscale, and even a degree of misreading.

Perhaps it would be germane, too, to record here just what such Polish airmen were doing serving under RAF Command, so far from their homeland.

In essence, when Britain declared war on Germany on 3 September 1939, it was because Germany had invaded Poland two days earlier, and Britain – like France – had guaranteed Poland 'all the support and assistance in its power' should that occur. The Poles, vainly expecting tangible Allied support from day one, had fought valiantly in the west. But just two weeks later Russia had unexpectedly invaded from the east. Overwhelmed by this the Polish armed forces had been ordered to cross into then-neutral Romania where certain pre-war contingency plans had been laid. After which, following a nominal period of internment, they were variously routed to France, but arrived only a short while before the French government capitulated.

Blindly, indeed blithely, ignoring this official capitulation the Royal Navy evacuated many of them to Britain where the arrival of such a large body raised the constitutional problem of having a foreign armed force on British soil. This was quickly resolved, however, and on 1 August 1940 the airmen among them were officially incorporated into 'The Polish Air Force under RAF Command'.

Becoming operational as the Battle of Britain heated up, their squadrons then fought with distinction throughout the war. Sadly, despite their gallantry, the Poles emerged the major losers from the near-global conflict, for with the communists dominating post-war Poland many of these 'Western-tainted' Poles were never able to safely return to their homeland.

Regarding Flight Lieutenant Aleksander Chelstowski's subsequent wartime career, the brash recommendation of his commanding officer that his subordinate should no longer fly as a pilot in view of his 'extreme negligence' was totally discounted by cooler heads. So it was that Flight Lieutenant Chelstowski flew on and finished the war having distinguished himself by gaining not only the Polish Cross of Valour three times over, but the fifth class of the highest of all Polish decorations, the *Virtuti Militari*.

Official records for other occupants of Anson N9853 which crashed that December day show that Flight Lieutenant Witold Siuda also earned the coveted *Virtuti Militari*, Class Five, together with three bars to a Cross of Valour and a Silver Cross of Merit; while Flight Sergeant Stefan Pasinski, promoted to warrant officer, left the Service bearing a bar to his Polish Cross for Valour.

The recovery team tumbled the remains of Anson N9853 into a convenient gully; in part because recovery was so difficult from such a remote site, in part to prevent the wreckage from misleading any future aerial searches. However, although there were still copious remains in 2006, the ground is so broken with groughs – as the region's minor water channels are known – that it may well be found necessary to cast around from even the best of locational references in order to discover the correct gully.

One of the wreckage pools of Anson N9853 in 2006.

## Avro Anson Mk.1 DJ680, Hollingworth Hall Moor, north-west of Glossop

SJ 99700 97710 313m

No.2 Pilots Advanced Flying Unit, RAF Millom (Broughton-in-Furness), No.25 Group, Flying Training Command

20 March 1944

Crew: five, injured:

Flight Sergeant H. Edward (Ted) Rimmer, pupil pilot, bruises and abrasions

Pilot Officer N. Kerr, pupil navigator, ankles broken

Flight Sergeant Alan Boyd, pupil wireless operator, bruises and abrasions

Sergeant Jacobs, instructor, bruises and abrasions

Sergeant D.J. Mance, instructor, badly concussed, subsequently grounded

On 20 March 1944, Anson DJ680 was engaged in a night navigational exercise when, at 0715 hours, in conditions of grudging first light, recently-promoted Flight Sergeant Ted Rimmer found himself forced to accept that he and his mainly-pupil crew were lost.

By that time they had been airborne for two and a quarter hours on a route that had required them to fly from Cumbria's RAF Millom to Anglesey and then Stafford before returning to base. Throughout the flight, however, thick rain-bearing clouds had hampered the navigator from determining his position; at the same time the intense static generated by these clouds had prevented the wireless operator from assisting with either radio fixes or bearings. But with the fuel state reducing towards the safe limit it became imperative that the aircraft's position be established, and seeing no alternative, Flight Sergeant Rimmer made the decision to descend below cloud.

Commencing his descent at 7,000 feet he eventually emerged into clear air, only to find the ground obscured by a still lower cloud layer. Cautiously edging yet further down, and with all available crew eyes alert for any surface feature that would afford a pinpoint, he re-entered cloud with 1,500 feet indicated on his altimeter; only to be faced, after descending for just a minute or two longer, with the sudden loom of solid ground.

Desperately heaving back on the stick he managed to raise the nose and indeed, to match the upward-rising slope, for although the Anson bellied into the ground, its structure suffered only superficial damage. Nevertheless the impact was violent enough to throw navigator, Pilot Officer Kerr, from the astrodome, causing him to break both his ankles, and to concuss Sergeant Mance, who was thrown forwards into an obstruction.

Having evacuated the aircraft, and with his stranded crew as settled as could be expected, Flight Sergeant Rimmer had barely begun to take stock when, just visible through the rain and mist, he saw a providential light. This gave him some orientation, and after he had picked his way downhill in the slowly paling darkness, brought him to a cottage belonging to Landslow Green Farm – not the sole example of such bad blackout practices in the Peakland area! Here he raised the alarm, got aid for his injured crew members, and discovered that his aircraft had come to ground on Hollingworth Hall Moor, some seventy-five miles from its Millom base.

Later, Flight Sergeant Rimmer would recall that on reaching 1,000 feet on his altimeter he had expected to have at least that much clear air beneath him, for Millom, where the altimeter had been set, was at sea level. Except that Hollingworth Hall Moor stands at an altitude of some 1,050 feet above sea level.

The court of enquiry could not afford to be overly generous in its findings, the flight having been authorised at a minimum altitude of 2,500 feet, and accordingly the members held Flight Sergeant Rimmer 'essentially to blame for the accident' in coming below that height. The summary of evidence then ordered against the Flight Sergeant (the normal precursor to a court martial) also found that he had been guilty of disobeying orders in descending below the safety height; but it did concede that bad weather had played a part. As a result the case was eventually dealt with at a lower level than court martial, Flight Sergeant Rimmer's flying log book being endorsed, 'Disobedience of orders'.

Impact area of Anson DJ680, looking towards Hollingworth Hall Farm

At the Hollingworth Hall site the recovery crew jacked the aircraft up, lowered the undercarriage, then rolled the machine down to the trees where the wings were detached prior to the whole assembly being taken off by road. The aircraft was soon returned to service. And after a short leave most crew members too were back in the air; but not the concussed Sergeant Mance, who was medically screened from further flying duties. Flight Sergeant 'Ted' Rimmer, for his part, went on to fly Wellingtons operationally, surviving the war, and finally leaving the Service as a Warrant Officer in 1946.

In 1992, however, in company with author Mr David W. Earl, and aviation artist and crash-site researcher Mr Alan Jones, Mr Rimmer returned to the area. He was able to point out the route taken as the Anson was rolled down to the road, but he had to confess that, as he had come to earth on a dark and misty pre-dawn, he was unable to say exactly whereabouts on the moor he had done so.

Fortunately, the same did not apply to researcher Mr Jones, for he remembered just where the aircraft had come into view as he had ascended Cow Lane on his initial visit as a schoolboy back in 1944; although, recalling that visit he discovered himself to be still chagrined at having been forced to stand at the barrier a hundred yards off, whereas a boy who had arrived just a little earlier had been permitted to climb into the cockpit. Another witness able to re-locate the site – conceivably that same to-be-envied boy – was Mr Arnold Willerton, of Hyde, who as a lad had cycled from home to view the aircraft the morning after it had put down and remembered with great clarity the maps, headsets, and other flight paraphernalia still strewn around the cockpit.

Both these remembrances notwithstanding, in 2006 the slope on Hollingworth Hall Moor produced no tangible evidence of this forcible – rather than forced – landing. But that was hardly to be wondered at considering the lapse of time; particularly as the machine was barely damaged and the site so easily accessible for the recovery team.


## Avro Anson Mk.9 NL185, The Cloughs (north-west of Upper Booth), Edale

SK 08903 86696 506m impact site
SK 08874 86586 476m engine site
Headquarters Bomber Command Communications Flight, RAF Halton, Aylesbury
23 November 1945

Pilot: killed:
Wing Commander Richard Douglas Speare, DSO, DFC and Bar, Croix de Guerre with Palm


Avro Anson NL185 was on the charge of the Communications Flight at RAF Halton as a station runabout when it crashed into The Cloughs, on Kinder Scout, on 23 November 1945, at a height of 1,700 feet above sea level.

The pilot, Wing Commander Richard Speare, was no stranger to the Anson having been a Service pilot for nine years. Nor had those years been uneventful, for he had enjoyed 'a good war' on

Wing Commander
Richard Speare, vice
Chris Speare

bombers, culminating in operating No.138 Squadron's special-duties Halifaxes from RAF Tempsford, delivering agents and supplies to the continent for the Special Operations Executive. Further, his outstanding operational service had gained him a Distinguished Service Order, a Distinguished Flying Cross (twice awarded), and a Croix de Guerre with Palm; all these following on from a well-earned Mention in Despatches.

Since training in 1936, Wing Commander Speare had flown some 2,800 hours, considerably more than the average Service pilot of that era. On this particular occasion, however, stowing aboard all his kit for an anticipated leave, he had submitted a flight plan to ferry a machine from Halton to Feltwell (near Ely), a distance of 70 miles on a north-easterly track (050°True). That the aircraft flew a north-*westerly* track (330°True) and crashed some 118 miles *north-west* of Halton, remains something of a mystery. Indeed it remained a lifetime source of disbelief to some who knew Wing Commander Speare's capabilities. But then a crash site is ineluctable, and once interpreted, cannot dissemble.

The court of inquiry found that the aircraft had indeed been vastly off course when it flew into cloud-covered high ground. The members did suggest that Wing Commander Speare might possibly have set the wrong compass course, but the RAF accident report summarising the investigation does not record whether investigators at the scene actually found the compass-setting ring locked to some north-westerly, rather than some north-easterly, heading. Just the same, mis-setting the required heading in this way was one of several only-too-common navigational compass errors.

A similar error was to misread the pre-calculated heading when setting the compass; as when the author interpreted his hand-printed 'three' as an 'eight' and flew 082° (easterly) instead of 032° (north-easterly). Indeed, so common were such errors that the 1941 RAF *Air Navigation* manual devoted an admonitory section to 'Setting Reverse or Incorrect Courses', directing that 'The Navigator must keep a wary eye on … the Pilot, who, for various reasons, may not be steering the requisite Course', and further, 'It is advisable to look repeatedly over the Pilot's shoulder at the course being steered …'; poor solo ferrying pilot then, with no one to look over his shoulder!

Aside from the directional error, however, there was poor visibility between Halton and Feltwell that day, a meteorological condition which suggests only light winds. It was also recorded that the actual and the flight-plan winds were virtually identical. Which meant that the seventy-mile flight to Feltwell would have taken an Anson only twenty-two minutes. Yet even when Wing Commander Speare made the decision to descend blind he must have been flying for a good fourteen minutes longer than that.

One might, of course, speculate that, compared to the operational machines Wing Commander Speare had become used to, the Avro Anson would have seemed undemanding of much care. On the other hand it is a matter of record that this particular machine had been stripped of all its radio equipment; which meant that besides a compass Wing Commander Speare had only his map and the pilot-navigation techniques of mental dead reckoning to assist him; little enough in cloudy, low-visibility conditions. Further, having spent the years since his basic training in 1936 on bombers, he would have become reliant upon a dedicated crew member for the navigation and would not have been at all well-versed in the demands of single-pilot operation.

The court of inquiry dutifully proffered the lack of radio equipment as a contributory factor. But whether Wing Commander Speare would have called for radio assistance had a radio been fitted seems problematical, it being far more likely that he never doubted himself to be anywhere but in the vicinity of Feltwell. Or not until the last instant, for it was clear from the disposition of the wreckage that he had seen the ground, and desperately tried to avoid it; 'but was too late', as the crash report has it.

In this instance then, the often fraught decision to let down through cloud must have seemed unexceptionable to Wing Commander Speare; for the terrain in the Feltwell area was flat, and nowhere much more than thirty feet above sea level, even had he – with his altimeter still registering against the 370-feet-above-sea-level datum set at Halton – flown on past his estimated time of arrival. So while the unyielding slopes that constitute the Derbyshire crash site send a shiver down the spine of anyone visualising those final cloud-shrouded moments, the last thing on earth – a suddenly sobering phrase – Wing Commander Speare would have expected was to fly into a hillside when his altimeter was still reading some 1,700 feet. Only in truth he was now a full ninety-five miles north-west of those safe, flat, sea-level fens around Feltwell.

Accordingly, his body, made singular by his multiple rank-braids and the colourful array of medal ribbons, was duly found beside the aircraft high on The Cloughs amid the boulder-strewn grasses, a scatter of wreckage, the tumbled contents of his personal suitcases, and his Service cap.

In August 2006 Mr Roy Cooper of Highfield Farm, Upper Booth, remembered the discovery being made. 'It was my brother, Gordon,' he explained, 'who found the Anson, and raised the alarm. I remember the pilot's cap was left beside the wreck for some time. It had his name in it, Speare, if I recall. Indeed I always wondered if leaving it there was some form of tradition.'

The crash site is located beside a watercourse high on the slopes below the Wool Packs, and directly opposite the stone-stepped feature of Jacob's Ladder. In 2006 a fair pool of collected debris still remained, together with a metal cross, evidently inscribed by an intimate, to the memory of 'Dickie' Speare. In addition, one of the Anson's two Armstrong Siddeley Cheetah Mk.9 engines rested in a reedy gully just a little way further downhill.

Mr Roy Cooper, of
Highfield Farm, 2006

Top left: 2005, the author at the
impact area of Anson NL185

Left: The Cheetah engine, looking
slightly north-eastwards towards the
Wool Packs

## Avro Anson Mk.1 N9912, Whitwell Moor, Stocksbridge

SK 24758 97491 345m
No.25 Operational Training Unit, RAF Finningley (Doncaster), No.7 Group, Bomber Command
31 March 1941

Crew: four, superficial injuries:
Pilot Officer Bernard Maurice Fournier, RAF Volunteer Reserve, pilot
Sergeant Duncan Henry Barrett, navigator
Sergeant Ernest Richard Palmer, wireless operator/air gunner
Sergeant Dennis Watson, wireless operator/air gunner

Pilot Officer Bernard Fournier's trainee crew had come together at the start of the No.25 Operational Training Unit's course at RAF Finningley, so that by 31 March 1941, when they were detailed to fly Anson N9912 on a night navigational exercise, each had learnt to rely upon the expertise of the next. On the return leg that night, however, they became uncertain of their aircraft's position.

Not only had thick cloud prevented their getting a visual pinpoint, but the wireless operator had been unable to obtain a course to steer for base. Further, and unknown to the navigator, the forecast wind had changed in both speed and direction since they had become airborne, so deflecting the machine from the intended track and also upsetting the navigational timing. Eventually, Pilot Officer Fournier was forced to accept that they were lost, and chose to descend through cloud in order to establish their whereabouts. In the course of doing so, however, he bellied into a gently sloping hillside at an altitude of 1,200 feet above sea level, providentially without serious injury to his crew.

The court of inquiry decided that the accident was due to inexperience, and was, therefore, relatively benign in its criticisms. The navigation, it found, had been faulty, but it conceded that the weather had prevented the navigator from getting the pinpoints necessary for reassessing the wind. It also felt that had the wireless operator/air gunner actually on watch been more capable as a wireless operator he would have managed to make contact, suspect though his set was claimed to be; but it noted too that all his productive flying to date had been in his dual-category role as an air gunner.

Pilot Officer Fournier, relatively experienced for the period, with 266 hours' total flying, and 135 hours on type, was mildly castigated for failing to confirm that the serviceability of the aircraft's wireless-telegraphy transmitter/receiver was checked before take-off, and there is the suggestion that the route, substituted at the last moment owing to the weather, was not wisely chosen in view of its proximity to high ground.

This mishap notwithstanding, the crew went on to complete the Operational Training Unit course, and having subsequently qualified on Handley Page Hampden bombers were duly posted to No.49 squadron at RAF Scampton. On 29 August 1941, however, all four died on the return from a raid on Duisburg when their aircraft was shot down by a night fighter and fell in flames into Holland's Waddenzee.

In August 2001, Mr Frank Shaw, of Stocksbridge, recorded his recollections of this crash in a letter to a local crash-site enthusiast, Mr Roy Ashby. 'The plane came from north to south,' he wrote, 'low over the village and crash landed 300 yards south of Long Lane, in the heather. I was still at school but on home time hundreds of us dashed to see it. Police were there and some RAF personnel trying to keep us away. I think it was a good forced landing, cushioned by the heather …'

In 2006 the Whitwell Moor site, a seasonal pool on a rock-strewn slope still thickly covered with heather, showed no evidence of the inadvertent 1941 landing. In 1981, however, debris fragments had enabled researcher Mr John Ownsworth to re-identify the site.

This is a location where, with rocks and heather abounding, and bearing in mind the latitude of error afforded by a GPS, it might be difficult to decide which of the seasonal pools marks the actual site: in 2006 it was the highest and longest of three pools, a prime marker being its particularly flourishing rushes.

Researcher Mr John Ownsworth, with debris, 1981

Wies White, drafted anorak, photo-matching, 2006

## Avro Avian Mk.3 G-EBVZ, Hough Hill, Stalybridge

SJ 96284 97461 192m
Lancashire Aero Club, Woodford
25 March 1928

Occupants:
Miss Winifred Sawley Brown, pilot, slight cut on chin
Mr Walter Samuel Browning, passenger, film salesman, private pilot, unhurt

Spectating children involved:
Master Jack (Jackie) Humphrey Hood, 7, killed, severe head injuries
Miss Edith Hood, 13, head wound and shock
Miss Margaret Walmsy, 17, shock
Miss Mary Taylor, 7, injuries to arm
Master Harry Downend, 14, slight head wound
Master William Brown, 8, injuries to left foot
Master James Poynter, 7, injury to left leg

Miss Winifred Sawley Brown,
and her Avro Avian Mk.3
birthday present.

Photograph by courtesy of
Osprey Publishing, Wendy Boase

The Avro Avian was a light sporting aircraft designed for long-range races and used to good effect by such celebrated fliers as Amelia Earhart and Bert Hinkler, but also by Mrs Emily-Lynn (Lady Mary Heath) who used the type for her record-setting Cape Town to London flight.

Another aviatrix to favour the Woodford-built Avian – hers was a birthday gift from her father – was Miss Winifred Sawley Brown, of Cheshire. In July 1930 Miss Brown was to beat all her male competitors (to 'actually' beat them, as a contemporary source had it) and win the prestigious King's Cup Air Race. This win, which drew praise from the world-famous Miss Earhart herself, entailed flying a 750-mile route around England, a feat which Miss Brown accomplished at an average speed of 102.7 miles an hour, winning comfortably, as the same source observes, 'by consistent rather than spectacular flying'.

But then perhaps Miss Brown had tasted to the full the bitterness inherent in any flying bordering on the spectacular after an incident which had occurred on Sunday, 25 March 1928, almost two years before her King's Cup triumph.

At that time Miss Brown, an international hockey star who had served with the Red Cross during the First World War, had already been among the foremost of Britain's women aviators – only the week before, at Croydon Aerodrome, she had been presented to reform-minded King Amanullah Kahn, of recently independent Afghanistan. On that fatal Sunday, however, she became embroiled in an infamously-mishandled publicity stunt in which a young boy was killed and six other children injured. Miss Brown was exonerated from all blame by the inquest jury; nonetheless, the trauma was evidently deep-seated.

The stunt had been conceived by Mr Milton W. Parker, the manager of the *New Prince's Cinema*, Stalybridge, to promote his premises by having a copy of the new First World War film, *What Price Glory?* flown from Woodford Aerodrome to a local venue. A film salesman, Mr Walter Samuel Browning, who, as a member of the Lancashire Aero Club, held a pilot's 'A' Licence (the modern Private Pilot's Licence), vetted the proposed venue, a field near Hunters' Tower, then a singular landmark on the Gorse Hall Estate at Hough Hill, Stalybridge, and having confirmed its suitability, agreed to do the job. Accordingly publicity arrangements were made which promised that after delivery the aircraft would 'engage in manoeuvres similar to those used in actual warfare'. In addition numerous placards directed spectators 'To the New Prince's Landing Ground'.

By the appointed time of two o'clock in the afternoon of the twenty-fifth, a foggy, virtually windless day, a crowd estimated at twenty thousand had gathered to view the spectacle. Only, ostensibly because of the fog, nothing happened. Until at three-thirty the aeroplane appeared briefly, but then disappeared once more. Predictably, as the still-unexplained delay became yet more protracted, so the chilled crowd dwindled. Just the same, at just after four o'clock, when the aircraft eventually returned and began to circle overhead, an estimated twelve thousand spectators still remained.

The venue was a roughly rectangular field, relatively narrow, and totally enclosed by drystone walls; indeed running across the narrow 'stop end' to the north there were two of them, set in parallel. These were part of the 430-yard-long border of the Victorian rifle range, the inner wall some four feet high, the far one, which also served as the Estate boundary, rising to seven feet. The crowd had gathered six-and-more deep along all the edging walls and many, despite 'Danger, Keep Out' notices and a Dukinfield Police Force presence, had clambered up to stand or sit on the walls themselves.

Unknown to the crowd, confusion had reigned for some time at Woodford Aerodrome. Mr Browning, having made a reconnaissance flight in a club aeroplane earlier that day, had decided against attempting the delivery himself. But now the man who had elected to fly in his stead, a Mr Cantrill, seemed unaccountably engrossed in something else. In the face of which Miss Winifred Brown, who had arrived on a purely social visit to the flying club, was approached, and on being told that the delivery was urgent, readily agree to do the flight in her own aircraft, taking Mr Browning in the front seat as her passenger.

Mr Browning, not without ostentation, suitably bestowed the precious film container, but once airborne was unable to locate the site in the prevailing poor visibility. However, after returning to Woodford Aerodrome, and having studied the map once more, he had Miss Brown take off again when, on locating the field, she was 'astonished' to see such a crowd assembled. Yet to convey this astonishment was impossible, for as her passenger later testified, 'being in a hurry I could not be bothered to rig the earphones into my own helmet', so that while he could talk to Miss Brown, she could not reply. For that matter, when he asked her to 'put on a bit of a show', she discounted the request, and doubtfully eyeing the landing site through the mist, circled the field a number of times, assessing the problems it posed, and only then beginning a first, tentative, landing approach.

For as she, in turn, testified later, she was well aware that this was a field smaller than any she had ever attempted to land upon. Further, it was one made yet more restrictive by the people craning upwards from the near-end wall whom she would have to overfly; indeed, before actually touching down she was to make six more trial approaches, putting on power on each occasion and climbing away.

Clearly she could not afford to merely skim the people-studded wall on the approach, therefore, as she positioned herself for the final time, she gave her tyres a handsome margin. But this forced a late touchdown; in consequence of which, owing to the dead calm near the surface, she floated even more and so was unable to put her brakeless wheels onto the ground until she was practically halfway into the field. Then, with throttle closed, and hardly a breath of headwind to slow her, she waited for the grass to retard the momentum of the machine. Only to realise, seconds later, that the speed was barely diminishing! Yet ahead of her loomed stone walls, and a further jam-packed line of spectators! As she later recorded, she momentarily considered swinging the aircraft – but to each side the spectators appeared to be thronging closer. So as the only alternative she put on full power and desperately heaved the nose skywards.

The spectators had already experienced a fair measure of the thrills they had anticipated, for during each trial approach the passenger had waved, at which 'they had cheered wildly, some throwing their hats into the air in excitement'. Now, as just yards from the crowd the power came on and the propeller blurred into a shining disk once more, they patently took to this to be part of the show. Indeed one of those present, local dignitary Councillor Ashton, was later to testify, 'What surprised me was that the people did not move away. They must have thought the airplane was like a motor car with brakes, and that it could be brought to a standstill immediately.'

As it was, with no headwind to assist it, the machine could not develop sufficient lift and drove nose-high through the first wall to impact heavily upon the second.

Within moments, as the wreckage stilled, Miss Brown, her chin welling blood from a cut occasioned as her lap-strap snapped, was helped from the aeroplane by cinema staff and bundled away towards Hunters' Tower.

'Was anyone hurt?' she desperately asked those surrounding her.

'No,' she was told. And only with that assurance, and having already seen her passenger scramble clear unaided, did she submit to having her chin attended to.

Only people *had* been hurt: seven children who had been sitting on the first wall and who had been unable to scramble out of the way; each of them injured, some by debris, some by the machine itself, albeit most only superficially hurt and all to be released from Ashton Infirmary immediately after treatment. But seven-year old Jack – Jackie – Hood had been killed outright, dying instantly – as the inquest would later be assured – from severe lacerations to the brain. So that his body, after being moved to a house near Hunters' Tower for examination by a doctor, was taken on to Dukinfield Mortuary.

Above: Avro Avian G-EBVZ, its nose buried in the higher of the two walls, photograph by courtesy of the *Tameside Reporter*, formerly *The Reporter*, Stalybridge

Right: Miss Winifred Sawley Brown

Back at the landing site a frenzy of excitement prevailed, with women pushing forwards to ascertain the identity of the injured children, fearing for their own, and with several of them fainting ...

At the funeral service the next week the presiding clergyman, the Reverend V.R. Smeed, vociferously spoke out against the practices of advertising. 'We need', he fulminated, 'another commandment, "Six days shalt thou advertise, but on the seventh remember the Lord thy God".' Adding, in a voice that only too vainly echoes down the years, 'Even in advertising the canons of good taste should be observed.'

Miss Brown would later give the newspapers her, evidently shock-hazed, impression of the final moments of her ill-fated landing attempt. As they quoted her: 'The whole affair is extremely regrettable, and I was horrified when I learnt the full extent of the tragedy. I had no intention whatever of flying when I went to Woodford on Sunday afternoon. On my arrival there I was told that it was a matter of the utmost urgency that Mr Browning should go to Stalybridge with certain films.'

She had therefore offered to make the flight in her machine, which was hangared at Woodford, and eventually made the fatal approach.

'I throttled down the engine, preparatory to landing, and under ordinary circumstances this, of course, would reduce the engine [aircraft] speed. The engine [aircraft], however, did not seem to slow down, and as I swept earthwards I saw a large crowd standing where I was about to land. There was only one thing to do to avoid the crowd, and I endeavoured to do it. I opened out the engine ... and tried to rise. The next thing I knew was that the machine had struck the wall and was lying across it.'

She was further quoted as attributing her inability to become airborne once more as 'due to the sheltered conditions created by the wall ... an absence of wind, which is the only braking power when landing.'

The tragedy struck across the whole community, and not least at the Hob Hill Day School where, on the morning after the accident, 'even the little infants were impressed by the sadness of the occurrence …' Where, also, the headmistress would remember that just days before, Jackie, as everyone knew him, had presented her with a pair of sprouting acorns, saying 'I've brought you two young oak trees …'

Miss Winifred Brown displayed fine sensitivity by not attending the funeral, where her presence could only have caused distress and given rise to renewed newspaper interest. Her floral tribute, however, bearing the expression 'With deepest sympathy', spoke for the grief which superseded the horror of learning what had been so briefly hidden from her.

But at the inquest on 7 April 1928, again as reported by the Stalybridge paper, *The Reporter*, it became obvious that this was not the only thing that been concealed from her.

Mr Browning, private pilot and film salesman, giving evidence before Mr J.A.K. Ferns, the District Coroner, initially described the incident as a 'piece of pure bad luck'. But he was not to get away so easily. The coroner listened as the witness explained that he had been unable to 'hear anything Miss Brown said, of course, on account of the roar of the machine, but as she circled so many times … [he] presumed she was doubtful about the desirability of landing in so small a field.'

Had Miss Brown, the coroner wanted to know, been told it was a small field surrounded by walls? 'I did not tell her,' Mr Browning replied blandly.

And when the coroner pressed, 'You seriously tell the jury that you considered a field 150 yards long on one side, and 190 on the other, and surrounded by stone walls, suitable for landing an aeroplane in?' Browning promptly asserted, 'I could have landed a machine there.'

Only to have the coroner snap, clearly referring to the original plan, under which Mr Browning would have been the pilot, 'Why didn't you?'

Following hard upon these exchanges Sergeant F. Wheatman of the Dukinfield Police Force supplied damning details of the landing site. From corner to corner along the landing approach was just 179 yards. From the point of the aeroplane's touchdown to the fatal wall was only 108 yards. The field was marked solely by a central white circle with white corner flags, and had no restraint against a surging crowd. Nor had any arrangement been made for signalling to the pilot from the ground.

But perhaps the most heinous aspect of the affair was yet to come out. For it transpired that the box carried in the aircraft by Mr Browning had been empty! That from the outset the intention had always been to deliver the film by road!

Miss Winifred Brown, questioned on this revelation, replied categorically, 'If I had thought it was an empty box I wouldn't have gone.'

Whereas Mr Browning, questioned in his turn, was almost patronising. 'It would have been *far* too dangerous to carry a celluloid film in an aeroplane.'

At which stage the coroner asked both the cinema manager and Mr Browning individually, 'So this was a publicity stunt to delude the public?' and 'A hoax on the public?' Receiving the answers, 'Precisely,' and, 'That is so. A publicity stunt.'

Such contrite admissions, however, did not save either from the coroner's acerbity. Tersely he sought and gained admissions that the salesman had never been a captain in the army, and had never been in the Royal Air Force (claims made, one must suppose). Also that he had little experience of landing aeroplanes other than at Woodford, with its spacious manoeuvring area. Following which the coroner once more addressed the jury, directing them to recognise that Miss Winifred Brown had had nothing to do with the scheme, indeed that she had been deliberately lied to concerning the film.

'You have seen Browning in the witness box,' he reminded the members. 'And you must judge for yourselves whether he is experienced enough for choosing a field.' After which he commented witheringly, 'I think his flying experience has been gained in an office but you might think otherwise …'

And outraged still by the revelation that the intention all along had been to delude the public, the jury reached their verdict, completely exonerating Miss Winifred Brown from all blame, and expressing their belief that she had done everything in her power to avoid a much more serious accident.

Horrific as the incident had been, and deeply as it had grieved her, the trauma had not irreparably blunted Miss Brown's zest for aviating. Indeed, as already seen, the following year, flying G-EBVZ once again, she entered the prestigious King's Cup Air Race, and as Amelia Earhart justifiably crowed in her 1932 book, became the only woman to have won it. Indeed it would be 1981 – fifty-one years – before her exploit was emulated; while in the interim Miss Brown, as a winner, would have been the sole woman entitled to eat her annual celebratory dinners at the Royal Aero Club.

Nine years later, in 1939, and despite having reached the age of forty, Miss Brown – Mrs Adams rather, for by then she had married her fiancé passenger in the King's Cup Air Race, Mr Ron Adams – might have seemed a prime contender for the wartime Air Transport Auxiliary, the civil organisation which delivered aircraft from the factories to operational airfields. But when war broke out she turned to the sea, and served instead as a coxswain at the Saunders-Roe flying-boat base at Beaumaris, Anglesey.

All those years earlier, at the 1928 inquest into the Stalybridge crash, the District Coroner, after consulting the attending Flight Lieutenant P.H. Davy of the Air Accidents Investigation Branch, had stressed the importance the Air Ministry attached to the inquiry, 'as affecting the safety of the public in the future in such cases as these.' A concern which is reflected in the stringent rules which have for so long been imposed upon all public flying displays.

By 2006 only vestigial evidence remained of even the site of the 1928 tragedy, for the drystone wall on the approach, over which Miss Brown had dared not merely skim, together with those on the sides of the field, had been demolished as housing estates proliferated, spreading, seemingly inexorably, from Stalybridge. Notwithstanding which, sections of the double wall of the rifle range still held back the urban flow. So it was that, although nothing remained to indicate the actual impact point, and no debris could have been expected, the spot could be deduced – as it has been here – by plotting out the known distances involved.

2005; local historian Mr Graham Brown, standing by the now slighted inner wall of the Victorian rifle-range, indicates the outer wall

Beyond the bungalows and the remnants of the rifle-range walls a commendably active Local Trust, in 2006 often fronted by its worthy representative Mr Graham Brown, capably preserved the Estate of the former Gorse Hall. The Hall was demolished in 1910, but was once the home of Beatrix Potter's grandmother where the young Beatrix spent several family holidays. Of more notoriety it was also the scene of the now celebrated unsolved Storrs murder of 1909. As for the area beyond the double walls upon which the attempted overshoot had foundered so tragically on that baleful day in 1928, that was regularly mown to provide, somewhat ironically perhaps, a safe, traffic-free playground for the local children.

## Boeing B-17G 43-37667, Meltham Moor (south-west of Huddersfield)

SE 07088 09526 426m
United States Eighth Army Air Force, 447th Bombardment Group,
709th Bombardment Squadron, AAF126 (RAF Rattlesden), Stowmarket, Suffolk
6 April 1945

Crew: five, United States Army Air Force, all injured, two seriously:
First Lieutenant Winston Johnson, pilot, fractured spine
Second Lieutenant Raymond W. Parks, co-pilot
Second Lieutenant Walter Vukelic, navigator, fractured spine
Sergeant Robert J. Schnug, flight engineer
Sergeant Robert J. Woodbeck, radio operator

All aircraft require periodic servicing, and on occasion relatively major modification as components approach the end of their useful life. So it was that on 6 April 1945 it became necessary to run in – the American term was to 'slow time' – two newly-fitted engines on B-17G 43-37667. This merely involved flying off a certain number of hours. So when he volunteered for the task First Lieutenant Winston Johnson stood down his four gunners and his bombardier, Second Lieutenant Dick Kinder, as surplus to the flight. For the rest of the crew the duty probably offered a relaxing break after the six missions (the RAF term was 'operations') they had flown over Germany since arriving in the United Kingdom a month before.

The truncated crew duly got airborne at 1730 hours, and after a while, to escape the monotony of simply cruising around the local area, decided to head off to Manchester. As they approached the Southern Pennines, however, the weather deteriorated, and with the visibility decreasing and the under-surface of the cloud forcing them ever lower in order to maintain visual contact with the ground, they suddenly realised that they were lost. Accordingly, First Lieutenant Johnson, with the aircraft flying in a rain-fringed cloud base that varied from just 400 to 600 feet above ground level, handed control to his co-pilot and joined the navigator in the nose in what proved to be a vain endeavour to obtain a visual fix.

First Lieutenant Johnson had just decided to resort to their Gee radar-lattice navigational aid, and so positively determine their position, when the co-pilot, suddenly seeing hills looming to one side, powered up into a climb. The machine at once entered cloud but before the co-pilot could fully settle onto instruments it flew into the moorland sloping upwards from below.

On impact the climbing B-17 slowed rapidly, shedding components in a lengthy uphill slide until a wingtip dug in and slewed it violently, bringing it to an abrupt halt, with fire breaking out just moments later. The co-pilot, the engineer and the radio operator, all only slightly injured, evacuated hurriedly; to discover that the pilot and the navigator, having been flung through the Plexiglas nose on impact, had suffered more grievous hurts.

The three most mobile having settled somewhat, and with two dinghies impressed into service to shelter the pilot and navigator from the elements, Second Lieutenant Raymond Parks, the co-pilot, set off into the drizzly darkness to seek aid. Initially he trekked downhill along the debris trail, then followed a stream until he eventually saw a light – these Peakland epics are studded with this fine disregard for blackout regulations which, on several occasions, guided survivors: although, in truth, by this time the European War had only a month to run, and blackout restrictions had been gradually lifted over the last year or so.

The co-pilot had actually come down between Brow Grain Hill and Bracken Hill, to the north-east of the crash site, and found succour at Brow Grain Cottage, then a Water Board property, where the resident waterman, Mr Tasker, raised the alarm.

The first band of rescuers brought in the radio operator and the flight engineer but were loath to move the pilot and navigator until a doctor had pronounced upon them; yet setting out following a doctor's arrival, and supplemented by two stretcher parties, the rescuers themselves ran into difficulties. Seeing none of the anticipated guidance flares, they got disorientated in a thickening mist and eventually had to return to Brow Grain Cottage. Indeed conditions had worsened so much that it then took Mr Tasker himself, supported by his dog, one and a half hours to lead them to the site. Even then the ordeal was not over for either rescued or rescuers, for the stretcher teams disagreed over the return routing, each eventually going its own way. Both, however, arrived back safely.

Shortly after dawn a salvage team arrived, and after specialists had sought to locate the then-secret Norden bombsight, they proceeded to dispose of, burn, and bury most of the wreckage.

The inquiry into the crash ruled that it had been caused by the pilot persisting in trying to maintain visual-contact flight in unsuitable weather conditions when lost over unknown, high-level terrain. Only as the co-pilot had actually been at the controls when the accident occurred, he – and not the aircraft commander – was the pilot charged with the accident!

Tragically, both First Lieutenant Johnson and Second Lieutenant Vukelic had suffered broken spines and were subsequently confined to wheelchairs. Indeed, when First Lieutenant Johnson died in 1961 it was held to be a direct result of the spinal injury received that night.

In 2005 Mrs Joyce Casseli, of Meltham – ten-year-old Joyce Hooley in 1945 – remembered the excitement the crash caused locally. 'At the time', she recalled, 'we lived in Marsden, and after the first few days, when nobody was allowed near – because of the danger, or secrecy, perhaps – it proved a great draw. And not only for us children, so grown-ups too used to bring souvenirs down: metal, Perspex and the like. But my mother refused to have anything from the plane in the house. So I didn't take anything.' Pressed about the Perspex, Joyce smiled. 'I did have a Perspex brooch during the war – but it wasn't from there …'

Perspex – or its kindred thermoplastic – had rather more significance for the regular bombardier of the crew, the erstwhile Second Lieutenant Dick Kinder, who had been stood down for the ill-fated flight. Later he became a close friend of author Ron Collier and his wife, Susan, making a particular visit at the launch of the second of the *Dark Peak Aircraft Wrecks* books in the 1980s where he met Park Ranger Peter Jackson. 'He was very well aware', remembered Mr Jackson, 'that had he been aboard and at his station he too would almost certainly have been thrown through the Plexiglas and seriously injured.'

Notwithstanding the diligence of the salvage party in burying the wreckage, much re-emerged over the years. Consequently, being in a relatively remote spot, and even in the brightest of weather vividly reflecting the difficulties facing both the shocked co-pilot and the rescue teams who had to traverse the moor on a rainy, mist-laden night, the crash site still displayed a substantial amount of surface debris in 2006.

Former bombardier Second Lieutenant Dick Kinder in the 1980s. By courtesy of Ranger Peter Jackson

Ranger Peter Jackson, 2006

The B-17G 43-37667 crash site in 2006, looking northwards, downslope, back along the line of flight

## Consolidated Vultee PB4Y-1 Liberator 63934, Broken Ground, east of Mossley

SE 00815 01666 429m
United States Navy, VB110 Bombing Squadron, AAF173 (RAF Dunkeswell), north-east of Exeter (VB: 'V' denotes aeroplane; 'B', a bomber; 'PB', denotes Patrol Bomber)
18 December 1943

Occupants: one passenger and ten crew, most US Naval Reserve, all parachuted, five suffered minor abrasions and contusions:
Lieutenant George H. Charno, Jr, pilot
Lieutenant Junior Grade Robert G. Wissman, co-pilot, injured
Ensign Cecil R. Colyer, navigator, injured
Aviation Radioman (ARM 3) Warren W. Olson, radio operator
Aviation Ordnanceman (AOM) Walter O. Levering, weapons
Aviation Machinist's Mate (AMM 3) Douglas S. Peterson, radio operator
Aviation Machinist's Mate (AMM 3) Archie P. Oliver, engineer, injured
Seaman 2nd Class Dewey M. Clark, gunner
Seaman 2nd Class Winston C. Ketchem, gunner
ACRM1 Boyd S. Barber, US Navy, injured, with shock
Seaman 2nd Class William J. Clayton, passenger, broken ribs

In early 1943 three American maritime squadrons were operating PB4Y-1s, the re-designated Liberator variants, from RAF Dunkeswell; among them Bombing Squadron 110, one of whose aircraft was to be abandoned by its crew in the vicinity of the Wash and to come down in the Peakland area.

This was PB4Y 63934, in which Lieutenant George Charno and his predominantly United States Naval Reserve crew were tasked to carry out an anti-submarine patrol in the area of Biscay. They had left RAF Dunkeswell, to the north-east of Exeter, at 0700 hours on 18 December 1943, having been briefed to expect an early recall due to an anticipated deterioration in the United Kingdom weather. The recall came at 1100 hours after a single radar sweep of their patrol area, high winds, turbulence, constant rain, and a solid 400 feet cloud base having nullified a visual-contact search. The recall order required them to arrive back at their Dunkeswell base by 1700 hours and must have been received in the spirit of a half-holiday award, letting them off, as it promised to, with just a twelve-hour flight.

Lieutenant Charno's established crew of specialists were accustomed to co-operating together on long-range maritime operations that invariably called for many hours of seemingly unproductive – and therefore frustrating – patrolling, often enough to be flown at low level and in such characteristically appalling weather conditions as those they were returning from. Which was just as well, for the British weather was to take no account of any holiday expectations; on the contrary, it was to set about taxing them to the very limit of their combined forbearance.

At first all went to order, and making use of a timely fix obtained by one of their W/T (wireless telegraphy: morse) operators, they accomplished a landfall at Bude, on the North Cornish coast, at 1600 hours, allowing them to penetrate inland while keeping visual contact below cloud at just 500 feet above ground level. The overland weather deterioration had set in earlier than expected, however, and on contacting No.19 Group, RAF, the controlling authority, and having already passed overhead the first possible bad-weather bolt hole, RAF Winkleigh, to the north-west of Exeter, they were ordered to overfly their Dunkeswell base and divert to RAF Beaulieu, in the New Forest, to the west of Southampton.

Lieutenant Charno would later record that, having looked down at both Winkleigh and Dunkeswell in passing, he could still have made a safe landing at either despite conditions already being marginal, with low ceiling, reduced visibility in drizzle, and high winds. As his Liberator was operating as an isolated unit, however, he was obliged to trust to Group's having its paternal eye on some bigger picture, and obediently held course for Beaulieu.

Navigation was aided by a series of headings obtained by W/T, despite the fact that with the manual direction-finding of the day, and the poor reception occasioned by heavy static on this particular late afternoon, such vital bearings, spelled out in morse, often took five minutes to arrive on the navigator's table. But even as they closed with the Beaulieu area the poor visibility was exacerbated by heavy rain so that Lieutenant Charno was forced to climb to 1,500 feet and revert to flight on instruments alone.

The initial approach, consequently, embarked upon with the aim of making visual contact with Beaulieu, saw them letting down on an easterly heading-to-steer obtained by W/T. They actually broke cloud at some 700 feet, but despite having lookouts positioned at every hatch, in addition to the eyes in the cockpit, they saw no sign of the airfield; indeed minutes later another bearing showed that they had passed it by. They duly commenced a westerly turn to take them back to the airfield area but as they did so the nearby barrage-balloon defences of Southampton were seen rearing to 5,000 feet above them. Prudent avoidance procedure called for a southerly turn, notwithstanding which, moments later, they began receiving balloon-hazard radio signals. Being in visual contact with the surface as these warnings sounded they were, happily, able to discount them as spurious, and some time later were able to fix themselves off the coast near Portsmouth, to the east of Southampton.

With the crew now positive of their position the co-pilot, Lieutenant Robert Wissman, referring to the topographical chart, then gave of his best in mapreading them to the mouth of the Beaulieu River, from which there was every chance of their making a successful visual approach. They were up against rapidly deteriorating visibility, however, and although Lieutenant Charno managed to make fleeting radio telephony (R/T: voice) contact with Beaulieu and requested full airfield lighting to assist them in locating the field, it was to be told that the lights had been fully on from the outset. At this crucial moment a hazard-warning-ahead advisory from the W/T operator necessitated a ninety-degree heading change, the attendant climb to a recommended 1,700 feet safe height taking them, willy-nilly, back into the turbulent overcast.

By then it was 1745 hours, December's daylight had long waned, the high winds and gusty conditions were making flight on instruments difficult, and with heavy rain now falling it became evident that contact flying, and continuing to attempt to make visual approaches without ground assistance, was no longer tenable. Nor was their own airborne radar able to assist in conditions so bumpy, accordingly Lieutenant Charno had the radioman currently at the wireless operator's station, Aviation Radioman Boyd Barber, call for a formal 'Controlled Descent Through Cloud' (CDTC).

In later years, when voice communication and automatic direction-finding would provide instantaneous headings to steer, the CDTC – or to use the handier, brevity-code terminology, the QGH – became the standard non-radar method of safely descending cloud-thwarted aircraft; when carried out using morse code and manual direction-finding, however, it was a very protracted procedure. Just the same, it was a relatively sure method of penetrating through to any reasonable cloud base, the ground controller routing the machine to clear all obstructions and high terrain. On this occasion, however, Lieutenant Charno, with a declared three hours of fuel still on board, was asked to hold off, for other, lower-endurance, aircraft, it transpired, were also endeavouring to make approaches.

Lieutenant Charno dutifully positioned himself to the north of Beaulieu, maintaining his 1,700 feet until the time came when those aircraft had completed their approaches and he was called back to commence his own let-down. Only the moment he turned onto the heading passed to home him to the overhead, balloon-hazard signals forced him to turn aside from it. Nor, for fear of collision in cloud with other still-dwelling aircraft, could he afford to climb above the hazard signals; had he been able to do so he would have re-descended to the 1,700 feet commencement height once ground control had ascertained that he was safely over Beaulieu. Except that, in mid-dilemma, the Liberator's main radio equipment broke down altogether, the heavy rain – as the two on-board operators had to assume – having earthed out the aerials.

In this extremity, cut off from any form of ground control, no matter how tenuous, flying through thick, turbulent cloud in an airspace congested not only with unseen aircraft milling about to no set pattern (in those days), but with balloon cables hungry for trade and indifferent to whether the customers were Allied or enemy, Lieutenant Charno initiated the first of a series of calls to the 'Darky' emergency-homing service on his limited-range voice radio. All he received, however, was one unintelligible response, after which nothing more was heard despite attempts which were continued throughout the remainder of the flight. He also had the 'Identification Friend or Foe' (IFF) equipment turned to 'Emergency', although this would have been more to conform with signals procedures rather than in expectation of ground radar stations actually seeing the singular alerting code and organising a shepherd aircraft to first locate him, and then guide him to a more suitable airfield. Just the same, at 1830 hours, it did seem as if Lieutenant Charno's crew had been granted a reprieve, for at this stage W/T contact with Beaulieu was regained, and another controlled descent begun. In the course of this, however, balloon hazard warnings started to come in once again, but this time Lieutenant Charno was satisfied that he was far enough north-west of Beaulieu to ignore them, and carried on descending. At which juncture the W/T finally cut out altogether, never to be restored.

Pragmatically accepting that they must now assume that they had been irretrievably cast upon their own resources, Lieutenant Charno continued his descent on the last received safe heading, with all aboard straining to sight either airfield lights or cloud-base-locating searchlights. Only nothing relieved the opacity as they nosed down from the cloud rack. But not long afterwards flares were seen; indeed, on two occasions, yet, although the aircraft was immediately turned towards them the crew then found only darkness. For a while, a little later, they all thought they had finally seen an airfield and even a flarepath, but after several low orbits had been made the navigator, Ensign Cecil Colyer, identified the hoped-for flarepath as nothing but the dimmed headlights of a lorry convoy.

Clearly there was nothing to be achieved by continuing to randomly hunt about at hazardously low level in such poor visibility, and so Lieutenant Charno commenced a spiral climb above this provenly safe area, and at 5,000 feet set a northerly heading. Their best hope now, it seemed evident, was to head towards the Midlands, an area where airfields abounded: not for nothing was wartime Britain talked of as an aircraft carrier moored off Europe.

Lieutenant Charno's was a reasoned course of action, yet as they progressed northwards, over persistently unbroken cloud above a blacked-out land, hopes of finding any useful clearance began to fade, and as time dragged on and the fuel gauges began demanding notice, it became clear that the aircraft might well have to be abandoned. There was at least one other alternative, of course, that of descending blind through cloud, and although by now quite uncertain of their position, taking the chance of breaking into clear air before hitting the ground; to his further credit Lieutenant Charno discounted this course out of hand.

Then again, when he purposefully broached the subject of abandoning by parachute, one crew member, no doubt impelled by the universal reluctance of aircrew to leave an aircraft by any other means than down its steps, did suggest that they might turn towards the sea – whether east or west did not signify, with Britain not being that wide – and put the aircraft onto the water. But it was a suggestion only tentatively made, for nobody on board had any illusions regarding the Liberator's ditching characteristics: parachutes it would have to be. Therefore, as yet more time passed, and still no gaps were seen in the cloud below, so preparations were set in hand. Radar Operator Douglas Peterson busied himself in ensuring that the radar dome was fully retracted and in destroying the still-secret components; Aviation Ordnanceman Warren Olson double-checked that his charges – mines and the very secret acoustic torpedoes – were indeed unarmed; and Aviation Radioman Boyd Barber, at the W/T set, persisted until the last in tapping away at his morse key, hoping that transmissions, at least, might be getting through, dead though reception was. But finally, with only an estimated fifteen minutes' fuel left in his tanks, Lieutenant Charno opened the bomb bay doors, the safest parachuting exit, and ordered the crew to jump.

The evacuation went like the pre-ordained drill, except that (as former-Aviation Radioman Douglas Peterson would recall in a 1995 letter) Aviation Ordnanceman Orville Levering snagged his ripcord handle on a projection, so that when his turn came he had to jump with his part-opened canopy hugged in his arms. Lieutenant Charno, with the auto-pilot set, waited until the last man, co-pilot Lieutenant Wissman, was clear, and then, turning the aircraft onto a heading just north of west, followed in his wake.

The abandonment was highly successful, and although there were a few superficial contusions, and a broken rib or two on landing, this was hardly surprising with a surface wind logged at 48 miles an hour and using parachutes of a type which, for many years afterwards, limited even paratroop training drops to a maximum surface wind strength of 10 miles an hour.

In his 1995 letter Mr Peterson described his own bale-out experience. 'I pulled the rip cord,' he wrote, 'and when the chute opened it knocked the wind out of me… I stopped and my flight boots kept right on going, so I landed in my socks. Being it was a blackout I didn't even see the ground when I hit it, a plowed and muddy field. I couldn't spill the [28 foot diameter] chute and was dragged a couple hundred feet before it spilled over a hedgerow.' Gathering his parachute he then walked some quarter of a mile to a house. 'The man let me in (I was covered in mud) and his wife laid a bunch of newspapers on the floor and I peeled the mud off and got out of my mae west and chute harness.' The man provided him with a pair of old shoes, and having taken him to the local pub, where he phoned his position through to base, took him back to the house where 'his wife made some bacon and eggs (which you didn't see much) and later a couple of bobbies came and took me to Boston (they had picked up 11 when I got there), and then to an RAF airfield where we had physicals. Next day we went to London and next day a Catalina flew us all back to base.'

As the crew had variously found out, the aircraft, acted upon throughout its northerly passage by the strong south-westerly wind, had actually been in the vicinity of the Wash, on the East Coast, when it was abandoned. But, while, in retrospect, it might seem that Lieutenant Charno would have been better advised to turn the aircraft onto an easterly heading this would be to take unfair advantage of hindsight, particularly with the British Isles being such a deceptive shape. (For example, steering northwards from Liverpool, does Edinburgh lie to the east or the west?) After all, having set a northerly course from the New Forest area, Lieutenant Charno might reasonably have expected to be abandoning in the Midlands, equally close to either coast. As for the ordnance left on board – the mines and the torpedoes – not having been armed, these presented no more of a threat than matériel of that nature ever does.

Left to its own devices, the machine, with its automatic pilot engaged and trimmed to straight flight – if commencing a steady descent once Lieutenant Charno had vacated – and with little fuel registering on the gauges, flew on westwards, heading, as it transpired, directly for the Ashton-under-Lyne area of Manchester. It had already reached a concerningly low altitude by the time it was seen over the Tame Valley. But at that juncture, it has to be assumed, a starboard engine ran out of fuel and cut; for when the Liberator was next seen, further north, over Mossley, it was heading eastwards, the drag of the windmilling propeller having pulled it into a wide curve to the right. Just a short while later, and providentially after clearing the built-up areas, it had descended so far that it struck the top of the barren, stone-littered, peat-surfaced plateau of Broken Ground at 1,400 feet above sea level. There was no fire on impact, nor did the safely unarmed ordnance explode.

The United States Navy's investigating board found that the pivotal communications failure was due to no apparently remediable cause, and consequently recorded the accident under the miscellaneous category: 10% attributable to radio failure, and 80% to weather.

Following this, Lieutenant Charno received a well-merited commendation for 'Taking correct and decisive action in an emergency and for the obvious good discipline of the crew'. Obvious, that is, in the sense that their good discipline illumined the whole episode. Additionally, what has to be reiterated is that here is one captain who, despite having seemingly pulled out all the stops in his protracted efforts to save his aircraft, did not then make the mistake made by so many others in this Peakland series: that of fatally hazarding his crew by descending blindly below cloud once they were no longer receiving radio-navigational assistance and had become hopelessly lost!

This account having very properly highlighted the exemplary conduct of each member of Lieutenant Charno's crew, it might be politic to declare the sources used in its compilation. These comprise the official statement submitted by Lieutenant Charno to the United States Navy's investigating board (the endearingly styled 'Trouble Board'); the Naval Accident Report, Form 339, entitled 'Aircraft Trouble Report'; two letters written by the former-Lieutenant Charno in August and October 1998 respectively; and the letter, previously referred to, written in 1995 by former-Aviation Radioman Douglas S. Peterson. All these documents were supplied to the present writer by the *Hell on High Ground* series author Mr David W. Earl (see bibliography) together with his permission to use them here.

Regrettably, in 1982, a journalistically-styled account was published which presented this estimable crew in an altogether less favourable light. The documents cited here prove that portrayal to have misinterpreted salient facts, thereby doing the crew a disservice that cannot sit easily with anyone who has ever flown professionally, whether Service or Civil; be it as a pilot, or as the member of an aircrew.

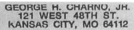

Left: sources, courtesy of former-Lieutenant Charno and author Mr David W. Earl

Above: Mr David W. Earl, author and veteran researcher

Left: 1998 letter extract from former-Lieutenant Charno, courtesy Mr David W. Earl

The write up about us bailing out was fairly accurate except the writer had a vivid imagination. I was the radioman plus radar on the flight. The air was toorough the radar was useless so I cranked it up (manually), as it was where the bottom turret would normally be and it sutck out quite a bit, and I didn't want that hanging down in case we had to leave the aircraft. There were two radiomen on the crew, one of us was on radar and the other on the radio, we took turns at operating each position. With the problems with the radio, which was not uncommon, my trying to get soemthing to work was not bordring on panic, but on frustration. Orville Levering, one of the mechs, did not pull the rip cord handle as the article states but it got caught on one of the nandles of the radar and it popped the chute. He held it in his arms and when he was clear of the aircraft he let go and it opened.

1995 letter extract from former-Aviation Radioman Douglas S. Peterson, courtesy Mr David W. Earl

The crash site of PB4Y-1 63934, at Broken Ground in 2006, looking towards Carrbrook and Ashton-under-Lyne

Certainly it was a portrayal refuted by both former-Lieutenant Charno and by former-Aviation Radioman Peterson; not that either, as generous American gentlemen, was anything but indulgent. Mr Peterson merely allowed that 'the writer had a vivid imagination'. The former-Lieutenant Charno, for his part, benignly saw the minor inaccuracies as 'the figment of someone's imagination', and attributed the most glaring to the writer's having 'extrapolated inaccurately, although of no particular moment in the course of history'. But he especially singled out the compiler's unfamiliarity with the word 'pilotage', which Lieutenant Charno had used in his 1943 report. For far from meaning that the co-pilot suddenly seized control, as the portrayal in question had it, the now somewhat arcane word, harking back as it does to the days of volplaning and joysticks, merely means to navigate by mapreading. Indeed, although seemingly dated, it was to be correctly employed by the up-to-the-mark crew of the Apollo 8 moonshot in 1968, who recorded having had 'difficulty in "pilotage", that is, in trying to plot our path on the map of the back side of the moon'.

Regarding the Liberator's impact site, veteran researcher Mr John Ownsworth remembered that the scrap dealer who recovered the wreckage utilised sections of it to fence off his lot. Notwithstanding which, two engines and the main-undercarriage members remained on the surface for many years. Then, in 2002, in a reciprocal arrangement with the landowner, one engine was removed while the other large items were buried at some remove. In 2006, therefore, there was little surface evidence left, just a minuscule pool of collected debris and a myriad scraps of metal littering a wide area of the pitch-black peat.

## Consolidated Vultee B-24H-20 Liberator 42-94841, Twizle Head Moss, Lightens Edge, Holme Moss

SE 10684 03573 500m impact point
SE 10670 03449 501m port gear
SE 10629 03383 505m terminal-run site
United States Eighth Army Air Force, 492nd Bombardment Group,
857th Bombardment Squadron, AAF 179 (RAF Harrington), west of Kettering, Northants
9 October 1944

Occupants: USAAF, two passengers and seven crew killed; one survivor:
First Lieutenant Elmer D. Pitsenbarger, pilot
Second Lieutenant James D. Nendal, co-pilot
Flight Officer Jack M. Bliss, navigator
Flight Officer Frank Cser, bombardier (survived impact for some hours)
Technical Sergeant Presley E. Farris, engineer
Technical Sergeant Joseph W. Zwinge, radio operator
Staff Sergeant Curtiss Anderson, waist gunner (survived, critical injuries)
Staff Sergeant Frank A. Villelli, tail gunner
Corporal Clarence S. Watson, passenger, non-aircrew rated
Corporal Charles T. Lowblad, passenger, non-aircrew rated

The Consolidated Vultee B-24 bomber had a healthy cruising speed exceeding 220 mph (190 knots) at low level but its rate of climb of only a thousand feet a minute meant that the determination of a safe height to fly was of particular importance. As was only too starkly demonstrated on 9 October 1944, when B-24 42-94841 was flown into Twizle Head Moss, above Holme.

Having arrived in England in early June 1944, just prior to the D-Day landings in occupied France, First Lieutenant Elmer Pitsenbarger's crew had been engaged in bombing raids over Germany, and later, in transport-support missions into France. On 9 October, following an acclimatisation course designed to further familiarise him with flying in temperate conditions over hilly terrain, First Lieutenant Pitsenbarger was detailed to air test a repaired aircraft which another crew was to fly on an operational mission later that day. The proving test was to be carried out as an integral part of a navigational exercise that was to route via Goole, Huddersfield, Stafford, Builth Wells, Worcester, Banbury, and so back to Harrington, the specific weather briefing being to remain in sight of the ground throughout. At 1415 hours, therefore, carrying just eight of his normal ten-man crew, but with two, joy-riding, non-aircrew passengers aboard, First Lieutenant Pitsenbarger took off in the aircraft its regular crew had christened 'Sad Sack'.

The first two legs were completed without undue incident, but then came the south-westerly leg from Huddersfield to Stafford. Another pilot, whose aircraft had preceded First Lieutenant Pitsenbarger's on the route by twenty minutes, later reported that low stratus was actually hanging on the high ground throughout this leg. Yet although the topographical map shows several spot heights of nearly two thousand feet bracketing the track, 'Sad Sack' was seen heading towards the cloud-shrouded 1,728-feet-above-sea-level Holme Moss at an altitude that alarmed onlookers. And their alarm was well justified, for shortly after the machine disappeared into the cloud they heard a dull thud, and knew that it had indeed crashed.

In fact, it had been within a mile of its intended track when it struck the ground just above the rim of 1,600-feet-above-sea-level Lightens Edge. On impact it had gouged a wide groove through the peat and then careered on for some two hundred yards, shedding pieces as it went. Then it had burst into flames.

It seems probable that both the co-pilot and the engineer, the latter positioned behind the captain's seat, actually saw the ground an instant before impact, for their arms were found to be lifted, as if to ward off the danger; the majority of the others, who would have been enjoying the low-level views, and were therefore not strapped in, were killed instantly. But two men survived to be taken off the moor. Flight Officer Frank Cser, the bombardier, was carried down to a hospital, only to die in the early hours of the next morning. But Staff Sergeant Curtiss Anderson – 'I'm from California,' he greeted rescuers – although suffering injuries that would involve him in surgery until late 1946, eventually made a reasonable recovery.

Rescuers were soon on the scene, but once they left the road they found actually crossing the moorland to be an arduous undertaking. Nor was their task made any easier as they neared the burning wreck by exploding bullets hazarding all comers. In 2005 Mr Kenneth Denton, of Holme, who as a youth of fifteen took his turn in helping with Staff Sergeant Anderson's stretcher, vividly remembered the sharp detonations punctuating the crackling of the engulfing flames. 'But I was too intent on the task in hand', he said, 'to be over-concerned.'

It was to prove a busy night for all those involved in the rescue effort, whether Police, Fire Service, Ambulance, or civilian volunteer helper, like Mr Denton; and even then the task was to be extended, because, when it was established that one of the passengers was still unaccounted for, a series of searches was mounted into the surrounding moors; searches which were only called off days later when a heavy section of wreckage was lifted for removal, to reveal the body of Corporal Clarence Watson underneath.

The Accident Investigation Committee had little to do, for they had the evidence of the pilot of the preceding aircraft regarding the cloud disposition, and witnesses who had seen First Lieutenant Pitsenbarger's aircraft flying at a fatally low altitude. In their summary, therefore, they were unequivocal in attributing the accident to 80% pilot error, finding that Lieutenant Pitsenbarger had shown poor judgement in not returning to base when such bad weather was encountered 'as this was not an operational flight'.

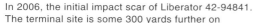

In 2006, the initial impact scar of Liberator 42-94841. The terminal site is some 300 yards further on

The terminal crash site, Twizle Head Moss, in 2006, looking north-west towards Holme Moss television mast.

In 2006 the crash site retained a distinctive scar where the machine struck Lightens Edge. Then came a two-hundred-and-twenty-yard stretch over which debris was strewn. Next, a minor, and eighty yards on, a major, location where the main body of the Liberator had burnt out, with two patches yet devoid of vegetation, in each of which an undercarriage leg and a mass of fragmented debris remained.

### Consolidated Vultee B-24J Liberator 42-52003, Mill Hill, Little Hayfield

SK 05844 90610 500m impact site
SK 05731 90583 490m gully site
United States Eighth Army Air Force, 27th Air Transport Group, 310th Ferrying Squadron, AAF582 (RAF Warton), near Preston, operating from AAF590 (RAF Burtonwood), near Liverpool
11 October 1944

Crew: two, United States Army Air Force, both survived, injured:
First Lieutenant Creighton R. Houpt, pilot; broken jaw, lacerations
Staff Sergeant Jerome M. Najvar, flight engineer; lacerations

When an American operational squadron required a replacement aircraft it was often delivered by an extempore ferry crew based at such aircraft storage and maintenance pools as the Base Air Depot at Burtonwood, sited within easy reach of the Liverpool docks. Accordingly, when B-24J 42-52003 was to be delivered to AAF104 (American Air Force Station 104, the American designation for RAF Hardwick), just south of Norwich, the task was assigned to a pilot and a flight engineer who had not flown together before, indeed who had never previously met. Not that this should have been any bar to a successful delivery, just so long as standard operating procedures were adhered to.

So it was that First Lieutenant Creighton Houpt, a ferry pilot with nearly two hundred hours on B-24s, and Staff Sergeant Jerome Najvar, a flight engineer-cum-pilot's assistant, with a year's experience in ferrying B-24s and other bomber types, were arbitrarily brought together for the flight which was to result in the total destruction of the aircraft when it was flown into Mill Hill at an altitude of 1,640 feet above mean sea level.

Half cloud cover (5/10) was forecast for the route with the main cloud base solid at 1,500 feet above the ground. In addition, there was a reduced visibility of 3,900 yards in haze despite a gusty surface wind of 24 knots, itself the presager of a considerably higher wind at altitude. Just the same, the flight clearance was that customarily issued for a ferry flight and required visual ground contact to be maintained throughout, the standard operating instructions for ferry crews being to go around areas of marginal weather, alternatively to put down at a suitable airfield, or to turn about altogether and return to base.

Having considered the conditions First Lieutenant Houpt elected to fly at 2,800 feet, 'figuring', as he later stated in his report, 'that according to the map the highest point on course was 2,080 feet, which would leave plenty of margin to clear the hills.' He also recorded that before take-off he had set his altimeter to airfield elevation, or 76 feet. But the proposed 2,800-feet flight altitude – had he indeed maintained that height – would have given him, at best, only 800 feet clearance, leaving little enough to compensate for the severe up- and down-draughts engendered by the strong wind.

On the other hand, in the same statement First Lieutenant Houpt declared that after taking off from Burtonwood he had set a south-easterly course; except that such a course would have taken him far south of the hills, and nearly twenty miles clear of the 2,080 feet of Kinder Scout – and equally, of nearby Mill Hill! But all his declarations notwithstanding, what he had to admit to was that, after a declared fifteen minutes' flying (representing about twenty-nine miles), he saw hills; the crash site at Mill Hill being just that far, twenty-nine miles, from Burtonwood, but directly *east* of it.

Leaving aside First Lieutenant Houpt's heading, however, and regardless of how his altimeter had been set, and even what height he actually maintained on that altimeter, just fifteen minutes out from base he found himself 'flying on instruments in very rough air and little visibility': so much for maintaining visual contact with the ground, as required by both his flight clearance and his standard operating procedures!

The flight engineer, acting as pilot's assistant, who is elsewhere quoted as having been uncomfortable from the outset – and later more than somewhat aggrieved – over the conduct of the flight, and who reportedly pointed out that the altimeter was only reading 1,500 feet, has little to say in the official report. He notes that he 'called the pilot's attention to the 2,080 foot mountain on course,' but nonetheless concedes that 'it seemed from the instruments that we had plenty of clearance.'

All they were afforded, however, was a momentary glimpse of a dark surface through a gap in the cloud, and although First Lieutenant Houpt immediately applied full power and pulled up, the aircraft struck the ground – to reiterate, at 1,640 feet above sea level, and with virtually that reading on his altimeter – long before either action had time to take effect.

Although the aircraft was totally destroyed it did not catch fire, and as neither man had suffered incapacitating injuries, both were able to stumble clear of the wreckage.

It must have been evident that they had crashed in a remote area, and that in the existing weather conditions any search would take some time to set in train. They decided, therefore, to make their own way down from the hills. As First Lieutenant Houpt reported, 'We walked downstream along a mountain creek until we hit a road.' Clearly they had descended the gully below the crash site and dropped into Hollingworth Clough, for eventually they reached the Hayfield–Glossop road, hitched a lift, and were taken to a public house where they phoned the tidings through to Burtonwood.

The Accident Committee could not fault either the aircraft or its instruments. They therefore found that First Lieutenant Houpt had been in error for 'holding the altitude of the ship at 2800 feet on instruments, which would allow as safety margin less than 800 feet clearance of the ridges.' Further, they could see no justification for his having even attempted to continue the flight beneath the overcast.

Both crew members were briefly hospitalised with minor lacerations, although First Lieutenant Houpt additionally suffered a fractured jaw; and his aggrieved flight engineer notwithstanding, who could doubt but that it was an injury occasioned by having impacted with something hard during the crash!

Because of the relative inaccessibility of the crash site it was decided to set fire to the wreckage. Nevertheless there are many stories of items being removed, and often utilised for many years afterwards, by locals; among other anecdotes being that recalled by Mr George Sherratt, of Glossop.

The impact site in 2006

The gully, south-west of the impact site; since 2000 skirted by a paved causey path

'My friend, Ken Bancroft,' he said, speaking in July 2006, 'came from a toolmaking family, but guns were always his passion. So on one visit to this crash site, he and another friend removed a machine gun. Along the way, however, they got tired of carrying it, and hid it; except that, despite searching for it on several occasions afterwards they could never find it again. But many years later, when Ken mentioned this to a keeper, it transpired that his collocutor had discovered its corroded remains, not that long before, and just where Ken had described secreting it.'

Notwithstanding such casual enterprise, even in 2006 a surprising amount of surface debris remained. Debris, at this juncture, almost continuously overflown by aircraft whose crews, unlike the hapless ferry duo, duly respect the Peaklands, and who fly at a safe height as they pass overhead in the process of letting down into Manchester's airport, just beyond the western skyline.

## Boeing F-13A (RB-29A Superfortress variant) *'Over Exposed!'* 44-61999, Higher Shelf Stones, Bleaklow

SK 09042 94912 612m

United States Air Force, Strategic Air Command, 311th Air Division, 91st Reconnaissance Group, 16th Photographic Reconnaissance Squadron, detached to RAF Scampton (north of Lincoln), from McGuire Air Force Base, Fort Dix, New Jersey
3 November 1948

Crew: thirteen, all United States Air Force, all killed:
Captain Landon Peter Tanner, pilot, designated airplane commander
Captain Harry A. Stroud, co-pilot
Captain Howard Keel, navigator
Sergeant Charles R. Wilbanks, flight engineer
Technical Sergeant Ralph W. Fields, radar operator
Staff Sergeant David D. Moore, radio operator
Staff Sergeant Gene A. Gartner, scanner
Corporal Clarence M. Franssen, scanner
Corporal George Ingram, Jr, photographer
Private First Class William M. Burrows, photographer
Staff Sergeant Robert I. Doyle, photographer
Technical Sergeant Saul R. Banks, camera crew
Sergeant Donald R. Abrogast, camera crew

During the 1948 Russian blockade of Berlin, the United States Air Force utilised B-29 Superfortresses of their Second Bomb Group to supplement the transport fleets. Among these bomber types, however, they interposed some of the F-13 photographic variant to secretly film Soviet-held territory; these F-13s, although ostensibly still B-29s, having been so modified as to require the change of designation. It was one of these covertly-employed machines, 44-61999, which, on 3 November 1948, having returned to its temporary UK base, and just days prior to its homeward passage to McGuire Air Force Base, New Jersey, was detailed for a delivery flight to the main American depot at Burtonwood, near Liverpool.

At 1015 hours on that day Captain Landon Tanner, later to be described as 'one of the most experienced of B-29 pilots', took off from RAF Scampton. The particular F-13 he was flying, inherited by his thirteen-man crew-complement for the duration of their European detachment, was a veteran in its own right, and much earlier in its photographic career had been named – with what was to become ironic prescience – *'Over Exposed!'*

The route-forecast for the flight reflected that there would be scattered cloud from 2,000 to 4,000 feet, and an overall visibility of four to six miles, reducing somewhat in occasional rain showers; in view of which Captain Tanner elected to fly under Visual Flight Rules; essentially, to maintain visual contact with the ground, keeping clear of cloud. The distance from Scampton to Burtonwood is just eighty-six miles, the track westerly, and at a conservative low-level cruising speed of 220 mph (191 knots) the aircraft should have arrived at Burtonwood some twenty-two minutes after take-off; except that, initially inexplicably, it failed to do so.

Concern would have grown only gradually, but when 44-61999 was a full hour overdue a contingency plan came into operation as a result of which a search aircraft reported burning wreckage on high ground some thirty-one miles short of Burtonwood.

Had there been survivors it would have been truly propitious that this sighting report was picked up by the RAF's Harpur Hill Mountain Rescue Team which was exercising in the area. As it was, there were none, and although members of the team reached the crash scene with commendable dispatch they found no one to aid. They located eight bodies before nightfall, but found no sign of life anywhere amid the burning wreckage.

The rescue effort truly got under way at first light the next morning, but although widening moorland searches were initiated, the bodies of the unaccounted-for crew members were eventually found amidst the debris at the scene.

In general, the findings of American air-accident investigations from that era tend to be more benign than those of their RAF counterparts. Certainly, in this case, the investigators seem to have done their best to avoid deciding upon a condemnatory cause, arguing that there were too few facts to enable them to reach any definite conclusion. The aircraft, they reported, had been found to be in alignment with, and just three miles north of, the direct track to Burtonwood; there had been no witnesses and no recorded emergency transmissions. Beyond this, a crew member's watch had been smashed while reading 1050 hours. Taking this as the time of impact, and calculating from the known take-off time to obtain the planned estimate for Burtonwood – around 1037 hours – they might well have reasoned that the crew had done some sightseeing before entering the cloud belt; a reasonable assumption in view of their imminent departure from the United Kingdom. As it was, the Accident Committee had no remit to speculate, and merely submitted that Captain Tanner and his crew had inexplicably flown into the high moors; that consequently they could make no recommendations.

Higher formations accepted this indecisive finding. Nevertheless, they expressed their concern that this appeared to be the type of accident that occurred when a pilot tried to maintain a Visual Flight Rules operation even when the weather conditions became marginal. An observation which, predictably enough, immediately drew avowals from all the Division's subordinate commanders that *their* pilots were constantly urged to re-file to an Instrument Flight Rules plan whenever such conditions were encountered.

The salvage team reduced the wreckage as far as possible, and yet in late 2006 a bewildering amount remained; indeed one might have said a monstrous amount. Certainly if anyone wished to make the case that such wreckage should be cleared once and for all, then this site might well be proffered as the prime example. That said, the writer had to confess to lingering by the adjacent Higher Shelf Stones trig column on two occasions prior to learning of the crash site, and having not the slightest inkling that the northerly aspect held anything but moorland, so well did the groughs conceal the remains.

A monument was subsequently brought to the site, and as late as 2006 a plethora of poppies and wooden commemorative crosses invariably lent colour to the almost aggressively sepulchral wreckage.

Two views of the terminal-area site in 2006

## Fairey Barracuda Mk.3 MD963, Redbrook Clough, Close Moss, Marsden

SE 02365 10445 367m
Royal Navy, Station Flight, Royal Naval Air Station Dunino, south-east of St Andrews
29 July 1945

Pilot: solo, killed:
Sub-Lieutenant George Henry Ambler, Royal Naval Air Service

The Barracuda was designed as a three-seater torpedo-bomber and reconnaissance aircraft for the Royal Navy. Although unprepossessing in appearance, and with its design performance degraded by the heavy components called for by the carrier-dictated Admiralty specification, the Barracuda was still a step up from the Swordfish and Albacore types it replaced and 2,572 saw service in some twenty-three operational squadrons. But while the Barracuda gave yeoman service there is the adage, variously expressed, but as old as aviation itself, which holds that those aeroplanes which fly good, invariably look good. Only surely even the Barracuda's own designer cannot have thought much of its looks! Although judging by the number of female ferry pilots photographed while operating the type there may be some element here of the beast attracting the beauty.

It is known that Fairey Barracuda MD963 was based at Royal Naval Air Station Dunino, south-east of St Andrews, Fife, when it was destroyed on 29 July 1945; also that, although the type normally accommodated three crew, Sub-Lieutenant George Ambler, the pilot, was on a solo detail.

Beyond this, however, nothing more was established regarding the prelude to this fatality.

But there was a witness to the final moments of the Barracuda's flight: a man who was walking on Close Moor when a very low-flying aeroplane suddenly appeared out of the overcast. His impression was that the pilot saw the ground and immediately began a tight, avoiding turn. As the aircraft banked, however, the walker was horrified to see it falter, then plummet into the ground, and explode in flames.

It is evident that Sub-Lieutenant Ambler, suddenly aware of his peril, pulled hard, away from the ground; but pulled too harshly, and straight into the judder of a high-speed stall, totally defeating his object as the turn rate faltered and a wing dropped. Restoration of the turn required the merest relaxation on the stick; only with a hillside looming that luxury was denied the hapless Sub-Lieutenant Ambler.

In 2006 the crash site retained a surprising amount of wreckage considering its proximity to a road; additionally a wooden commemorative cross had appeared. However, such proximity notwithstanding, and as the site is just off the northern edge of the

An Air Transport Auxiliary ferry pilot about to fly the beast, literally 'by the book'. Note the sturdy undercarriage (on the Barracuda) and the Fairey-Youngman flaps which helped make the Barracuda so heavy.

ATA pilot Maureen Dunlop in a Barracuda.

Both photographs by courtesy of Osprey Books, Wendy Boase, and the Radio Times Hulton Picture Library

Carriage House Pub

2006, the crash site of Barracuda MD963, looking towards the Carriage House Pub popular Dark Peak map, it might be of use to walkers to know that a track, starting opposite the Carriage House pub (which then, at least, gladly made available its spacious customer-only car park), bridged Redbrook Clough and led directly to the site. The alternative, parking on the nearest lay-by down the A62 (Marsden to Oldham Road), necessitated either an unpleasant juggernaut-braving roadside trek, or an even more unpleasant trackless negotiation of the steep-sided Clough and its boggy hummock grass.

## Fairey Battle, Penistone

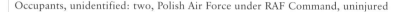

SE 25287 04013 225m
Polish Air Force under RAF Command, RAF Bramcote (south-east of Nuneaton),
No.6 (Training) Group, Bomber Command
*c.*1940

Occupants, unidentified: two, Polish Air Force under RAF Command, uninjured

Between July and August 1940, four Polish Fairey Battle light-bomber squadrons were raised at RAF Bramcote, in Warwickshire. The crews were initially converted onto Battles by a cadre of Poles trained at RAF Hucknall, in Nottinghamshire, but by November 1940, with the Battle having proved so disastrous in operations, all four squadrons had been re-equipped with Wellingtons. By mid-1941, however, Polish pupil pilots, having started from scratch in Britain, were flying Battles as advanced trainers from RAF Newton, near Nottingham itself; notwithstanding which, it was almost certainly before November 1940 that a Polish Battle was destroyed in making a forced landing to the north-east of Penistone. The aircraft struck a kinked, drystone wall – shown on the 2002 edition of the 1:25,000 Ordnance Survey map – and had to be written off, although the two Polish occupants were uninjured.

In the 1980s the incumbents of two immediately-adjacent farms, High Lee and High Lea [*sic*, Lee and Lea!], described the occurrence to researcher Mr John Ownsworth. By 2006, however, nobody could be found who knew of it, and even the drystone wall in question had been demolished, leaving a single spacious field. Prior to that the wall ran uphill from SE 14100 03890 208m, via SE 24150 03950, thence to the reference given.

2006, the line of the erstwhile wall. The background includes the Penistone Viaduct

## De Havilland (Canada) L-20A Beaver 52-6145, Bramah Edge, east of Glossop

SK 05531 97589 399m
United States Air Force, 81st Fighter Bomber Wing, 7519th Air Support Group,
Operations Squadron, RAF Sculthorpe, near Fakenham, Norfolk
5 December 1956

Occupants: pilot and passenger, both killed:
First Lieutenant John Rossman Tinklepaugh, USAF, pilot
First Lieutenant Guy B. Waller, USAF, passengering pilot

The L-20A Beaver was manufactured by de Havillands of Canada between 1952 and 1960, the type being used by, among many other agencies, Britain's Army Air Corps in Malaya and elsewhere. But the United States Air Force operated two hundred as liaison and light-transports, one of which, Beaver 52-6145, was on the strength of the 7519th Air Support Group Operations Squadron when it made its last flight on 5 December 1956.

It was flown on that occasion by First Lieutenant John Tinklepaugh, who had been detailed to transport fighter pilot First Lieutenant Guy B. Waller from Sculthorpe (east of The Wash) to the

American base at Burtonwood (Liverpool), to pick up an F-84 jet fighter. A straightforward enough task which merely required First Lieutenant Tinklepaugh to conform to an initial-departure routing, then fly 140 miles to the radio beacon at Oldham where he would turn south-westwards for a radar pick-up and descent into Burtonwood.

As significant medium-level cloud cover was forecast, and being aware of the high ground obtaining as far as Oldham, First Lieutenant Tinklepaugh filed an instrument flight plan for an altitude of 4,500 feet. Additionally, using the forecast weather, he calculated that his flight would be slowed by a headwind of 20 knots, resulting in a groundspeed which would bring him overhead Oldham some one hour and twenty minutes after take-off, and over Burtonwood sixteen minutes later.

What was to remain unknown to him was that, because of an approaching cold front, the headwind had more than doubled in strength. Which meant that it would now take him an additional thirty minutes to reach Oldham, and an additional six minutes to reach Burtonwood; such unallowed-for extensions to his expected journey times setting the scene for the tragedy about to be played out.

And very unusually, a tragedy in which mistakes were not only to be made by the man in the air, but also by the controllers on the ground. Perhaps, therefore, it would be germane to recap on the procedure for the acceptance of an aircraft by Air Traffic Control radars in those far distant days.

For many years since, identification of a target aircraft has been made by its on-board transponder equipment automatically responding with a dedicated code to any interrogating radar; this code (or 'squawk') being assigned by air traffic control before take-off. Indeed, even back in the 1950s some aircraft would have carried the transponder's predecessor 'Identification-Friend-or-Foe' (IFF) – codenamed 'Parrot', from which the still current 'squawk' procedural words survive – but clearly Beaver 6145 was one of the many which did not.

In those days, accordingly, the pilot would advise radar of his estimated position and heading. Radar would then monitor any targets showing on the screen in that vicinity which seemed to correspond, at the same time instructing the aircraft to turn through thirty degrees for identification. And provided a target on the screen complied, and turned back again when so directed, positive identification was assumed and radar control was established, such identification being reinforced as the target continued to reflect radar's acknowledged instructions.

Regarding the radio-navigational aids fitted to this Beaver, it is not known whether First Lieutenant Tinklepaugh had the benefit of a (serviceable) radio compass to tell him when he was overhead the Oldham beacon, although it can be deduced from subsequent events that this facility was lacking. Further, it should be appreciated that in the fifties even a communications radio was a relatively low priority.

Reflecting upon what is known of the conduct of the flight itself, First Lieutenant Tinklepaugh's departure clearance required him to make a sizeable dog-leg after take-off in order to avoid The Wash danger areas, then to call when he was overhead RAF Marham. In the event he did not call, as a result of which, it was later held, he could not be passed the updated en-route weather, including the significantly-increased upper-wind speeds. However, it is a matter of record that he subsequently obtained a position line from a directional facility abeam his track by means of which, as evidenced by his later estimates, he realised, to some extent at least, that he was falling behind his planned timing. Unfortunately, his calculations failed to show him just how far behind.

The flight path from then on becomes peripatetically complex, but by using the air traffic record to back-plot from the crash site, a reasonably clear picture emerges.

At 1213 hours, after unknowingly combating a greatly increased headwind for an hour and twenty-six minutes, First Lieutenant Tinklepaugh reported that he was overhead the Oldham beacon. As previously said, what navigational means he employed to determine this is not known, but, on the strength of his call, Air Traffic cleared him down to 3,500 feet towards Burtonwood. In fact, he would have been nearer Holme, reasonably on track from Marham, but still some eight miles short of the Oldham facility.

As directed, he then contacted Burtonwood, advising that he was now at 3,500 feet, and inbound to Burtonwood on a south-westerly heading. Subsequent to which Burtonwood radar, tracking likely-looking targets approaching from the Oldham beacon area, twice ordered him to make identifying turns. On each occasion, however, as the target on the screen failed to respond, First Lieutenant

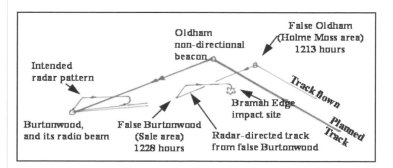

Schematic routing of Beaver 52-6145 having falsely called overhead Oldham

Tinklepaugh was directed to resume his own navigation for Burtonwood, with the additional anticipatory instruction that, having reached it, he should turn onto a north-easterly heading.

No positive radar identification was made, but at 1228 hours First Lieutenant Tinklepaugh reported that he was overhead Burtonwood and turning north-east; in fact, he was most probably in the Sale area. But on the radar screen a target was seen to be moving to the north-east from Burtonwood, and when, a minute or so later, First Lieutenant Tinklepaugh acknowledged (and obeyed!) the instruction to turn easterly – onto what was intended to be a long, downwind leg – this target did the same. Later investigation would prove this target to have been an aircraft coincidentally flying a visual downwind leg below the 1,600-foot cloud base; and on the Burtonwood tower frequency, not on the radar frequency. The reality was that First Lieutenant Tinklepaugh had been steered, initially north-eastwards towards Salford, then eastwards to the Crowden area.

Some minutes later, radar, now convinced that this was a positive identification, ordered a wide right turn intended to bring Beaver 6145 back to line up with the Burtonwood runway, clearing it to descend in the turn to 1,500 feet. Only although First Lieutenant Tinklepaugh immediately acknowledged that he was conforming, the target on the screen did not turn! Instead it continued to track eastwards.

Initially just a little puzzled, radar then made a querying call to which First Lieutenant Tinklepaugh promptly responded, confirming that he had indeed made the right turn and was well into the descent to 1,500 feet.

More hurriedly now, radar advised him to hold 2,000 feet and re-home to Burtonwood. But the only response to this instruction was First Lieutenant Tinklepaugh's startled, and abruptly truncated exclamation, 'What –!' Then silence.

And in that silence the misidentified target on the screen continued on its way, fading from sight as it reached ten miles east of Burtonwood.

But a full *thirty* miles east of Burtonwood, Beaver 6145 was now a burning mass amidst the boulders 1,300 feet up on Bramah Edge, and both its occupants were dead.

Above: the crash site in 2006; on Bramah Edge, above the Rhodeswood Reservoir and the Longdendale Trail

Left: contemporary United States Air Force photograph, courtesy of Mike Stowe

Mulling over the failure of the pilot, albeit with just 550 hours' experience, to fully utilise his in-flight track-check to more accurately revise his groundspeed, it is noted that his passenger, seated in the right-hand seat alongside him, was a jet-fighter pilot. An ebullient breed, and prone to indulge in raillery when passengering aboard a slow transport. Certainly a formula, if not for disaster, then certainly for distraction. But after all, where was the need for undue concentration? 4,500 feet was a safe height. And once in the vicinity of the Oldham beacon, Burtonwood radar would safely gather them in …

In 2006 a small cache of debris remained at the crash site on Bramah Edge, high above the Rhodeswood Reservoir and the Longdendale Trail; but this is one of those sites where, given the most trusty of references, a visual cast-about will probably be called for, in this case because of the proliferation of overhanging boulders.

## Bristol Blenheim Mk.1 L1476, Sykes Moor, Torside Clough

SK 08295 97035 481m
No.64 Squadron, No.12 Group, Fighter Command, RAF Church Fenton (York)
30 January 1939

Occupants: both killed:
Pilot Officer Stanley John Daly Robinson, pilot
Acting Pilot Officer Jack Elliott Thomas, passengering pilot

First flown in early 1935, the Bristol Type 142 was developed as the Blenheim bomber, the RAF receiving the type in March 1937. Nearly two years later, however, on 30 January 1939, with the type well established in the Service, Blenheim Mk.1 L1476 disappeared with its two South African occupants, Pilot Officer Stanley Robinson, and passengering pilot Acting Pilot Officer Jack Thomas, both of whom had been engaged in a local-area familiarisation flight from RAF Church Fenton: 'Local flying and sector knowledge', as the RAF accident summary specified. Although a search was mounted it was redirected at an early stage, and eventually called off, following a report – subsequently found to be false – that an aircraft had crashed into the sea. Indeed the missing Blenheim was not discovered until thirteen days later, on Sunday, 12 February 1939, when a chance walker, identified by the *Glossop Chronicle* as Mr Richard Robert Bridge, came upon its wreckage.

The senior officer appointed to investigate the crash, Squadron Leader Heber-Percy, from RAF Church Fenton, found a sizeable crater suggestive of a high-velocity impact, with debris thrown outwards over 'a couple of acres' by the exploding fuel tanks and with both engines detached, one being a hundred yards from the impact point. The *Glossop Chronicle's* account catalogued the condition of the bodies, in what, even then, it is be hoped, some must have felt was unnecessarily lurid detail. In essence, however (and as the Glossop Coroner's Court was told), Pilot Officer Robinson, together with his streamed – but undeployed – parachute, was found six hundred yards from 'the main wreck', while Acting Pilot Officer Thomas lay within two hundred yards of his designated captain, in a direct line from the tail. [Showing that Pilot Officer Robinson had ordered an abandonment and that both men had jumped; but at far too low a level.] Variously questioned by the coroner, Mr. G.H. Wilson, and also by Police Sergeant Clarke, of New Mills, Squadron Leader Heber-Percy gave it as his opinion that it was not unusual after a high-speed impact for the fuel tanks to have exploded without catching fire, the explosion not even staining the aircraft's fabric, but merely scattering the debris.

Significant witness evidence was given by a Mr

The Sykes Moor crash site. Left: Squadron Leader Heber-Percy and Police Sergeant Clarke of New Mills. Right, Constable Clark, of Charlesworth. Photo by courtesy of Mrs Margaret Buxton-Doyle, vice her father, Mr Harry Buxton, *Glossop Chronicle*

Thomas Ingledew Hardcastle, of Hillside Cottage, Glossop, who told the court how, on the day of the crash, with the moorland tops in mist, 'the sound of an aeroplane with the engines making a loud noise' had caused him to run up a field in a vain attempt to see what was happening. He described how the engine noise had then 'suddenly stopped'.

Notwithstanding all of which Squadron Leader Heber-Percy was obliged to advise the court that although all the indications were of a high-velocity impact with engines running, no definite cause for the loss of control leading to the crash had so far been determined. Nor does the RAF accident-card-summary, raised subsequent to the inquest hearing, record any cause. It might be ventured, nonetheless, that either disorientation in cloud, or failure to contain an engine-out condition – real, or purposefully entered into as a drill –, or indeed, both in conjunction, were all likely causes; particularly as Pilot Officer Robinson, the aircraft captain, could claim only ten hours' flying on multi-engined types. True, he had amassed a reasonable enough 363 hours in his two years as a pilot, but (having trained in South Africa) few of these would have been gained in the temperate-zone weather conditions of a British winter. Of course, such 'venturing' without the benefit of any contemporary deliberations, can only be speculative opinion; but – the appeal might be made – this is neither more nor less speculative than similar 'venturings' exercised, as a professional duty, in the course of several of the boards of inquiry served upon by the author.

The years have passed, both since those boards, and since the crash in question; but notwithstanding that the Sykes Moor crash was pre-Second World War – and as such, still free of wartime press-muzzling – the aircraft type involved does usher one forward into the era of that so-seminal conflict. In contrast, another facet of this accident takes one backwards, as to a bygone age. For when the chance walker, Mr Bridge, descended the moors to Reaps Farm, above Torside Bridge, it was to find that the incumbent, Mr Bert Crossland, had no telephone. The bleak news, therefore, had to be passed via 'a railway telephonic message' (*Glossop Chronicle*) from the nearby Torside railway signal-box to the railway controller at Manchester, who was able to alert the Glossop Borough police; so that, in his turn, the Derbyshire County Police Force officer responsible for the moorland area of Charlesworth Parish, a Constable Clark, was detailed to attend.

On the day following the discovery, once the site had been thoroughly scrutinised by his team, Squadron Leader Heber-Percy gave permission for the bodies to be stretchered down to Reaps Farm and taken to the mortuary at Glossop; thence to RAF Church Fenton. And by the third day, with the investigators' deliberations complete, and with the salvage team having camped on site, much of the wreckage had already been buried in a gully adjacent to the impact point. Long before 2006, however, much of this had surfaced. Just the same, the moor is relatively flat in the area, deeply heather-covered, and fretted by many watercourses, so that, despite the abundance of debris it may well be necessary to scout around from the reference in order to actually locate the gully and the memorial pillar.

The crash site of Blenheim L1476 in 2006, looking towards Torside Reservoir

## Bristol Blenheim Mk.1F K7172, Woolley Bridge, Glossop

SK 00395 95661 135m touchdown area
SK 00480 95555 128m termination point
No.29 Squadron, RAF Digby (north-east of Cranwell), Lincolnshire, No.12 Group, Fighter Command
3 December 1940

Pilot: solo, uninjured:
Pilot Officer Donald Anderson

Although impressive when its prototype first flew in April 1935, by 1940 the Mark One Blenheim had largely been relegated to training and trials duties. Indeed this was the role being fulfilled by Blenheim K7172 on the evening of 3 December 1940.

Flying K7172, Pilot Officer Donald 'Don' Anderson had been detached from RAF Digby (Lincolnshire) to RAF Cranage (north-east of Northwich, Chester), and was liaising with the Cranage radio station in carrying out communications trials; at that period various radio facilities were under either test or development, not least the High Frequency Direction-Finding service. It was unfortunate, therefore, for Pilot Officer Anderson, that towards the end of his duty, as his fuel state became a matter of concern, as the low cloud thickened below him, and as the light faded, so too did the signals from the Cranage facility.

Suddenly very lost, Pilot Officer Anderson took a calculated chance and, not without trepidation, blindly penetrated cloud. Providentially he emerged in a wide valley, which, it would transpire, lay to the east of Manchester. However, now even more aware of the mist-capped high ground all about him, he decided that one such chance taken was enough and prepared to make a precautionary landing before fuel became a real problem and darkness further exacerbated his predicament.

Selecting a suitable field in the area he would later learn was Woolley Bridge, on the outskirts of Glossop, Pilot Officer Anderson made his approach. Except that, on attempting to touch down, he realised that appearances had been deceptive and that (as a site inspection shows), the ground initially fell away before him so markedly that, regardless of his flaps, it was some time before he was able to set his wheels down and begin to kill his speed. Evidently deciding that he was committed to the landing – although his fuel state had not yet become critical, and another pilot might well have gone round again! – he persisted, but then, at the very beginning of his ground run, and certainly before his tailwheel made contact, a distinct change of gradient, previously undetectable, proved to conceal a field division, part-fence, part-hedgerow. In what he afterwards conceded was essentially due to over-hasty braking as he landed off the resulting bounce, the nose went down, the tail came up – then flipped all the way over. And the Blenheim landed heavily on its back.

Although the aircraft was initially judged to be economically repairable it was subsequently scrapped. Pilot Officer Anderson, on the other hand, was far more fortunate, for, despite finishing up inverted in his seat, he was able to release his straps, tumble onto the roof without breaking his neck, then extricate himself by way of an emergency exit; nor did the machine catch fire.

Despite his relative lack of experience – he had well under three hundred flying hours – the court of inquiry felt that Pilot Officer Anderson should have handled the situation more competently; accordingly an endorsement of 'lack of judgement' was duly entered into his flying log book; an endorsement which was to form a source of rancour to him until his death, in the year 2000.

After the Woolley Bridge crash, Pilot Officer Anderson – he would leave the Service in 1946 as a flight lieutenant – went on to serve throughout the war, although mainly as a ground-based fighter-controller after the loss of his medical category during a posting to the Middle East. Not the luckiest of wartime careers, but many years later, in 1977, he returned to visit the spot near Woolley Bridge where he had twice chanced his luck in the course of a single evening; and where it had twice held up.

In 2005 Mr Colin Gregory, of Home Farm, Woolley Bridge, was able to cast his mind back to that 1940 arrival. 'He came down, then hit a rough patch and went over,' he said. But further pressed to confirm the direction of approach he snapped tersely, 'Who knows? He didn't tell us he was coming.' He readily recalled the sightseers, however. 'People came from all round. Crowds of them. And airmen, soldiers – even sailors. [Glossop was home to an in-part hush-hush Royal Naval supply depot!] But they left soldiers to guard it. And guard it they did …' Adding then, the twinkle in his eyes momentarily belying his abruptness, 'from the pub, the moment everyone had gone.' Finally, ascertaining that the intention of the enquiries was to write a book on local aircraft crashes, Mr Gregory demanded devastatingly, 'Why?'

The author's overall mentor for the crashes in this area, Mr Arnold Willerton, of Hyde, visiting as a schoolboy, had seen the machine from the Glossop Road and in 2005 was able to point out the general location of the crash. This was later refined with the assistance of Mr Gregory and his sons, David, and Geoffrey. Then Mr Alan Jones, aviation artist and aircraft crash-site researcher, on being taken to the site as a very young child, had watched a guard idly lifting and dropping the elevator, leaving him with the [correct] impression that the machine had not been particularly fragmented. Mr Wright Cooper, of Tintwistle, who was a youth at the time of his 1940 visit, concurred with this impression: 'The Blenheim was on its back, of course, but after the RAF lifted it onto its wheels with a crane it seemed pretty whole. They took the wings off then, and carted the whole lot away on one of their long low-loaders.'

The lack of debris meant that there was little chance of determining exactly where the aircraft had finished up; certainly several site visits, and a cursory metal-detector search, had resolved nothing. But in mid-2006 Mr Mike Brown, of the Glossop Heritage Centre, unearthed the photograph of the Blenheim on-site reproduced here, taken by Mr Entwistle, a celebrated Glossop photographer, and inherited by his nephew, Mr Stanley Parker, of Glossop, by whose courtesy it is included.

Notwithstanding the clarity of the print, it has to be admitted that the author spent over an hour sidestepping across various fields, photograph in hand, vainly gazing eastwards the while, before being hailed by Farmer John Bower (and licked by Labrador Judy), of Carr House Farm. Mr Bower rapidly assimilated what the photograph showed, and firmly faced about – to the north! After which, identifying a mill – altered, sans chimney, and totally blotted from view by sixty-six years of tree-growth besides –; also recalling the location of a long-demolished gasometer; above all, knowing that the field pattern had remained unchanged; Mr Bower took only moments to successfully photo-match the precise spot.

The author having had such able assistance, it then became clear that, back in 1940, Pilot Officer Anderson had made his approach from the north-west, had touched down in the slightly-higher adjoining field (at approximately the reference supplied here), found his landing run upset by the still-evident abrupt change of gradient, and having run through the intervening fence (in 2006, mostly mature hedgerow), had stabbed too hard on the brakes, and so, somersaulted his machine. As the photograph shows, a nasty smash. And although Pilot Officer Anderson later resented the RAF criticizing his (mis)handling of what he had intended to be a precautionary landing, he must, nevertheless, have taken heart from the dual satisfaction of not having flown into a misty hilltop, and of surviving what was clearly a potentially-fatal crash.

Blenheim K7172 on Woolley Flats. Courtesy of Mr Stanley Parker, vice photographer Mr Entwistle, both of Glossop

Change of gradient and fence-cum-hedgerow

Direction of approach

Mr John Bower, of Carr House Farm (and Lucy), having photo-matched the site, July 2006

### Bristol Blenheim Mk.4 Z5870, Crowden Tower area, Edale Moor

**SK 09441 86962** 581m area of the speculative initial impact point
**SK 09143 87075** 619m area of the terminal crash site (330 yards on)
No.12 Group Anti-Aircraft Cooperation Flight, RAF Digby (north-east of Cranwell), Fighter Command
3 July 1941

Occupants: crew and passengers, all killed:
Sergeant Nicodem Plotek, Polish Air Force under RAF Command, pilot
Aircraftman Second Class Wilfred Cottom, RAF, wireless operator/air gunner
Aircraftman Ron Place, RAF, passenger
Aircraftman William Franklin Kidd, Royal Canadian Air Force, passenger

One of the roles undertaken by the Blenheim after being withdrawn from active operations was that of providing an exercise target for the guns, searchlights and radars of Anti-Aircraft Command. On 3 July 1941, however, Blenheim Mk.4 Z5870 was merely being ferried to the maintenance unit at RAF Ringway (Manchester) for an overhaul; in view of which its pilot, Sergeant Nicodem Plotek, agreed to take along two airmen for the ride.

Sergeant Pilot Plotek, a member of the Polish Air Force under RAF Command, had served with the Polish Third Air Force Regiment before the invasion of Poland and was, therefore, relatively experienced for the time with a total of 542 flying hours, 147 of which had been on Blenheims. Before being posted to an operational squadron in the United Kingdom, however, he was being given the opportunity to become familiar with RAF techniques and the English language.

Blenheim Z5870 was to be flown from RAF Digby (north-east of Cranwell) to RAF Ringway, an eighty-mile flight which would have taken under thirty minutes. As it was, the aircraft crashed near Crowden Tower, Edale, just four miles or so to the right of its straight-line track.

The wreck was discovered by Gunner John Hamer, of the Royal Artillery, who spotted it while out walking; escaping, as was his off-duty wont, from his searchlight post beside the mouth of the Cowburn Tunnel. As he was to tell researcher Mr Alan Jones, in a letter dated January 2000, he had ascended the track of Chapel Gate from Barber Booth and was making his way around the head of the valley via Colborne and Brown Knoll, when he saw the aircraft high on the distant moor. Accordingly, on approaching the Edale Cross area, instead of descending to Lee Farm by the Jacob's Ladder track, as had been his intention, he had continued around the northern rim and in due time had come upon the Blenheim. He remembered that although it had gouged a grassy north-westerly furrow into the heavily fissured peat of the plateau, it had seemed virtually intact. Just the same, all four of its occupants, it was to transpire, were dead.

The official investigators were unable to determine a definite cause for the crash, and although engine failure was considered it was eventually discounted as unlikely. It was held, therefore, that the pilot had encountered lowering cloud, and being unfamiliar with the area, had descended with the cloud base in a vain attempt to maintain visual contact with the ground.

Because the aircraft had largely retained its basic integrity there would have been little of the airframe shed; just the same, in research extending to July 2006, the author had failed to trace any authoritative record of debris ever being found relating to this crash. Indeed it became obvious that uncertainty had existed for many years regarding the actual location, with enthusiasts unrewardedly searching both the moor above the rock formation of Crowden Tower – 'moor' being the term local farmers habitually reserve for the upland plateau – and the grassy slope below it. It has to be said, therefore, that no definitive initial-impact site can be proffered; that the map references given here, while arrived at by collating all the evidence uncovered during research, must be, in the continued absence of debris, only an approximation.

The earliest extant evidence of location came from Police Constable J.A. Coleman, of Hope, who testified to the coroner, just days after the crash, that the Blenheim was found 'approximately 300 yards west of Crowden Tower, Edale', a position which, strictly plotted, would have been below the line of sight of former-gunner Mr John Hamer as he traversed the Colborne–Brown Knoll ridge. A slight adjustment to the south of west, however, gives the reference tendered here (SK 09143 87075

619m), which, being on slightly higher ground, nearer the rim, would certainly have caught Gunner Hamer's attention – but not, significantly, that of anyone crossing the lower, far more frequented, Jacob's Ladder col near Edale Cross. In which context it is noteworthy that the fractionally different map reference supplied by Mr Ron Collier (Collier/Wilkinson, 1979, p.153: 092 871, that is, SK 09200 87100) seems to have been taken from the policeman's report, for it too falls below the line of sight from the Brown Knoll heights.

The same applies to a reference furnished to the present author in 2005 by former part-time ranger Mr Ron Townsend, who not only visited the crashed Blenheim while it was in situ but led others to it on more than one occasion. However, while the location he picked out on the map from memory (plotted out as SK 09250 87610 620m) is on a ridge to the north of the Tower, it proved to be similarly unsighted from the Colborne–Brown Knoll track; although a confirmatory visit would, at least, have brought the grough-scrambler to within a hundred yards of what was arguably the moor's only conifer! (And still flourishing in October 2006)

The RAF summary crash report is more than usually unhelpful in the Blenheim's case, for although the location originally given was 'Crowden Tower' – location being a notoriously unreliable element in such reports – a contemporaneously handwritten amendment alters this to read 'Lee Farm'; not only this, but the summary records that the aircraft hit a hill at 2,800 feet, whereas Kinder Scout Summit itself lifts to only 2,088 feet.

Notwithstanding this, there was other evidence of location to be gleaned from the coroner's court; particularly that given by a Gunner Sydney Becket, who testified to the time it took to walk from the battery to the crash site, his timing according well with Police Constable Coleman's statement that the aircraft lay 'approximately two and a half miles from where the road ends at The Lee Farm, Edale'; for routing from Lee Farm and the Jacob's Ladder path to gain the northern rim towards Crowden Tower gives just that distance. At which point it is probably pertinent to observe that, approaching the wrecked Blenheim from the west, as Gunner Hamer and the initial locating and salvage parties did, Crowden Tower itself – for all that its name figures prominently on the map – cannot be seen, being on a level with the moor. With this in mind, therefore, it seems very possible that those making the initial report might well have mistaken the interposing 619m outlier of the Wool Packs for Crowden Tower (The Tower being located, incidentally, at SK 09441 87107 613m): a likely reason for the amendment to the RAF crash report; although one might have thought that Pym Chair or Wool Packs would have been more meaningful features to choose than either the Tower or Lee Farm!

Although the above details seem to furnish proof enough that the Blenheim was found on the rim of the upland moor, there are leads which suggest that the initial impact might have occurred below the rim. Author Mr Ron Collier, for example, despite giving an 'on the moor' location (Collier/ Wilkinson, 1979, p.153 see bibliography), prefaced his map reference with the rather equivocal statement that the aircraft 'crashed below Crowden Tower'. Further, in the eighties, part-time ranger Mr Ron Weeks told researcher Mr John Ownsworth that the aircraft crashed 'on The Pike' – a location which, in 2006, retired Area-Ranger Gordon Miller confirmed was the local name for the spur leading down from Crowden Tower to Lee Farm; Mr Weeks also held that what debris there was had been removed by enthusiasts between 1970 and 1971. Certainly Ranger Miller, who had set Mr Weeks on as a ranger, with something about debris striking a chord in his memory, could not altogether dismiss his erstwhile subordinate's claim.

Veteran Ranger John Campion 'Campy' Barrows, on the other hand, to whom the present author had been directed as another who could vouch for below-Tower debris, demurred. 'I've been asked about the Blenheim', he declared, 'countless times, but I never did see any trace of it, above or below the Tower.' Nor could Mrs Milly Heardman, long resident in the Edale valley, throw any light on wreckage being seen in either area, for all that she and her late husband, the redoubtable Dalesman, Mr Fred Heardman, had become familiar with all the other local crash sites.

Fortunately, additional confirmation for the upper-moorland terminal location was provided by former-Gunner Mr John Hamer himself. In January 2000, prior to a personal visit by researcher Mr Alan Jones, Mr Hamer had written two letters to him – details from which are used here by the courtesy of Mr Jones – in which he apologised for being so relatively vague about the Blenheim's

2006, former Area Ranger Gordon Miller

February 2000, Mr John Hamer (right), reminiscing with Mr Alan Jones

location, explaining that in the twenty-odd years since he had talked about his discovery to Mr Ron Collier, the details had simply slipped from his mind. By August 2005, when the present author approached him, Mr Hamer was in poor health, but in a telephone conversation he was able to indicate the answers to questions asked about the content of his letters. Supplementing the above reference to a failing memory, he had written, 'I fear that I am unable to pinpoint the position of the Blenheim. As you will appreciate 60 years ago is a long time to remember much of a trackless, featureless wilderness as exists on the moors.'

He had then explained that in the days after the crash had been located, he and the other young soldiers detailed for sentry duty had not bothered using the Jacob's Ladder path. 'Instead,' he wrote, 'we would go by lorry to Upper Booth and then continue on up a track until we came to a place where a high bank was on the right … Up this we scrambled, and took off across the moors. I have the impression it was not too far to the crash site [from the top], say 400–500 yards.' In a clarifying second letter, written just a day later, he amplified, 'The distance I gave in yards was arbitrary, just to emphasize that I do not remember …' And significantly, he noted, 'The ground was fairly level and it must have been grassy for I have no feeling of heather.' [Indeed there is little heather either above or below the Tower, the vegetation being predominantly bilberry and coarse grasses.]

In the above context, Mr Hamer observed, 'Lee Farm does not ring a bell, so maybe we turned off before reaching it'; which suggests that when bound for sentry duty they probably utilised The Pike, breasting the rim to the west of the looming Crowden Tower to reach the wreck which the policeman, it will be recalled, had described as lying approximately three hundred yards distant from the Tower.

Additionally Mr Hamer had offered, 'The aircraft was more or less in one piece. I have the distinct impression the RAF recovered it working from Hayfield. Less the Horlicks tablets, and the compass which someone pinched.' And his impression about the recovery being made to Hayfield seems reasonable, for the salvage crew would have wanted to maintain their height around the rim, after which the westbound track offered vehicular access from the region of Edale Cross.

In the absence of debris, anything further has to be speculation. It seems to the author, however, that there is no fundamental conflict between wreckage having existed on The Pike, with a terminal site on the rim, just above it. Indeed there seems every chance that the Blenheim, pursuing its track of 'west-by-north', its speed enhanced by its cruise-powered descent, could have struck The Pike, scattered some debris, and with the grassy slope falling away before it – and not inconceivably, with both throttles hastily jammed open after the unexpected impact – soared onwards until it bellied onto the peaty upland rim. Certainly the distance from speculative impact to almost certainly-determined terminal point is no more than similar leaps from cruising flight made by other aircraft in this series – Liberator 42-94841 on Twizle Head Moss comes to mind (as does a NATO-exercise vignette: of a *Luftwaffe* Nordatlas touching down woefully short of Decimomannu's runway in a cloud of Sardinian dust, then making a far longer and much higher leap past the nose of the author's Argosy to bang down with momentarily-splayed undercarriage onto the threshold). For the Blenheim, however, the location tendered to represent such a speculative initial impact point may be taken as SK 09441 86962 581m.

'The Pike', the speculative impact site and subsequent flight path, below Crowden Tower

Supporting this speculative scenario of a 'touch-and-soar', Mr Weeks told Mr John Ownsworth, speaking of the actual crash site, 'it was grassy, and there were no rock formations on the skyline beyond it'; hardly the description of a location on The Pike, from which Crowden Tower is such a marked feature on the skyline; in every way, however, matching the description of the upper-moor terminal site.

What seems likely, and indeed is a tenet held by crash-site delvers of all persuasions, is that debris will remain, minutiae though it be (and in this instance, despite the surface clearance in the 1970s); so that, for all that this Blenheim retained much of its integrity, someday someone will turn it up; and hopefully – the author having taken the speculative stance he has – on both the upper-moor to the west of Crowden Tower and on the grassy shoulder of The Pike, high above Lee Farm!

For completeness, it might be added that the coroner's court referred to was that held upon the Blenheim's wireless operator, given therein as Aircraftman Second Class Wilfred 'Cottam'. Commonwealth War Graves, however, with their records derived from official documentation, have the surname 'Cottom', the version adopted in the crew list above.

### Bristol Blenheim Mk.4 T1884, Harrop Edge, south-east of Stalybridge

SJ 98118 96494 259m
No.105 Squadron, RAF Swanton Morley (East Dereham, Norfolk), No.2 Group, Bomber Command
28 November 1940

Crew: baled out successfully:
Sergeant E.A. Costello-Bowan, pilot
Sergeant Broom, navigator
Sergeant Cameron, wireless operator/air gunner

When the more powerfully-engined Mk.4 Blenheim took over the operational task from the obsolescent Mk.1, No.105 Squadron was among the seventy squadrons which would eventually be equipped with the new version, receiving its first Mk.4 on 28 June 1940. Only at that time nobody on the squadron was qualified to fly it and it was not until early July that squadron pilots could be checked out on the type. Six months later, however, on 28 November 1940, with that mortifyingly too-early delivery well behind them, No.105 was to encounter a hiatus of a different sort.

On that November night, during a particularly foggy period, the squadron's fighter-bombers, among them Sergeant Costello-Bowan's T1884, raided Cologne, bombing the city, and strafing on opportunity during the return flight. In their absence, however, the fog had thickened over the United Kingdom, and particularly over their base at Swanton Morley, just north of East Dereham, in Norfolk.

In such conditions just one of the returning raiders managed to scrape into Swanton Morley. Another actually overflew the airfield, but then crashed. The crew of Blenheim T1884, however, lost above cloud, finally fixed themselves over Liverpool, turned

The impact site, looking back along the approach towards Wrigleyfold Farm; site-proving debris, subsequently re-interred, is shown on the rucksack

inland, and at 0100 hours, with the fuel very low, baled out, the navigator and wireless operator/air gunner landing near Ashton-under-Lyne, and pilot Sergeant Costello-Bowan near Stalybridge. Left to its own devices the aircraft flew on, twice menacing Wrigleyfold Farm in its circling descent before crashing into Harrop Edge, just beyond, and burning out.

Being close to roads, and on working farmland, the site was cleared within a matter of days, ostensibly by the RAF, but arguably just as much by such scavenging children as the enterprising young souvenir-hunter, Arnold Willerton, of Hyde, who visited the crash scene on his bicycle. What other debris may have been left behind on this pasture had, by 2006, long since been ploughed under; consequently there was nothing to be seen. Despite the lapse of years, however, both Mr Willerton and Mr Ellis Summerscale, who had farmed the area all his life, were able to indicate the impact point, following which metal-detector searches turned up items that positively identified the crash site as that of a Blenheim.

## Blackburn Botha Mk.1 W5103, Round Hill, Black Moss, Bleaklow

SK 11073 97536 559m
No.7 Ferry Pilots Pool, RAF Sherburn-in-Elmet (east of Leeds), Air Transport Auxiliary
10 December 1941

Pilot: solo, killed:
First Officer Thomas William Rogers, Air Transport Auxiliary

Throughout the history of aviation there have been British designs which were really not quite the thing, and the Blackburn Botha must surely be reckoned among the foremost of these. Over 400 were ordered in 1936 to provide Coastal Command with a modern torpedo-bomber/reconnaissance machine. However, because priority in engines was given elsewhere, the Botha introduced into RAF service in December 1939 proved unacceptably underpowered for an operational machine. Yet an under-rated engine was only one of the Botha's problems, for it was also prone to certain control complications and was soon relegated to the training role; only even there, albeit with a more power-ful engine being fitted, it was found to be unsatisfactory, and eventually ended up as a target tug.

On 10 December 1941, First Officer Thomas Rogers, a ferry pilot with the Air Transport Auxiliary (effectively, the 1938 Civil Air Guard, as reconstituted in 1939), was charged with delivering a new Botha from the Blackburn factory at Sherburn-in-Elmet, just east of Leeds, to No.48 Maintenance Unit at RAF Hawarden, near Chester. It was an eighty-mile flight and should have taken the Botha in the order of thirty minutes. However, the machine never did arrive, and when its wreckage was discovered by a sheep farmer the next day it was five miles south of its planned track, although less than halfway along the route.

Botha W5103, Round Hill, Bleaklow, in 2006

1968. Officer cadets from the RAF Technical College, Henlow; and the Botha engine which fell off their sledge into a grough. Courtesy of *Air Clues*, the RAF flight safety magazine

The wreck was found at 1,800 feet above sea level on Bleaklow's Round Hill, inverted, and with the pilot's body suspended in his harness. Yet notwithstanding the Botha's high accident rate, and after a painstaking examination, the investigators were unable to fault the aircraft. What they could be clear about was that First Officer Rogers had definitely crashed, as opposed to being compelled to make a forced landing. Therefore, as Air Transport Auxiliary pilots were generally constrained to maintain visual ground contact, and were often restricted to a maximum height, the conclusion had to be that First Officer Rogers had encountered cloud on the hills, and keen on getting the job done, had felt that by edging aside somewhat he could ease between the mist and the moor; as it turned out, a fatally erroneous feeling.

There was still a substantial amount of debris to be seen in 2006 despite the fact that in 1968 the engines were removed from the moor as a project for officer cadets from the RAF Technical College at Henlow; and also that years of subsequent unofficial scavenging had taken their toll.

## Reims Cessna 150M G-BFRP, Broadlee Bank Tor, Edale

SK 11390 86120 490m
BTJ Aviation Group (Transgap Limited), Ringway, Manchester
23 October 1983

Occupants: instructor and student, both survived:
Mr Barry Bryant, pilot, instructor
Mr John Steward Bateson, student pilot

Cessna 150M G-BFRP was being homed towards Manchester after a night training flight when it was caught in a lee-wave downdraft and crashed into the mid-slopes of Broadlee Bank Tor, above Edale village. Initially it struck near the top of a steep gully, then toppled backwards to come to rest inverted. The aircraft was destroyed but although both Mr Barry Bryant, the instructor, and Mr Steward Bateson, his student, suffered bruising on letting themselves fall from their seatbelts, they were able to walk down to Edale to report the accident.

The investigation found that Mr Bryant, a private pilot with 2,500 hours' flying, over 1,000 of which had been on Cessnas, had accepted radar assistance under Special Visual Flight Rules; two conditions of which required that he did not exceed 3,000 feet, and that he remained responsible for terrain clearance. When he was duly turned westwards onto an intercepting heading for an instrument approach onto Manchester's south-westerly runway, he was at 3,000 feet, near Edale, over ground rising to 2,000 feet, and significantly, to the lee (downwind) of the 2,088 feet-above-sea-level Kinder plateau. Significantly, because it had become evident that a 52 mph (45 knot) north-

Cessna G-BFRP, photographed by Area Ranger Gordon Miller

westerly wind was blowing at near right angles to the plateau; ideal conditions, as the meteorological authorities later confirmed, for the formation of mountain or lee waves. Mr Bryant acknowledged a refining heading, but shortly afterwards reported that he was in a severe downdraft and unable to maintain height. The radar controller immediately instructed him to resume his own navigation in order to keep clear of high ground, but not even a full-power maximum-rate climb could diminish the descent, and calling that he was 'going down at 1,000 feet per minute', Mr Bryant duly declared an emergency, striking the ground at 1,640 feet above sea level.

Mr Gordon Miller, in 2006 the globe-trotting Executive Director of the International Ranger Federation, but who had served as a Peak Park Ranger for thirty-five years and who, at the time of the crash, held the title, 'Area Ranger for Kinder – including Edale, Castleton, and Hayfield', remembered that it had been a wild and gusty evening. He actually saw the Cessna hit the hill as he drove home, but when its hitherto steady lights suddenly rotated he decided he must have been eyeing a hovering helicopter. Subsequently, driving into an Edale full of blue flashing lights, he realised that he had indeed seen a fixed-wing aircraft crash.

He was ready to fear the worst, but even as he joined the rescue forces gathering in the village centre he became aware of two men pushing through the crowd and into the Nag's Head Inn; the pilot and his student, it transpired.

A police guard was mounted overnight but at first light Area Ranger Miller, together with Chief Ranger Ken Drabble, Area Ranger Brian Jones, and a supporting team, began clearing the wreckage, being especially anxious to obviate damage to the drystone wall separating the upper moorland from the lower pastures should spectacle-seekers be tempted to leave the footpaths and clamber over it. What struck Area Ranger Miller most forcibly, he remembered, was how insubstantial the aircraft's structure appeared to be. 'We took the wings off,' he explained, 'then dropped them over the wall, and dragged the fuselage bodily. The heaviest thing was the power plant, and we put that on a Thompson stretcher – a locally-developed adjunct to the mountain rescue task – and lowered it down.'

In 2006 the thick grasses, bracken, and bilberry of the hillside bore no trace of the accident, but the site could readily be identified thanks to contemporary photographs taken by Mr Miller.

2006, the Cessna crash site

Salvaging the engine. Chief Ranger Ken Drabble, left, and Area Ranger Gordon Miller, right, with Area Ranger Brian Jones belaying. By courtesy of Mr Miller

## De Havilland Chipmunk TMk.10 WB579, Arnfield Moor, Tintwistle

SK 02738 99870 407m
No.2 Reserve Flying School, RAF Flying Training Command, Barton (west of Manchester)
3 July 1951

Pilot: unhurt:
Pilot Officer Harry Bate Wright, RAF Volunteer Reserve

The Chipmunk was the worthy replacement for the redoubtable Tiger Moth biplane trainer and became the mainstay of the RAF's Volunteer Reserve units. However, although easy to fly in a general way, it was a very demanding machine to operate with precision. Always lurking too was a spin characteristic which could – and on occasion did – bite, retrospective anti-spin modifications notwithstanding. But such characteristics aside, it was among the most pleasant of aircraft to fly, as Pilot Officer Harry Wright of the Volunteer Reserve was well aware when he got airborne from Barton, near Manchester, on 3 July 1951.

With an authorisation that included low flying he set off intent on carrying out a local-area detail to the east of Barton, only to find that, having overflown a layer of cloud, he could discover no breaks. At which stage, suddenly uncertain of his position, but believing himself to be far nearer the airfield than he actually was, he carried out an unassisted let-down, emerging into rain. The rain drastically reduced the below-cloud visibility, so that, even as he looked into the cockpit to refer to his compass, so he flew into rising moorland, the fixed undercarriage somersaulting the Chipmunk onto its back to leave Pilot Officer Wright dangling upside down in his straps.

Although uninjured Pilot Officer Wright experienced some difficulty in safely extricating himself from his inverted cockpit. Having done so, however, he then made his way down the moor to what he was to discover was Arnfield Farm, a mile and a half from the wreck of his aircraft, and fifteen miles east of his Barton base. The incumbent, tenant farmer Mr John Highley, told the *Glossop Chronicle* that Pilot Officer Wright had said it had seemed like hours before he had been able to dig his way out of the peat blocking the cockpit, while a Mrs Thompson ('one of the residents', as the

Chipmunk WB579, on Arnfield Moor, photo courtesy of Mrs Margaret Buxton-Doyle, vice her father, Mr Harry Buxton, *Glossop Chronicle*

paper coyly put it) made the point that the shocked pilot had been so mired with peat that it had been hard to tell that he was in uniform. Once the wreck was discovered, as the *Chronicle* faithfully recorded, it was dealt with by airmen from the RAF Maintenance Unit at Bowlee, Manchester.

The board of inquiry – for by 1951 'court' of inquiry had given place to 'board' – found that Pilot Officer Wright had entered cloud rather than turning back on encountering it, as his Unit Flying Orders required. Additionally it found that he had let down blind rather than climbing up until he had altitude enough to ensure that he could obtain a radio homing to base. He was also called to account for not taking sufficient note of compass-turning errors, or alternatively for lack of care in setting his directional indicator against his compass; the argument being that having adopted the correct procedure for either would have freed his eyes from the cockpit at the critical time.

Speaking of the incident in July 2006, Mr Wright Cooper (Wright being a long-cherished Christian name locally), of the neighbouring Townhead Farm, picked up on the fact that the hapless pilot had escaped injury despite his machine being inverted. 'Johnny Highley,' he said heavily, 'my lifelong friend, didn't have the same luck some years later when his tractor tipped over on him ...' And Mrs Thompson? One of the residents? Mr Cooper immediately brightened. 'That was Katey, Johnny's girl friend, though the papers wouldn't like to say so at the time.' He paused, and then added warmly, 'She was flighty –, but Oh! what a *bonny* girl.'

On the afternoon of the crash, mist and drizzle had prevented the salvage party from locating the wreck, but the next day, with clear weather, the aircraft had been sighted without difficulty. A circumstance which, it might be felt, had set a pattern, for although in 2006 a small pool of wreckage still remained to mark the impact site, yet with the ground being so broken and with heather abounding, there have been some good-weather searchers – certainly this one – who, having approached from Tintwistle Knarr and the shooting cabins, actually reached the reference given, yet went away frustrated; only to see the site from half-a-mile off next time, on approaching from Arnfield.

The crash site in 2006, looking southwest; Arnfield is off to the left

### Airspeed Consul TF-RPM, Crow Stones Edge, north of Howden Reservoir

SK 17403 96616 483m
Icelandic Airlines
12 April 1951

Occupants: two crew and one passenger, all killed:
Captain Pall Magnusson, Icelandic Airlines, pilot
Mr Alexander Watson, Morton Aviation, Croydon, wireless operator
Mr Johann Rist, passenger

The twin-engined, six-passenger Airspeed Consul was the civilian conversion of the RAF's wartime Oxford trainer. It filled a need after the Second World War with many airlines, particularly emergent companies, welcoming the relatively inexpensive machine. So it was that TF-RPM, a conversion which had been built as Oxford Mk.1 HN471 and released after RAF service, was painted in the livery of Icelandic Airways when, on returning to Iceland after a Certificate of Airworthiness renewal at Croydon Airport, it crashed on Howden Moor, killing all three on board.

Captain Pall Magnusson had planned a visual flight with refuelling stops at both Liverpool and Prestwick en route to Iceland. On reporting for departure at Croydon, however, he learnt that the weather pattern was such that westerly winds of up to sixty knots were driving low clouds before them; conditions which made it unlikely that visual ground contact could be maintained. On the other hand the direct route for Liverpool, crossing Birmingham and then the Cheshire Plain, would not require overflying high ground of any significance. Accordingly, and notwithstanding the unpropitious weather, Captain Magnusson duly departed on a visual flight plan.

What happened after that has to be, in part, a matter of conjecture. For the Consul's wreckage was discovered forty miles to the right of the direct track and in the very centre of the high moors of the Peak District, moors which lift to nearly two thousand feet above sea level.

The air accident investigators must have deliberated over the time and distance flown along track. The planned distance to Liverpool was some 185 miles – or about one hour and ten minutes at the Consul's 163 mph (140 knots) still-air cruise. The distance to the crash site they would have plotted at 160 miles, or one hour's lapse time; in planning terms, just when Captain Magnusson must have expected to be abeam Chester or thereabouts, and so, a very reasonable time at which to think of edging down to re-establish visual ground contact before commencing an approach to land; that is, had the aircraft flown its planned track of approximately 320° rather than its more north-easterly actual track of 335°.

But what had taken it so far to the right of track? The extremely strong westerly wind blowing from the left? Or a compass – or compass-setting – error?

Turning away from what, for the author, could only be speculation, the accident investigators could find no sign of either structural or mechanical failure; indeed they established that both engines had been under power when the aircraft struck. Their submission simply stated, therefore, that the pilot had strayed markedly off course, and after cruising above a cloud layer, and believing himself to be approaching Liverpool, had maintained cruising speed as he had descended blindly through cloud. Except that he had descended into the cloud-obscured high ground of a rock-strewn grouse moor, striking at nearly 1,600 feet above sea level when his altimeter – soullessly registering heights above the near sea-level datum to which it was set – would have persuaded him that he still had more than adequate clear air below.

In September 1996, researcher Mr Alan Jones unearthed a poignant survival from the 1951 crash in the form of the Aerad Company's radio-facilities booklet which Captain Magnusson would next have referred to when making his approach to Liverpool. As Captain Magnusson had failed to get that far, the booklet remained as he had stowed it, enfolded between two newspapers; the three documents remaining perfectly legible for all their 45-year entombment in the peat.

Aerad (radio facilities) chart for Liverpool, recovered September 1996 from Consul TF-RPM. By courtesy of Mr Alan Jones

The crash site in 2006, looking north-westerly, with No.7 shooting butt on the left

Even in 2006 the crash site, a severe mile's walk north of Howden Reservoir's Slippery Stones Bridge, retained a surprising abundance of wreckage in a heather-fringed gully which bent around shooting butt number seven, the relevant line of butts being numbered uphill towards Broadhead Clough Head.

### Douglas Dakota G-AHCY, Wimberry Stones Brow, Chew Valley

SE 01556 02451 447m impact site
SE 01494 02686 342m undercarriage member
British European Airways (BEA)
19 April 1949

Occupants: 21 passengers and 3 crew died; 8 passengers survived.
These died:
Captain Frank Whartley Pinkerton
First Officer George Holt
Radio Officer Richard Willis Haig

Mrs Edith Barclay, Miss Jean Barclay, Mr Ashton, Mrs Davies, Mr Hubert Lea, Mr Cyril Beenstock, Miss Brimelow, Mr Clarke, Master Roger Evans, Miss Bridget Ann Farrell, Mr George S. Gisby, Miss Ivy Gwendoline Jones, Mrs E. Schofield, Mrs Beatrice Siddall, Mrs Edna Vickery, Master David Vickery, Mrs Joan Prestwich, Mr Henry Bryce Prestwich, Miss Elizabeth Anne Prestwich, Miss Jane Caroline Prestwich, Mrs Baird.

These passengers, though injured, survived:
Mr Robert Ashton, Mr Horace Evans, Mrs Ruth Evans, Master Stephen Evans, Miss Kitty McMahon, Master Michael Prestwich, Mr Arthur Frank Vickery, Mr Christopher Watt.

The loss of twenty-four lives on 19 April 1949, when BEA Dakota G-AHCY crashed on the heights of the Chew Valley, sixteen miles north-east of Manchester Airport, was found to be caused by the failure of the crew to correctly establish their position on the radio beam designed to get them down safely through cloud. It might be apposite, therefore, to consider some core aspects of the bad-weather aid-to-landing system then in use.

In essence this 'Standard Beam Approach System' (SBA) transmitted a thirty-mile-long, very narrow radio beam down the extended centreline of the runway. This told a pilot receiving the aural 'on-the-beam' signal that he was somewhere along the projected centre line of the runway.

To furnish an exact location *along* the beam, an 'Outer Marker' radio beacon was sited three miles from touchdown. This sent a coded signal vertically upwards to tell an inbound pilot that he had three miles to go and should commence his final descent to land.

Such marker-beacon signals, however, were not designed to cause the needle of a radio compass to point towards them. This meant that, in order to positively

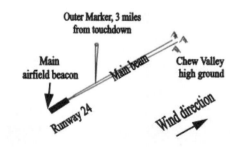

Essential elements of the Standard Beam Approach System (SBA) at Manchester, landing south-westerly

ascertain his position before establishing himself on the beam, a pilot would normally have to home to the main airfield beacon – to which the needle did point – a commercially wasteful procedure. On the other hand, it was perfectly permissible to navigate directly to the Outer Marker by independent means. And this is what Captain Frank Pinkerton elected to do.

On this occasion G-AHCY, inbound from Belfast, was already on a reasonable heading for the Outer Marker, but to refine his track Captain Pinkerton obtained a radar fix. This showed that he was presently heading somewhat wide of the Outer Marker, indeed aiming towards the high ground of the Chew Valley, so that a minor – but essential – change of heading to the right was necessary. A change that was duly declared to have been carried out. Except that Captain Pinkerton never did make that vital correcting turn!

Trying to determine why the turn was never made would engage the air accident investigators in much deliberation. Notwithstanding which the fact remains that, despite the accurate fix obtained, G-AHCY continued to be flown directly towards the high ground.

Patently, in Captain Pinkerton's mind, the turn had actually been made, leaving him convinced that he was now heading directly for the Outer Marker. After which the rest would have been plain sailing, for he had made nearly ninety landings at Manchester

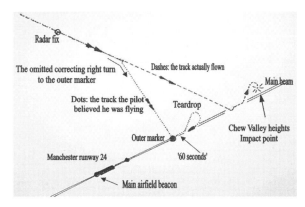

Schematic plan of the routing intended, and that actually flown, by Dakota G-AHCY

in the previous two years, a fair proportion of which must have been in poor visibility, and with the aid of its beam approach.

What Captain Pinkerton envisaged doing from then on, therefore, was to maintain the 'new' heading until he heard the coding of the Outer Marker. The procedure would then require him to turn smartly left and fly the beam *away* from the runway for a timed sixty seconds. With that time up he must then fly a stylised teardrop-shaped 'procedural turn' designed to bring him back on to the beam again, but inbound now, towards the runway, with the Outer Marker ahead, dutifully waiting to tell him when to commence his final approach from his cleared 1,500 feet.

Except that, as Captain Pinkerton was never to know, when he first intercepted the beam he was not overhead the Outer Marker, but some eleven miles downwind from it. In his own mind, however, although he could not hear the coding, he would have 'known' that he was very close to its overhead. So he turned anyway, timed his sixty seconds away from the airfield, then embarked upon the teardrop-shaped 'procedural turn': first left, spacing him from the beam, then a long, steady, right turn all the way around, to gradually establish on the beam inbound. Only, in reality, he was flying out this procedure with reference to a phantom marker. And it was in the course of this protracted right-hand turn that he flew his passengers and crew into the only too real 1,500-foot elevation of Wimberry Stones Brow.

Fortunately, rescuers reached the shattered wreckage with surprising speed and were able to carry eight survivors to safety, having saved at least one from the encroaching flames.

Facing uphill, by courtesy of the *Tameside Reporter*, formerly *The Reporter*, Stalybridge

Nothing could be done, however, for the other twenty-one passengers, for Captain Pinkerton, or for his crew.

Contemporary photographs of the scene show rescuers swarming on the steep, debris-scattered slopes of the clough. By 2006, however, nothing whatsoever showed of the tragedy enacted above this scenically-rich ravine; indeed even a metal-detector search, cursory though it was, produced no results. Yet the site is more remote than two others nearby where surface debris still remained from much smaller aeroplanes. The conclusion to be drawn being that, even then, back in 1949, no civil company wanted to perpetuate its mistakes, but rather took pains to ensure that not a trace was left.

As it was, contemporary photographs made identifying the impact point a straightforward task; additionally one undercarriage frame which somehow escaped the salvage operation still rested far downhill near the foot of the clough. It was, however, particularly gratifying to discover, by a chance sighting, one tiny fragment of molten aluminium among the scree of the rim footpath; a fragment now secreted at the site to continue to bear mute witness.

2006. The undercarriage member, near the foot of the clough

The crash site in 2006, looking north, towards Dovestone Reservoir. Inset: the single fragment found (and subsequently replaced) in a visual search

In the course of that 2006 visit, Mr James Bradbury, farming Kinder Intake, below the clough, was able to throw some light, at least, on how the site was cleared. 'Everything was snaked down by Frank Shockton,' he smiled. 'He wasn't a scrap dealer, as such, but Frank'd never miss a trick if there was money in it.'

And as a footnote, poignant rather than ironic, Captain Pinkerton had been a keen walker, and the Chew Valley one of his favourite haunts.

## Boulton-Paul Defiant N3378, at Near Bleaklow Stones, Bleaklow

SK 10610 96957 574m, impact point
SK 10649 96948 594m, terminal point
SK 10624 97052 595m, gully
No.255 Squadron, RAF Hibaldstow (Brigg), No.12
Group, Fighter Command
29 August 1941

Occupants: both killed:
Pilot Officer James Craig, pilot
Aircraftman Second Class George Daniel Hempstead, passenger

After its, at best, patchy career as a day fighter, the Defiant fared much better as a night fighter, its Airborne Interception radar (AI) enabling it to intercept and shoot down enemy aircraft as no other contemporary night fighter was able to. Losses occurred, nonetheless, as when Defiant N3378 failed to arrive after an innocuous-seeming non-operational positioning trip on 29 August 1941.

N3378 was the machine Pilot Officer James Craig had been detailed to take from RAF Turnhouse, Edinburgh, on the 200-mile – say 45 minute – flight to his base at RAF Hibaldstow, effectively, if not yet in fact, the satellite of busy RAF Kirton on Lindsey, both south-west of Brigg. Nothing seemed untoward, indeed thirty-six minutes after taking off with an airman passenger, Aircraftman Second Class George Hempstead (identified by the *Glossop Chronicle* as Bolton's golf professional in civil life), Pilot Officer Craig transmitted the routine advisory that he was in contact with RAF Kirton in Lindsey and inbound to his base; Hibaldstow being located abeam Kirton and just six miles nearer Brigg. After that, however, there was no further contact and indeed no trace of N3378 or its two occupants until a month later, when its wreckage was discovered at Near Bleaklow Stones, a remote moorland location just below Bleaklow Head, and forty-six miles off its intended track.

The preliminary court of inquiry was held while the aircraft was still listed as 'missing', Pilot Officer Craig's puzzled commanding officer writing, 'Flying experience of pilot makes disappearance difficult to understand'. And clearly, in the month before it was found, the disappearance of Pilot Officer Craig's aircraft was indeed something of a mystery, for the visibility on his planned route had been good, notwithstanding that cloud was known to have moved in over the high moorlands to the south-west. It should be stressed, however, that for all Pilot Officer Craig's relative experience – 630 hours' total flying time and 100 on type – the true source of puzzlement was not that he had crashed, but that his aircraft had not been found. Certainly, when the court was re-convened, after the missing airmen had been located and the wreckage inspected, any difficulty in comprehension was dispelled. Accordingly, the finding added to the summary report recorded that Pilot Officer Craig had attempted to blindly penetrate low cloud – in direct contravention of the controlling No.12 Group's order forbidding such a risky practice – and had flown into a hillside.

Puzzlement, in fact, was replaced by poignancy, the discovery of the wrecked machine having revealed that, although seriously injured, the occupants had survived the actual crash, for they were found seated outside the aircraft, beneath the cockpit; only both had died long before succour arrived. A tragedy like so many others recorded in this Peakland series; and once the wreckage was found, another whose cause the re-convened court of inquiry had no difficulty in determining.

Over the years, however, and with a fine disregard, at the very least, of the significance of the radio traffic logged between Pilot Officer Craig and various ground stations, enthusiasts would speculate upon more sensational causes.

One of these was that Pilot Officer Craig had indulged a whim to overfly a house holding members of his family in Wakefield; except that Wakefield would have only have taken him some twenty miles off track, while the Bleaklow crash site is more like forty miles displaced, as well as being fifteen miles further down the planned-track distance than Wakefield. Nor is any record proffered of the aircraft having been seen over Wakefield, or the house having been buzzed.

An alternative hare started by the mystery-at-any-cost lobby, was that the Defiant had been misidentified and shot down by Spitfires 'near Bishop Aukland': not that any Spitfire incident-reports are furnished in support. The enthusiast claim also lends significance, with equal lack of substantiation, to reports that bullet holes were subsequently found in the wrecked Defiant's radiator cowling. But with Pilot Officer Craig's routinely-phrased radio call having been made some fifty miles south of Bishop Aukland one might have thought he would have mentioned, even in passing, being attacked, and indeed, damaged; particularly by Spitfires: easy enough to be bounced by unseen fighters at their footpad nefariousness, but damage to the engine panel out on his nose could hardly have gone unremarked. As it happens, in July 2006, Mr Mike Brown, of Glossop, in the course of mutually regretting the scourge of – often paranormal – moorland myths which had arisen in recent years, commented upon this shooting-down aspect of the Defiant crash. Mr Brown, a retired schoolteacher who began visiting local crash sites as early as 1958, was encountered at the Glossop Heritage Centre. 'The whole moorland where the Defiant came down,' he reasoned, 'was used for battle training; you've found 0.303 inch calibre cartridges, both unused and spent; as I have. And what better target to loose off at in such featureless terrain than a wrecked aircraft?'

In a bid to course this particular 'mystery' hare, at least, a corrective note might be constructively applied to its most influential perpetuator, *Dark Peak Aircraft Wrecks 1* p31 (see bibliography). In all good faith the Collier/Wilkinson coverage, reprising the 1941 event from the late seventies, records that '*it was claimed* [of an army unit] *that they had discovered bullet holes in the wreckage and the theory was put forward that the Defiant had been shot down …*' The passage, however, then takes both claim and theory, adds a rumour, then launches out on speculation: as, of course, is its prerogative. On the other hand, when it observes, '*their existence* [the bullet holes] *was denied in an official report of the day – the official comment on the accident stands at: "Aircraft flew into a hillside in low cloud"*', this – and particularly the expositive dash – is quite mischievously misleading. For the RAF summary crash report, the document in question, denies nothing, makes no official 'comment' but, in accordance with its function, baldly states the finding of the court of inquiry, the exact quote being, 'Flew into hill side in low cloud (Group ban)'. The corollary of the official finding being that when the RAF investigators inspected the site there were no bullet holes in evidence; nothing whatsoever, therefore, to deny. [It might be borne in mind by any 'cover-up' lobbyist that, RAF investigators being junior officers, reports to their seniors admitted of no latitude; apart from which, being fliers all, it was in everyone's interest to both determine and disseminate within the RAF the cause of any given crash.]

What remains a true mystery is that with the multitude of causes that would take a single-crew aircraft off track, anyone should bother subscribing to fanciful embroideries. After all, a track error of just fifteen or so degrees would place the aircraft over the Bleaklow crash site, whether caused by an inadequately compensated-for drift or an inaccurate met wind – either very likely to be undetected, bearing in mind the known cloud encroachment; by an incorrectly set compass course; by a faultily-set, or too infrequently reset, directional gyro; by erroneous mental dead-reckoning in pilot-navigation; or even by sheer, everyday human complacency.

What is clear, from his last radio call, is that Pilot Officer Craig believed that he was nearing his destination; which means that, shortly after making the call, he would have begun a powered descent, expecting to break cloud in the vicinity of Hibaldstow. For the crash site is indeed just twenty or so miles short of the planned along-track distance to Hibaldstow, just right for commencing such a descent; had it only been 33-feet-above-sea-level Hibaldstow on Pilot Officer Craig's nose and not a Bleaklow moorland elevated to some 1,900 feet above sea level: the delusory height his altimeter would have been showing him when he struck. Truly, with such facts in evidence, only the most dedicated sensationalist would find the need to look any further.

Defiant N3378, at Near Bleaklow Stones, 2006

As late as July 2006, a considerable amount of debris was gathered about a tastefully-modest tribute placed at the terminal point in the mid-1990s; additionally there was wreckage at the impact point and many scattered fragments in adjoining gullies.

The centrepiece of the tribute had taken the form of a well-conceived commemorative tile, but in 2003 this was maliciously smashed.

### Boulton-Paul Defiant N1766, Rowlee Pasture, west of Derwent Reservoir

**SK 15286 90495** 448m

No.96 Squadron, RAF Cranage (south-east of Northwich, Cheshire), No.9 Group, Fighter Command
13 April 1941

Crew: baled out safely:
Flight Lieutenant Paul W. Rabone, New Zealand, pilot
Flying Officer John Ritchie, air gunner

By August 1940 the Defiant's mediocre performance had led to its being withdrawn from daytime operations. When re-employed as a night fighter, however, it did rather better, and it was during this second phase of its operational life, on the night of 12 April 1941, that Flight Lieutenant Paul Rabone, a New Zealander serving with the RAF, was detailed to carry out a navigational exercise. The round-trip route was planned to take him and his gunner from RAF Cranage (seven miles south-east of Northwich, Cheshire) to RAF Digby (north-east of Cranwell, Lincolnshire), and return.

The outbound leg to Digby was uneventful, but on the return, when the cloud lowered, Flight Lieutenant Rabone, being mindful of the region's high ground, increased his altitude, and called for a radio homing to Cranage. He received no intelligible response, however, and although he persisted in trying to make contact, the wireless set eventually died altogether. On top of which he was becoming increasingly concerned about the engine; indeed the subsequent inquiry, exonerating him from all blame in the loss of the aircraft, records that it actually cut out. But evidently before that could happen, and having discussed the situation with his air gunner, the decision was taken to bale out.

Indeed there was no other sensible option. They were lost, in the dark – and with a wartime blackout below – deprived of radio assistance, uneasy about the engine, above solid cloud, and with hungry high ground awaiting should they seek to penetrate that cloud in a blind descent. Accordingly, as Flight Lieutenant Rabone subsequently stated in his report, he climbed the machine until his altimeter indicated 3,000 feet, then ordered Flying Officer Ritchie to abandon; after which both of them made successful parachute descents.

Flight Lieutenant Rabone himself was no stranger to parachuting, having previously baled out five times from both Fairey Battles and Hawker Hurricanes; three times after being shot down, once with engine problems, and once having lost control in a storm cloud at 22,000 feet. Flying Officer Ritchie, on the other hand, was a novice jumper, but he too landed safely. On seeing a light, however, and making his way to a farmhouse, he had some difficulty in convincing the shotgun-wielding farmer that his thick Scottish accent was not German. [In view of the number of survivors who reported being guided by lighted windows, it is clear that blackout regulations in country areas were relatively lax. Nor was Ritchie the only Scottish survivor to be faced with suspicion by Peakland locals.]

It was to Flight Lieutenant Rabone's credit, then, that he did not fall into the only too common trap of 'pressing on regardless' and of descending blind when lost above high ground. Nor, despite this being his sixth abandoned aircraft, was there any pusillanimity about his caution. On the contrary, for by the time of this Rowlee Pasture episode he had already proved himself a successful – and enterprising – fighter pilot, having survived the debacles of the Maastricht and the Seine bridges. Indeed, by the time he went missing in July 1944, during a cross-Channel daylight sweep, he would have had the downing of ten enemy aircraft attributed to him.

Notwithstanding that the crash site was excavated in 1980, when the Rolls-Royce Merlin Three engine was removed, a reasonable amount of wreckage remained in 2006; at which time, it was understood, the recovered engine was displayed at the South Yorkshire Air Museum in Doncaster.

The crash site of Defiant N1766, Rowlee Pastures, in 2006

## De Havilland DH9 F2751, The Mudd, Lower Mudd Farm, Mottram

SJ 99590 94696 223m
No.38 Training Depot Station, RAF Tadcaster (before July 1918,
RFC/RAF Bramham Moor)
18 January 1919

Pilot: forced landed, uninjured:
Second Lieutenant William Henry Carr Robson, RAF

On 18 January 1919, Second Lieutenant William Henry Carr Robson, RAF, was detailed to deliver newly-manufactured de Havilland DH9 F2751 from Seahouses (Berwick-on-Tweed) to No.38 Training Depot Station, his home unit, then located at RAF Bramham Moor (Headley Hall Farm), Tadcaster. It seems likely that the sortie was utilised as a multi-legged navigational exercise, for a straight-line ferry, flown at a representative cruising speed for the DH9 of 100 mph (87 knots), would have covered the 170 miles in not much more than an hour and forty minutes. As it was, it was only after being airborne for some three and a half hours that the machine's 230-horsepower Siddeley Puma engine began to cause concern, forcing Second Lieutenant Robson to set down in a field thirty miles west of Tadcaster, at Lower Mudd Farm, Mottram, at that time under the tenancy of Mr Joseph James.

The precautionary landing being successful, Second Lieutenant Robson placed his machine under local police protection, then made his way to the Alexandra Park Aerodrome to obtain assistance and an RAF guard. [The aerodrome was sited at SJ 83500 95000 between the Whalley Range and Moss Side areas of Manchester]

The guard appointed took the form of two airmen, Corporal Walter Jennings and Aircraftsman

Second Class Percy Ruffle, who duly took over from the police. Second Lieutenant Robson found himself accommodation in Mottram village, while the two airmen, requiring a base closer to their charge, were granted billeting facilities by Mr George Henry Roebuck and his wife, Margaret, at Parsonage Farm, Mottram.

Corporal Jennings set up a schedule by which he and his fellow airman would each be able to have supper and some rest, leaving the other to guard the machine. However, at about midnight, feeling that Aircraftsman Second Class Ruffle was overstaying his break somewhat, Corporal Jennings left the aircraft to fend for itself while he walked up to Parsonage Farm; to find that, after his supper, Aircraftsman Second Class Ruffle had gone upstairs and dozed off on a bed. 'I've been out all day,' the miscreant excused himself. At which juncture the whole household was alarmed by a clamorous knocking on the door, and the news, delivered by Mr Fred James, the student son of the Lower Mudd Farm tenant, that the aircraft was ablaze.

Corporal Jennings at once rushed back, via the yard of Lower Mudd Farm, to the aircraft, but found that it was beyond saving, with the engine having collapsed onto the ground, and only the tailplane and the wing tips recognisable.

A month later, both airmen would testify before the local magistrates' court when Mr Fred James was arraigned, charged with setting fire to the aircraft in the course of attempting to siphon off fuel by the light of a storm lantern. At the time of their appearance as witnesses, both airmen were themselves awaiting courts martial, charged with deserting their posts while on guard. Corporal Jennings was clearly sensible of the gravity of the offence, ruefully telling the magistrate, 'I was in charge of the guard'. Aircraftsman Second Class Ruffle, on the other hand, comes across as the

archetypical irresponsible 'erk' (The air arm's irreverent, but always respectfully-affectionate, term for the lowest rank of airman; 'airk', from *airc*raftsman; their equivalent of Bairnsfather's Old Bill, the always-put-upon-private). Asked by the defence solicitor how concerned he had been on seeing the state of the aircraft, Aircraftsman Second Class Ruffle replied, 'Not very much. I treated it more as a joke than anything. I wasn't going to burn my fingers'; an incorrigible attitude which makes it doubly regrettable that his subsequent court-martial findings have not come to hand.

The hearing at the magistrates' court lasted for some nine hours, the newspaper reports of the day being unearthed in 2006 by the independent diligence of Mr Arnold Willerton, of Hyde, and Mr Bill Johnson, of Mottram. The court was to hear that an RAF inquiry, chaired by the Officer Commanding of the Alexandra Park Aerodrome, Major George Williamson, MC, had been convened at Mottram the day after the conflagration, during which the activities of Mr Fred James had come under close scrutiny.

At the magistrates' hearing Mr James was charged with stealing 30 gallons of aviation spirit, valued at £5, as well as causing malicious damage to an aircraft valued at 'over £2,000'. On the night of the conflagration, it was recorded, he had been treated for burns by the local GP, Doctor Awburn, and still had bandages on his head, his face, and both hands, in the courtroom; additionally, a motoring coat he had been wearing was shown to be burned through. It transpired that when the aircraft's engine had been moved by the RAF investigators a broken storm lantern, which Mr James claimed he had used only to tend to the cattle, had been found beneath it. It was also discovered that one of the two fuel-drain plugs on the engine had been unscrewed, and was missing, and that a spanner which fitted the plugs lay nearby. Further, in the farm's motor-shed a capless fuel can showed signs of scorching. Mr Fred James' defence – 'I ran towards it to put out the blaze' – was to be strenuously maintained in court, but the facts were clear enough for the case to be sent on to the Assizes.

The Assizes duly opened on 25 February 1919, the case occupying the whole of the Wednesday and the Thursday. At length, the jury, having been absent for some while, found the accused 'not guilty' on both accounts, and Mr James was discharged. The acquittal, as the newspaper recorded, was greeted with applause. And why not!

Regarding the identification of the aircraft involved as DH9 (or DH9A) F2751, it should be noted that no DH9s are recorded as having been on the strength of No.38 Training Depot Squadron, which seems to have been equipped with over seventy SE5As and Avro 504s as well as a Sopwith Pup. Indeed, Air Historian Mr Malcolm Barrass – Air Historian being a distinction far too commonly bestowed in the enthusiast world of *soi-disant* appellations, but applied unreservedly in this case – advised that the only Training Depot Squadron to have DH9s was No.10 TDS at Harling Road (north-east of Thetford) in Norfolk. On the other hand, during the next fifty-plus years, and certainly as late as 1973 in the author's case, it was common enough for an RAF pilot to fly aircraft from units other than his own.

Air Historian Mr Malcolm Barrass

The map reference for the occurrence given here was based upon testimony in the court proceedings which located the aircraft in the next-but-one field to Lower Mudd, but out of sight of the farm. In 2006 a rather cursory metal-detector scan was carried out during a site visit made in company with artist and researcher Mr Alan Jones, but nothing aircraft-related was found; nor was anecdotal evidence forthcoming. Indeed, until Mr Johnson's delving into the old newspapers stirred recollections, there had been virtually no local awareness that the incident had ever occurred.

The newspaper reporting of the day is of additional interest in showing both the public's conception of the Service in 1919, and the transitional state of the RAF itself, at that time slightly less than a year old. Indeed, as Mr Barrass pointed out, the new RAF ranks were not to be introduced until August 1919, seven months later, so that the term 'military', rather than 'RAF', is applied, while a mix of army ranks and tentative air-force variants are still used by both court officials and the serving personnel themselves: hence major, lieutenant, and 'second aircraftsman'; in fact, on one occasion the defending solicitor evidently believed he was indeed dealing with the army, while elsewhere the unrepentant Aircraftsman Second Class Ruffle was actually referred to as *Private* Ruffle.

The field at Lower Mudd Farm where the setdown and conflagration occurred: Mr Alan Jones, having carried out a 2006 metal-detector search

## De Havilland DH9A, Rollick Stone, above Torside Reservoir

**SK 08137 98602** 359m
RAF, on delivery from No.2 Northern Aircraft Repair Depot, Coal Aston (south of Sheffield); also known as Norton
17 October 1919

Crew: two, both injured:
Lieutenant A.S.M. Meydrick-Jones, RAF (the most likely identity)
Observer, presently unidentified

Little enough is known about this crash; about the identification of the individual de Havilland DH9A involved; about its crew – both of whom are said to have been injured; or of the purpose of the flight which ended when the machine crashed into the rocky shoulder below Rollick Stone, to the west of Fair Vage Clough, and high above the junction of the Torside and Woodhead Reservoirs.

Unsubstantiated enthusiast references, which is all the author found to work from, hold that this DH9A was on a delivery flight to Liverpool from No.2 Northern Aircraft Repair Depot at Norton – alternatively known as Coal Aston – near Sheffield; that it ran into low cloud, and was destroyed in the course of attempting either a setdown or a cloud-penetration.

That, apart from the October 1919 dating, is the total substance of such sources. Archive research from 2003 to 2006 turned up nothing more, and although the crash occurred long enough after the Armistice of November 1918 to be free of wartime reporting restrictions, no reference to the incident was found in contemporary newspapers.

What seems pertinent to some degree, however, is a reference in the almost invariably dependable Air Britain series of publications to another DH9A crashing at about this time. This reference has DH9A F2751 being forced-landed at Mottram, '*where it was seemingly inexplicably burnt later that night*'. But in demonstrable contravention of the facts established in the court proceedings dealing with the Mottram burning (see the previous narrative in this book), the Air Britain entry has the subsequently-burnt machine piloted by Lieutenant A.S.M. Meydrick-Jones in company with an observer. Further, it has the DH9A on delivery from No.6 Air Issue Section to No.205 Squadron; except that, at the time, No.6 Air Issue Section was at Tourignies, while No.205 Squadron, the Armistice notwithstanding, was still stationed at La Louveterie, also in Northern France. It seems highly likely, therefore, that the details of two DH9 (or the variant DH9A) crashes, occurring within a few miles of each other, in the same year, and so many years since, have become admixed.

Finally, to record a snippet which just might prove useful for future research, in the 1980s Waterman Harold Done, held to have been reputable regarding other crashes, told researcher Mr Alan Jones that the Mudd machine had been 'one of three DH9A aircraft in the flight'.

Notwithstanding the sparseness of reliable detail for this early crash, the location itself was supplied to researchers Mr John Ownsworth and Mr Jim Chatterton by Mr John Davies, in 1970 the incumbent of Railway Cottages, Woodhead. Standing outside his house Mr Davies pointed to a distant peaty patch on the heights where the researchers found an abundance of wood minutiae but also retrieved a brass petrol cap stamped by the Aeronautical Inspectorate Directorate, so verifying it as an aircraft part.

Mr Jim Chatterton, veteran researcher

A subsequent knee condition prevented Mr Ownsworth from revisiting the site, but in 1995 Mr Chatterton retraced his steps in company with Mr Alan Jones. Although easily able to relocate the relevant peaty patch, however, neither could find any trace of the crash itself.

A series of visits by the author in 2005 and 2006 proved no more successful, even though during the final one, made in company with Mr Jones, another comprehensive visual search was backed up with two metal detectors. It was concluded, therefore, that as time has characteristically altered the peat fringe, so the wood minutiae evident in 1970 has been either overlain or washed away down the slope. [The degree to which the Peakland peat fringe both retreats and advances had been dramatically shown by aerial photographs taken over the years and used by police searchers in an early-2000's attempt to find the (then) last unaccounted-for victim of the Moors murderers, Brady and Hindley.]

Since the DH9A crash site was pointed out by Mr Davies in 1970, indeed since the second visit made by Mr Chatterton in 1995, the direct route of access has been blocked to walkers by the extensive holding of the Boar Pigeon Shoot, any 'Right to Roam' legislation being officially set aside on the grounds of public safety. In 2006, then, the barbed wire fence delineating the southern boundary of the holding (running essentially east–west at SK 08134 98610

2006. Researcher Mr Alan Jones vainly searching for the minutiae still extant in 1970 above the boundary fence of the pigeon-shoot. Showing too the junction of Torside and Woodhead Reservoirs, Railway Cottages, and the old paper mill, since become the Boar Pigeon Shoot

345m) actually clipped the lower edge of the peat patch of the site, conveniently marking it.

In general, the author does not take it upon himself to patronise the walker by recommending routes to crash sites, but on this occasion, having become only too well aware of the countless, bracken-shrouded boulder masses on all the slopes below the site (outside the proscribed area – naturally!), it is suggested that the easiest route is to start from the limited parking that, in 2006, existed at Railway Cottages [SK 08245 99360], and then follow the shooting-range fence. Of course, the most straightforward way would be to obtain prior permission from the operator of the shoot to utilise the range's access tracks.

## De Havilland DH90 Dragonfly, Thornseat Delf, Bradfield Moors

SK 22972 92717 429m
Civil aircraft impressed to RAF duty
c.1941

The twin-engined, five-seater, de Havilland DH90 Dragonfly cabin biplane, the luxury version of the de Havilland Dragon Rapide, was one of many civil communications and transport types to be impressed into RAF service during the Second World War. When one of these crashed at Thornseat Delf, above Emlin Dike, on the Bradfield Moors, Corporal Charles D. 'Taffy' Austin, BEM, was a member of the attending Harpur Hill Mountain Rescue Team. Mr John Ownsworth, his confidant in the 1970s, was able to vouch for the location supplied to him by Mr Austin; a location substantiated by Mr Alwyn Haigh of West Nab Farm, Bradfield, when Mr Ownsworth contacted him in the 1980s.

In 2006 Mr Haigh reconfirmed the location from the ridge above his farm. 'I would have been about twelve,' he told the author, 'which would make it about 1941. I had no idea what type it was, for it wasn't one of the crashes we went to, but we could clearly see its tail sticking up from the top of the bank [hillside] just as if it had nose-dived in.'

The Dragonfly site indicated by Mr Haigh is on the brow of the ridge just above – but by virtue of the convex slope, unsighted from – the two shooting cabins in Small Dale; in slight contrast, Mr Austin is understood to have described seeing a tail sticking up 'from a marsh'. No trace of marsh, however, was found during visits up to 2006, nor had local residents any notion of one ever existing; accordingly, Mr Haigh's description has been taken as the definitive one. Up to publication date nothing had come to light of the Dragonfly itself, although, in view of the comparative accessibility of the area, that was hardly to wondered at.

Drawing upon his intimate local knowledge, Mr Haigh proffered, 'Some crashes, like the Margery Hill Stirling and Broomhead Wellington, weren't even guarded, the wrecks just lying there until they were eventually dragged away. But the moor itself was restricted, with sentries on the roads. For as well as training grounds, they had one of the decoy-Sheffield sites – piles of old tyres – on Broomhead,

The area of the crash of the de Havilland DH.90 Dragonfly.

Farmer Mr Alwyn Haigh, witness

which they set fire to during raids. But after Lord Haw Haw said he knew where it was, it was taken away: probably it proved too good a marker for the real Sheffield.' [Lord Haw Haw: the Nazi propagandist broadcaster and English traitor, William Joyce, American-born, Irish-nurtured, and duly hanged.]

A marked map feature at the end of the Thornseat Road, the most direct approach to the Dragonfly site, is what appears to be a substantial building; this however, had long gone by 2006. Finally, it might be of passing interest that 'Delf', as in Thornseat Delf, refers to a drain, ditch or excavation.

### Gloster Gamecock J7920, Diglea Farm, Diggle

SE 01316 01712 459m
No.43 Squadron, RAF Tangmere
19 May 1927

Pilot: unhurt:
Flying Officer Bertram William Trelawney Hare

In the course of a detached duty from their home station of RAF Tangmere, near Chichester, four Gloster Gamecocks of No.43 Squadron, having departed from RAF Sealand, near Chester, ran into a substantial amount of cloud as they approached the high ground at Standedge. Realising the danger of attempting to penetrate the build-up, the leader judiciously turned away. However, on casting his eye over the formation, preparatory to signalling his intentions, he discovered that one of his quartet, Flying Officer Bertram Hare, was no longer keeping station. At once he directed his two remaining machines to support him in an area search. But although watchers saw the three aircraft circle for some time it was clear that they found no sign of their colleague, for eventually they were seen to form into a 'Vee', and pass out of sight into the mist.

As it transpired, and as people in Diggle, just to the south of the highest ground, were already aware, Flying Officer Hare, presumably having suffered some engine malfunction, had found it necessary to set his machine down. The field he chose was a large pasture at Diglea Farm, on Boat Lane, just to the north-east of the Diggle Hotel. By mischance he undershot his approach and clipped the top of a drystone wall with his propeller, the impact flipping the machine over, leaving Flying Officer Hare suspended in his inverted cockpit. There was no fire, however, and the aviator was soon pulled clear of the wreckage having suffered little more than a good shaking.

In September 2005 Mr Jack Taylor, of Diglea, was the only person encountered who knew anything of the incident, although to collect his thoughts he went even further back to a world that had already been radically changed by 1927. 'I was born in Petrograd,' he smiled, 'where my father was installing textile looms for the Russians. But just after I was born, in 1915, with the Russian Revolution boiling up, he had to send my mother and us three children home, not leaving himself until after the trouble had erupted.' He pointed outside. 'Regarding the plane – a Gamecock, it was said – it put

Mr Jack Taylor, witness, photographed in late 2005, describes the 1927 setdown

down in what they called the Cricket Field, although its real name is Broad Meadow. It's rough now, but it was smooth enough back then, for the Wriggly Mill School played on it; although I only actually saw one match. On the day of the crash, though, a great crowd gathered around at the wall where the plane had finished up, so I haven't retained any clear impression of it. Then they cleared it away.'

Little enough, but gratifying in the extreme, sufficing, as it did, to confirm just where this relatively minor upset had occurred. Concurring with Mr Taylor, the local newspaper commented that 'hundreds of sightseers visited the scene of the accident during the evening', recording too that Flying Officer Hare had been accommodated for the night by a Mr Marsden of Dobcross, a mile or so south-west of Diggle.

By late 2006 no RAF accident report had been found regarding this incident, and nothing related to the upset was visible at the site; although by then Boat Lane had long become that section of the walkers' Standedge Trail paralleling the southern end of the Standedge rail and canal tunnels. Yet if nothing came to light regarding the technical reason which forced Flying Officer Hare to make a landing, rather than continue to hold his place with the formation; and while nothing was known of the findings of the inquiry; records do exist of Flying Officer Hare's subsequent career. Air historian Mr Malcolm Barrass, having referred to contemporary Air Force Lists, established that Flying Officer Hare had joined No.43 Squadron on 1 July 1925, subsequently becoming their pilotage [navigation] officer. He had remained with them until 30 September 1927, when he had been posted to No.11 Squadron, being promoted to flight lieutenant on 1 January 1928.

In attempting to determine which of No.43 Squadron's Gamecocks was involved, records showed that of those on the establishment both J7920 and J7904 left the squadron in 1927 'after being damaged'; both subsequently re-appearing with other units. As J7920 left in May, and the setdown occurred on 19 May, this would seem to be the particular Gamecock in question.

For completeness, and for posterity, it should be recorded that an unidentified enthusiast source held that the date was 28 March 1927, and the aircraft an Avro 504K, of No.5 Flying Training School, RAF Sealand; the aerodrome from which the flight had been operating on that leg of its progress. A parallel search of Avro 504K accident reports, however, proved as fruitless as that for the Gamecock, so that positive determination will have to await future archival research.

The 'Cricket Field', site of the precautionary landing, and the upsetting collision with the wall. Boat Lane forms the left-hand boundary of the field

## Gloster Gladiator K6133, Hermit House Farm, Gawber, near Barnsley

SE 31967 06999 118m
No. 72 Squadron, RAF Church Fenton, No.12 (Fighter) Group, Fighter Command
23 July 1937

Pilot: solo, killed:
Acting Pilot Officer Philip Hughes Crompton

On 23 July 1937, Acting Pilot Officer Philip Crompton, of No.72 Squadron, with just under 200 hours' experience, was flying one of the RAF's first-line fighters, the newly developed Gloster Gladiator, from RAF Sealand, near Chester, to RAF Church Fenton, in Yorkshire. In the course of the flight he ran into bad visibility and crashed at Hermit House Farm, Gawber, near Barnsley. Acting Pilot Officer Crompton did not survive the impact.

Witnesses reported that they had heard the aircraft circling around and flying very low. 'Almost immediately,' one would tell the coroner, 'there was a loud bang and the plane burst into flames and burnt.' Others would relate how a man in the road rushed into the field to endeavour to help but was unable to do so owing to the extreme heat; and how people from the farm rushed with buckets of water hoping to extinguish the fire, only to find their efforts unavailing as the aircraft burnt itself out.

The crash site. Photograph from Mr Wainright, vice *Times Past in Gawber* by Mr Gerald Bradbury

Examination of the wreckage by RAF investigators showed that the aircraft had impacted at high speed, from which it was concluded that the machine had hit the ground on being dived through low cloud. Particular care was taken to stress that Acting Pilot Officer Crompton had died from multiple injuries, and not from the fire.

It also emerged that, although the Officer Commanding at RAF Church Fenton, advised of deteriorating weather, had tried to stop the flight taking off from Sealand, communications had been such that the cancellation messages did not get through in time. Wireless telegraphy (morse) links had not been available, it transpired, while telephone communication had been 'exceedingly unsatisfactory'. Indeed it was determined that only a telegram had got through; and that far too tardily. Accordingly much rethinking was done regarding the local signals facilities at both Church Fenton and Sealand.

The inquiry was bound to observe, however, that this failing in communications was not the prime cause of the accident; that Acting Pilot Officer Crompton should have turned back to Sealand on encountering the bad weather. In an attempt to obviate such accidents in the future, therefore, procedures were instituted to ensure that pilots would henceforth be able to obtain both actual-weather reports and route forecasts from the Church Fenton meteorological office before they took off from Sealand. It was also to be a requirement that the Officer Commanding himself would have to authorise the departure of all such flights.

As contemporary photographs show, debris was widespread, with pieces being found up to 80 yards from the point of impact. The police were swiftly on the scene and cordoned the area off, shortly after which airmen from RAF Finningley arrived. In early 2006, with the field having been in continuous use, there was, of course, no visual evidence of the crash.

Far left: Mr John Butterfield, at the impact point, photo-matching the site from *Times Past in Gawber*

Left: in 2006 John's mother, Mrs Sandra Butterfield, at the impact point, with sheds where her farmhouse home formerly stood: demolished following mining subsidence

## Handley Page Halifax Mk.2 HR727, Blackden Edge (near the 590m trig column)

SK 13082 87632 585m impact point
SK 13039 87745 586m terminal point
No.51 Squadron, RAF Snaith (south of Selby), No.4 Group, Bomber Command
5 October 1943

Crew: seven; five killed, two survived:
Killed:
Sergeant Ernest Hatfield Fenning, RAF, pilot
Warrant Officer Class Two, Jean Gilbert Felix Fortin, Royal Canadian Air Force, navigator
Sergeant Eric George Lane, RAFVR, flight engineer, survived briefly
Sergeant Frank Squibbs, RAFVR, wireless operator
Sergeant Boris Carl Short, RAFVR, mid-upper gunner

Survived:
Sergeant Victor Garland, RAF, bomb-aimer, injured
Sergeant Jimmy Mack, RAF, air gunner, injured

The Halifax was the second of Britain's four-engined heavy bombers, entering service after the Stirling, but becoming available a year before the Lancaster. However, although it has since lived in the shadow of the Lancaster, it showed itself to be an extremely versatile aircraft, additionally serving in such roles as transport, glider-tug, maritime reconnaissance, and clandestine delivery vehicle for both the dropping and the landing of agents and supplies. When Frankfurt-bound Halifax HR727 took off from its base at RAF Snaith, near Selby, on the night of 4 October 1943, however, it was operating in its design role of heavy bomber.

Sergeant Ernest Fenning and his crew had just bombed their target when they were coned – hedged about – by searchlights and then attacked by a night fighter, their left-inner engine sustaining damage and catching fire. Just the same, after successfully evading their assailant they were able to stop the engine, extinguish the fire, and, having feathered the windmilling propeller – that is, turned its blades edge-on into the airstream to minimise the drag – to continue flight on three engines.

It was soon discovered, however, that one of their fuel tanks had been holed; after which the flight engineer began minimising the wastage by making the damaged tank the priority fuel source for the three remaining engines. Meanwhile the aircraft, now asymmetrically powered, was settled onto the pre-calculated and tactically-designed circuitous return course that would first bring the crew safely over the south of England defences, then take them north to their Yorkshire base.

The rough course having been set, the crew were then faced with a nice problem of navigation and fuel endurance. Having done his calculations, however, and having liaised with the navigator, the flight engineer was soon able to assure Sergeant Pilot Fenning that it would be four hours before they ran out of fuel; which must have been a relief to the pilot as he re-trimmed the rudder yet again to ease the strain on his right foot, for by the navigator's estimate they would have landed at Snaith long before that.

The besetting problem thereafter was to update the weather last obtained many hours before, and in particular the winds affecting them. The wireless operator, unhappily, was unable to supply this information, a failure which forced the navigator back upon his air plot, a draughtsmanlike form of navigation – some would say, esoteric – which, by its nature, grows in error the longer it runs.

Fortunately, visual fixes were obtained over Beachy Head, and again over Reading, each allowing the air plot to be restarted from a known point, and permitting the updating of both headings and estimates for RAF Snaith. At which juncture, having utilised all but 20 gallons in the damaged tank, the flight engineer began restoring the normal fuel feed to the three remaining engines.

Except that at this stage the crew's problems took a turn for the worse. For with thick cloud now widespread ahead of them, the aircraft's communications equipment failed altogether, cutting them off even from the emergency aid available through the ground stations of the 'Darky' homing organisation. Additionally, and unknown to any of them, despite the recent pinpoints furnished to the navigator, they were drifting inexorably to the left of track. What became only too apparent, however, was that the fuel gauges were suddenly seen to be reading unaccountably, and very alarmingly, low.

Now faced with the imminent, and hitherto totally unexpected, threat of running out of fuel, Sergeant Fenning decided upon letting down in a gradual descent, hoping that on breaking cloud they could pin-point themselves once more; after all, he would have reasoned, the navigator's revised heading from Reading took them well to the east of any high ground, while Snaith itself lay at very nearly sea level. Only abruptly, with some 2,000 feet still reading on its altimeter, the Halifax impacted heavily into solid ground, breaking apart and instantly killing four of the crew, Sergeant Pilot Fenning among them.

Sergeant Jimmy Mack, the rear gunner, and Sergeant Victor Garland, the bomb aimer, gathered concernedly about flight engineer Sergeant Eric Lane, finding him in a bad way. In fact, within a matter of hours Sergeant Lane was to die of internal injuries. But having tried to make him comfortable, and leaving him in the care of Sergeant Garland, whose injured ankles prevented him from walking, Sergeant Mack set out to seek aid.

Blundering his way back along the debris trail over waterlogged and hummock-hagged grasses, then down near-precipitous slopes through stygian darkness, it was only when he eventually reached a cottage in the Woodlands Valley and raised the alarm that Sergeant Mack discovered that their

Halifax had crashed above Blackden Edge, 1,600 feet up on high Derbyshire moorland, over fifteen hundred feet above, and a full thirty-five miles from, their low-lying aerodrome at Snaith.

The joint causes of the accident settled upon by the court of inquiry were lack of fuel and faulty navigation. The flight engineer was singled out for particular blame, both for miscalculating the fuel endurance and for failing to keep a check of the fuel actually being used until the state had become critical; blame upheld by the various senior commanders who declared him primarily responsible. Sergeant Pilot Fenning, for his part, was found to have made an error in captaincy in letting down through cloud when uncertain of his position, and also in guilelessly taking the flight engineer's fuel-endurance estimate on trust.

The reproofs may appear harsh, yet the reality that would have been recognised by all aircrew, including the reporting officers – many experienced in, or resting from, operational tours themselves – was that if, like most returnees of the bomber force engaged that night, the crew had brought their damaged aircraft safely back to a base – any base – there would have been acclamations all round for a job well done. As it was, avoidable errors had prevented them from doing so, and in consequence, Halifax HR727, both valuable and costly, lay a worthless wreck upon a Derbyshire peat bog; while dead amidst its wreckage lay five of its crew.

In mid-2006, Mr Maurice Cotterell, of Hayridge Farm, in the Woodlands Valley, remembered the equally grim aftermath. 'I was at Gillot Hey Farm at the time,' he recalled, 'and the plane hit the top between our place and Edale. The bodies were brought down to our little chapel.'

Another local resident with personal reminiscences of the crash was jauntily-ninety-plus Mrs Milly Heardman, of Edale, who, also in 2006, remembered that, before RAF personnel arrived, her then-fiancé, Fred, had stood guard over the wreck with a stalwart, if somewhat hidebound, policeman who had pedalled over from Hope: 'He wouldn't even allow Fred into the fuselage to shelter from the rain.' Despite the policeman's august presence, however, Mrs Heardman recalled, too, that when the second party of RAF recovery men begged a supply of hot drinks up at the site, her fiancé suggested that they bring down the sturdy vacuum flasks he had seen in the fuselage. 'Oh!' he was assured, 'they've long gone.'

But clearly, hot drinks or not, the salvage teams did not do that thorough a job, for in 2006 a considerable amount of debris still remained. Perhaps that was not so surprising, though, for as veteran ranger John Campion 'Campy' Barrows was to observe, despite retaining much of its integrity, the Halifax had nevertheless shed a considerable amount of debris in the course of a relatively lengthy slide; indeed in the 1980s Mr Alan Jones found tools dropped by the salvage parties within two hundred yards of the trig column, that is, well over one hundred yards from the initial impact point.

Above: Ranger John Campion 'Campy' Barrows. Inset, 'Campy' in July 2006

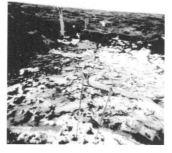

Left: the impact point of Halifax HR727 in 2006, looking north-west

Left: the terminal point, with the 590m trig column to the north-west

[Mrs Heardman, whose late husband had been a Moorland man of large repute, took the opportunity to clarify some issues with family names. 'They call me Milly', she explained, 'from my maiden surname; though my real name is Nancy. As for my husband, Fred, that's what it said over the doors of both the Edale pubs he came to own, but it was Bill, or "Bloody Bill, the bog trotter", otherwise.']

As a footnote to the cost of such bomber accidents, the Air Officer Commanding-in-Chief of Bomber Command, 1942–1945, later to become Marshal of the Royal Air Force Sir Arthur Harris, is quoted as saying that an aircrew paid for its training, and its aircraft, if lost after two successful operations having bombed its target on the third (Ollis, see bibliography). Ollis himself observes, 'A credit tick, and all for the price of seven telegrams.'

## Handley Page Halifax (probably spurious), Cartworth Moor, above Holmfirth

Reference to this crash is found in two enthusiast lists. Canvassing the farms on the plateau in September 2005, however, turned up nobody, even among the oldest and longest-term residents, who knew anything of this reputed crash; nor was anything discovered in the archives. Had the report held the aircraft to be either a Lancaster or Spitfire – the Allied types so commonly attributed to any crashed machine – then one might well be dismissive about this site. The Halifax, however, is hardly a common type to settle on; accordingly this reference is recorded with an open mind.

## Handley Page Hampden Mk.1 AE381, Cluther Rocks, Kinder Scout

SK 07793 87485 614m

No.50 Squadron, RAF Skellingthorpe (west of Lincoln), No.5 Group,
Bomber Command
21 January 1942

Crew: all killed:
Sergeant Royal George Heron, Royal Australian Air Force, pilot
Sergeant Walter Chantler Williams, Royal Australian Air Force, navigator
Sergeant William Thomas Tromans, RAF, wireless operator
Sergeant Sidney Albert Peters, RAF, wireless operator/air gunner

At its manufacturer's declared maximum speed of 254 mph (221 knots), the Hampden was the fastest bomber of its time, but once war had broken out, it proved too vulnerable in the face of enemy fighters and was quickly switched to night bombing. It did serve, just the same, as the platform for the first two Bomber Command VCs in late 1940. For Sergeant Pilot Royal Heron and his crew, however, airborne on the night of 21 January 1942, there was to be no such kudos.

Having taken off on a night cross-country exercise from RAF Skellingthorpe, near Lincoln, a satellite airfield of RAF Swinderby, they ran into blizzard conditions, became lost, and crashed into Cluther Rocks on the western rim of Kinder Scout, fifty miles off their planned course. There were no survivors.

Sergeant Heron had been trained in Canada under the Empire Air Training Scheme, and would hardly have been fully acclimatised to United Kingdom conditions; nor was his navigator, Sergeant Walter Williams, a fellow Australian, all that experienced. Offsetting this, the court of inquiry was assured that before take-off the crew had been fully briefed on radio beacons, also in obtaining such emergency in-flight navigational assistance as 'Darky'; that additionally the use of occulting – essentially, direction-indicating – searchlights had been covered. In fact, inexperience notwithstanding, on accepting that they were lost Sergeant Heron sensibly had Sergeant William Tromans, his wireless operator, contact the direction-finding (D/F) facility at Ringway (subsequently Manchester International Airport) for a series of bearings, obtained and relayed by morse code, which enabled them to be homed towards that airfield.

A popular account from 1979 (Collier/Wilkinson, *Dark Peak Wrecks*, 1, p.106) has former airman Mr Herbert Ward making reference to a radio beam. And it is possible that, with the products of both the Avro and Fairey factories to be flown off locally, to say nothing of its increasingly important paratroop commitment, Ringway might well have received a Standard Beam Approach (SBA) installation that early on. Yet even had the facility existed, it hardly seems likely that this particular crew would have had the training necessary to utilise it. One suspects, rather, that the former airman – by his own admission only getting the gist of things from wireless-operator colleagues – introduced the knowledgeable-sounding term 'beam' to add verisimilitude to his account, and that this crew, with 'neither pilot nor navigator very experienced', as the RAF investigators observed, never so much as attempted to access a radio beam.

The beam issue aside, the homing Hampden was eventually heard passing overhead Ringway; at which point Sergeant Heron would have received the customary advisory, 'Engines overhead'; a call which would have immediately relieved his crew of their uncertainties regarding their location, while at the same time requiring them to assimilate the fact that they were a full fifty miles from their intended track.

It is not known what decision Sergeant Heron made at this juncture. He could well have decided that enough was enough, and elected to land at Ringway. But that would have meant embarking upon a cloud-break procedure, or alternatively, given that SBA was indeed available, upon a full-blown beam approach, neither one a sinecure in the blizzard conditions obtaining. Then again, giving up and landing at Ringway would have meant his crew facing the bantering derision of their peers on their eventual return to base; best, surely, for Sergeant Williams, the navigator, to simply plot a revised course for Skellingthorpe, where the weather could hardly be worse, and where they would arrive, if a little late, yet with no suspicion cast that they had ever got themselves quite so totally lost.

The navigational problem facing them was straightforward enough, for as Sergeant Heron battled the gusts, Sergeant Williams would have ruled off a track from overhead Ringway to Skellingthorpe of some 100° True – eastish – at a distance of 43 nautical miles. Given a workaday cruising speed for the Hampden, and adding on the healthy south-westerly (tail) wind ahead of the blizzard, something less than twenty minutes' flying time.

Whatever on-board decision was made, however, deliberations must have taken an appreciable time, for after a while the tower, mindful of the high ground to the north and east of Ringway, and aware that the aircraft was flying at only 2,000 feet, directed it to turn about and return to the overhead; except that nothing more was heard from the Hampden.

Discounting the possibility that this had indeed been a beam-trained crew who fatally mishandled the inbound procedural turn – no anachronism there, for both procedure and terminology date back to 1938! – then two other scenarios present themselves. The first is that, having been homed to the overhead, the Hampden crew merely maintained the last-directed heading; which had to be something rather more easterly than north-east. The second, and the kindest, is that they had, in fact, reassessed their position, and had already turned onto a roughly-estimated easterly heading for Skellingthorpe, intending to refine this as they neared their base. Except that the final result of all three possibilities was the same, for with just 2,000 feet showing on their altimeter – undoubtedly then regarded as an adequate height for their original route, and which, on track for Skellingthorpe from actually overhead Ringway, would still have been safe enough! – the Kinder Massif, at 2,088 feet, and Cluther Rocks, only slightly lower, lay directly in their path.

The crew died in the intense fire caused on

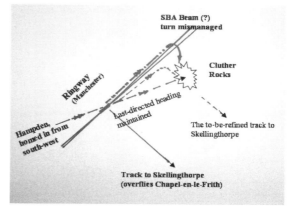

Schematic diagram of the alternative courses to disaster

impact, as rescuers who had struggled through the blizzard – including the impressed Airman Herbert Ward – were dismayed to discover. But another discovery, reported by the farmer from Hill House Farm (just east of the Bowden Bridge car park), was a widespread scatter of propaganda leaflets, a find which understandably gave rise to the belief that the aircraft had just returned from a leaflet-dropping operation. Only air-dropped leaflets have a propensity for not only plastering themselves over the aircraft employed, but secreting themselves in and about it; and these proved to be the detritus from some previous sortie.

By 2006 the crash site was marked by two rock-fringed pools of wreckage, but also a myriad molten fragments amid the boulders, just above Kinder's rim path. For many years there was a wooden *in memoriam* cross, with an inscribed metal plate; but this was smashed in 2003, the vandals making off with the plate.

Back in 1991 in contrast, and more pleasingly in sympathy with the site, aviation enthusiast Mr John Fairbrother, from Stalybridge, was 'just poking about among the rocks with a stick', as he told the present writer, when he came upon the remains of a watch engraved *'R.G. Heron, RAAF'*. After much perseverance by aviation author Mr David W. Earl, this was eventually returned to the pilot's family in Australia, undoubtedly furnishing some tangible closure to the loss they had suffered all those years before.

As an equally heartening footnote, in February 2005 a memorial plaque was placed in position by a member of the wireless operator/air gunner's family: albeit totally ignoring the traditional crew hierarchy in listing the names. But it is to be hoped that the plaque itself, being of heavy slate, proves substantial enough to escape the attentions of those who have chosen to desecrate so many memorials in the Peaklands.

2006. The Cluther Rocks crash site, looking over the rim path towards Kinder Reservoir

## Handley Page Hampden Mk.1 L4055, Holme, Round Hill

SE 09958 05715 394m
No.83 Squadron, RAF Scampton (north of Lincoln), No.5 Group, Bomber Command
23 May 1940

Crew: all killed:
Sergeant Stanley William Jenkins, pilot
Sergeant Peter Josse, observer
Aircraftman William Thornton, wireless operator
Sergeant Alan Marsh, air gunner

When war broke out in September 1939, the Handley-Page Hampden quickly ran into trouble as a day bomber, with five out of eleven reconnoitring Hampdens being shot down during just one encounter in that first month. Understandably the type was quickly transferred to night bombing; the task Sergeant Stanley Jenkins and his crew had been engaging in, when, in the pre-dawn of 23 May 1940, their Hampden bomber was flown into Round Hill, above the village of Holme.

The crew were returning from raiding the German rail network at Mönchen-Gladbach, west of Düsseldorf. Yet in that early-war period of disillusional trial and error for both the planners and the aircrews of the RAF, such a night operation must surely have aimed to mildly disrupt rather than to cause substantial damage. Certainly it had not aspired to act as a meaningful interdiction measure against the German armies even then closing in around Dunkirk. Indeed the harsh reality was that Hampden L4055 had accomplished no operational purpose whatsoever, because, unable to find a worthwhile legitimate target in Germany, Sergeant Jenkins had brought his bomb load back with him – it was, after all, very early in the war!

Compounding the situation for the crew, in the hours since the No.83 Squadron force had departed from RAF Scampton, the weather in Lincolnshire had deteriorated below operating limits; accordingly the returning bombers were diverted to RAF stations in Norfolk. Regrettably, Sergeant Jenkins did not receive the diversion message, although brief contact was made with his aircraft when it was interrogated on coasting-in over over Skegness.

Backplotting from the Holme crash site on a straight-line track to Mönchen-Gladbach – a routing not unlikely at that early stage of the war – it would seem that Sergeant Jenkins had actually passed overhead his Scampton base; only the speed of the along-track wind must have changed with the deterioration of weather because he overshot Scampton by fifty-five miles, a substantial error, although representing just twelve minutes in a one-hour-twenty-five-minute return leg.

That lapse time, however, during which the crew would have been assiduously searching for a pinpoint, took them over the high ground of the Peak District, and having let down to 1,300 feet – safe enough had they indeed been over flat, largely sea-level Lincolnshire – they flew directly into Round Hill where their bomb load exploded, the impact, the explosion, and the resulting fire, killing all four of them.

The explosion shattered the peace of sleeping Holme. Mr Derek Noble, approached in 2005, remembered that his mother sprang from her bed so hastily that she sprained her ankle; only to be disturbed again, even as she bathed the damaged member, by a thunderous knocking on the door as farmer Jack Gill of Lane Head Farm (the erstwhile Peacock Inn) arrived at a run.

'They're coming! They're coming!' he yelled, all the invasion-alarm rumours taking shape in his mind. ('Yes – *that* was my brother,' Mr John Gill, the 2005 incumbent smiled fondly.)

An Air-Raid Precautions warden, Mrs Doris Haigh, was one of those earliest on the scene, but found that nothing could be done; indeed until first light sheer discretion forced her to shelter behind a drystone wall as ammunition from the burning aircraft zipped around her.

The wreckage was left on the site for some months before being cleared, but in the interim those bombs which had not been detonated on impact were exploded by a bomb-disposal team. The crater this left was still visible in 2006, but although enough debris was detected to verify the terminal point, the crater was the only surface evidence of the crash. Apart from the wall through which the aircraft ploughed, that is, although this had long since fallen into so ruinous a state as to afford meagre shelter from the winds; let alone from exploding 0.303-inch calibre machine-gun ammunition.

2006, the Round Hill crash site, looking south-east, over the Holme Moss road, and over the drystone wall the machine ploughed through

## Handley Page Hampden Mk.1 X3154, Rushup Edge

SK 10418 82999 511m
No.106 Squadron, RAF Finningley (near Doncaster), No.5 Group, Bomber Command
21 December 1940

Crew: all killed:
Pilot Officer Michael Hubbard, pilot
Sergeant Kenneth Walsingham Boyd Perkins, pilot, acting as navigator
Sergeant Derrick Joseph Davey, wireless operator/air gunner
Sergeant David William Smith, wireless operator/air gunner

Although crews found the Hampden cramped it was generally well liked and especially by pilots, who deemed it pleasant to handle and to whom it afforded a good view. But any affection for the type had to be despite its shortcomings as an operational aircraft. Only, the best being the enemy of the good, as 'Father of the Royal Air Force' Trenchard was so fond of pointing out, it was what they had, and what they had to go to war with. And the job of No.106 Squadron was to teach crews how to do that in the Hampden.

At this period of the war, in late 1940, No.106 Squadron had two functions: that of flying operational sorties, most often mining harbours in France and Norway where the Germans were readying invasion barges; and that of training. Later, the training function was to be undertaken by specialist 'Operational Training Units'. But before this happened No.106 Squadron would have lost six of its aircraft, two of them on navigational training in the Peakland area, one of the latter being Hampden X3154.

When Pilot Officer Michael Hubbard took off in Hampden X3154 on 21 December 1940, he had flown just 23 hours on the type out of a moderate 310 hours' total flying. It is not known, however, what experience Sergeant Kenneth Perkins, a pilot, had in the role of navigator – even observers being commonly styled navigators at the time, although the aircraft category of Navigator, with its 'N' brevet, was not to be instituted until 1942. What is known is that they crashed fifty miles off their intended track.

The crew had been engaged on a night navigational exercise from RAF Finningley which had sent them into the Midlands area, surely enough, but on a route designed to avoid its high ground. Yet even though it was a clear night the aircraft was seen to approach from the Eldon Hill Quarry area to the south, and to fly without deviating into Rushup Edge, striking and bursting into flames at just 1,700 feet above sea level.

The official inquiry would castigate both Pilot Officer Hubbard and Sergeant Perkins (effectively pilot and navigator) on three counts: for being lost so far off track – and over high ground – without realising it; for flying so low; and finally, for their failure to utilise their W/T set (wireless-telegraphy: morse) which would have furnished true bearings, courses to steer, and fixes. As an outcome, jolted, perhaps, at this second such crash from his unit within three months, the squadron commander seems to have reacted rather precipitately, proposing to discontinue navigation exercises over England altogether, routing them instead over the North Sea.

Although the crew had seemed unaware of danger as they approached Rushup Edge, some early would-be rescuers formed the impression that one crew member had attempted to jump before impact, for his body was found some way short of the crash site. Others discounted this, however, pointing to the extreme steepness of the slope. Indeed in 2005 Mr Billy Dakin, who farmed the area at the time of the crash, remembered that when a rope broke during the salvage operation even a heavy engine careered all the way down to the road to hazard the salvage vehicles parked below.

By 2006 the site had long since returned to rough pasture and harboured just a few chunks of molten metal, one with a heat-exploded 0.303-calibre cartridge-case embedded. Such detail aside, the debris was very similar to that still to be found on Black Edge, near Buxton, where another No.106 Squadron Hampden, L4189, had crashed some three months earlier than X3154.

Witness Mr Billy Dakin, 2005

The crash site, overlooking Rushup Edge Farm. Inset: a heat-detonated cartridge

### Hawker Hart K4423, Peacock Lodge Farm, Wentworth

SK 40000 96700 55m
No.9 Flying Training School, RAF Thornaby (Stockton on Tees),
No.23(Training) Group, Training Command
23 July 1937

Pilot: solo, uninjured:
Flight Sergeant Raymond Middleton

On 23 July 1937, Flight Sergeant Raymond Middleton, carrying out service training in a Hawker Hart of No.9 Flying Training School, RAF Thornaby, near Stockton on Tees, ran into bad weather en route from RAF Hullavington, Wiltshire. He was on track at the time, but feeling that it was politic to set down, he made a forced landing near Peacock Lodge in Wentworth Park, Greasbrough. Flight Sergeant Middleton was unhurt when, at the end of the landing run, he struck a fence which damaged both wings of the machine.

As a point of interest for that relatively early period, the RAF Accident Report shows that at the time of the setdown Flight Sergeant Middleton had been a pilot for nine years, and that he had begun training at the then-advanced age of 24, after which he had amassed nearly 2,200 hours, 343 being on Harts.

The accident was reported in the *Sheffield Telegraph*, but by early 2006 nobody in the area could be found who remembered the incident. The fields below the farmhouse, however, seemed eminently well suited to making a forced landing.

The fields below Peacock Lodge Farm

### North American Harvard Mk.2B FT415, The Cloughs/Wool Packs, Edale

SK 08888 86897 580m impact point
SK 08895 86835 560m wreckage pool
No.22 Flying Training School, RAF Syerston (Newark), No.23 Group,
Flying Training Command
14 January 1952

Pilot: killed:
Midshipman Brian Farley, Royal Naval Air Service, pupil pilot

Of the 17,000 Harvards built during the course of the Second World War the Royal Navy acquired 236, receiving its first in 1943. Even before that, however, Naval pilots had been trained on the type in various Dominion countries under the Empire Air Training Scheme. Indeed the Harvard was still the prime advanced trainer in 1952, when pupil pilot Midshipman Brian Farley was on his wings course at RAF Syerston, near Newark, in Nottinghamshire.

On 14 January 1952, Midshipman Farley was briefed to fly a multi-legged navigational cross-country exercise from RAF Syerston which would include landing away from base at RAF Kemble, near Cirencester, Gloucestershire. But Midshipman Farley's machine did not arrive at Kemble and nothing was found of it by an air search which widely bracketed the prescribed route.

It was not until six days later that Gamekeeper Arthur Lowe discovered its wreckage high on The Cloughs, in Derbyshire's Vale of Edale, a location so far off the track set for the navigational exercise that the search had failed to cover it; the aircraft had crashed and burnt on impact, killing Midshipman Farley. In later years, as Farmer Mr Roy Cooper of Highfield Farm, Upper Booth would verify, 'Arthur would talk of finding the pilot still strapped into the cockpit. "He was totally mummified," he would say, "more like a dummy than a man."'

Mr Cooper had himself, in fact, seen the Harvard 'flying very low indeed, up the railway line towards the tunnel', but had not been called upon by the investigators. Another witness, however, told the inquiry that as the Harvard had approached the Cowburn Tunnel it had abruptly pulled up into a steep climb. This witness's impression had been that the pilot had not known that the railway entered a tunnel; that on realising it he had been forced to start a climbing turn. The tragedy being that anything other than a complete reversal of direction faced Midshipman Farley with ridges demanding a fifteen-hundred-foot zoom to clear their summits. Clearly unaware of this, the luckless student pilot opted for a moderate right turn; then ran out of space and rate-of-climb alike, and impacted just below the ridge.

The members of the inquiry discovered that Midshipman Farley, with just forty-one hours of solo experience, had not submitted his flight plan to an instructor before flight. Further, in view of the fact that he was so far off track, and heading for Manchester, they reasoned that, rather than adhering to his authorised route, he had decided to seize the opportunity of overflying Stockport, his home town. Not the first pilot to do so, and very far from the last. But most transgressors do not kill themselves, or destroy their aircraft.

By 2006 there were just a few pieces of wreckage in a pool some seventy yards below the impact point. There was also an inscribed cross, and some associated chiselling by a member of the salvage team on a flat rock nearby. Little enough to show for all the exuberance and high ambition so suddenly extinguished on that brisk January day.

The salvage team at work, courtesy of Crown Copyright, vice Mr Alan Jones

The impact site of Harvard FT415 in 2006

The debris pool, seventy yards beneath the impact point

## Miles Hawk (RAF Magister) G-AJSF, Kinderlow End, Kinder Scout

SK 07368 86688 594m
Blackpool Aero Club
29 July 1957

Pilot: killed:
Mr William Warburton Hall

The Magister trainer, developed from the Miles Hawk, and the first of the low-winged monoplane trainers in the RAF, briefly reversed contemporary trends, being constructed of wood with a ply skinning, as opposed to metal. Entering RAF service in May 1937, it was to remain on strength until 1948. This was not the end of the type's usefulness, however, for once released from the Service several were taken over by flying clubs; as was the case with the Magister which became Miles Hawk G-AJSF of the Blackpool Aero Club, and was to be destroyed on Kinderlow End on 29 July 1957.

On the day in question, aero-club member Mr William Hall, an ex-RAF wartime pilot, took off from Squires Gate, Blackpool, for the thirty-four mile flight to Manchester's Barton airfield. Although the sky was cloudy the sun was breaking through in places, and as he envisaged only just over a fifteen-minute flight at the Hawk's cruising speed, Mr. Hall did not bother formally consulting the meteorological service; even so he must surely have taken some note of the strong wind, when lining up for take-off, at the very least.

However, his Hawk was next seen by a couple who were walking near the summit of Kinder Scout. It suddenly came into view, flying just below the cloud which covered the high ground, yet even as they watched they saw it pull into a steeply banked turn which took it safely aside from Kinder proper, but as they were well aware, directly towards the cloud-covered, outlying ridge of Kinderlow End. Thereafter, just moments later, the cloud having once more shrouded the machine from their sight, they heard the sound of a heavy impact.

The crash site is nearly twenty miles beyond Mr Hall's intended destination. Therefore, unless he had decided to deviate from his declared straight-line track and do a little sightseeing – he was on a pleasure flight, after all – it has to be assumed that the strong tail wind had considerably increased his anticipated groundspeed and that cloud had unsighted him from the ground features uncharacteristically speeding by below. But if that was so, there must have been an equally strong westerly component to the wind, for the crash point is also a full eight miles off that direct-line track.

Whichever the actual case, it is clear that the high ground near Kinder Summit had suddenly appeared as Mr Hall broke cloud, certainly far closer to him than he had expected, and that he had hastily banked away; only to have the projecting spur of Kinderlow End fatally interpose itself.

But to interpose itself so 'only just' that, standing on this crash site in particular, just feet from the end of the summit ridge, the oft-experienced reflection comes to mind more poignantly still: so near – and yet …

Despite the remoteness of the crash site the Hawk was a very small machine and easy to salvage, so that in 2006 no trace seemed to have remained. Indeed all that had ever come to light for the writer, despite assiduous searches, and even when aided by attentive sheep, was a tiny fleck of yellow canvas that was blown from a peaty finger moments before it could be photographed.

The crash site of Miles Hawk G-AJSF in 2006, looking towards Kinder Reservoir

## Handley Page Heyford K6875, Broadlee Bank Tor, Edale

**SK 11092 86013** 530m
No.166 Squadron, RAF Leconfield (north of Hull), No.4 Group, Bomber Command
22 July 1937

Crew: all killed:
Sergeant Newton W. Baker, pilot
Sergeant C.P.D. McMillan, second-pilot
Sergeant Jim W. Barker, pilot (navigating)
Aircraftman First Class Harold Gray, wireless operator
Aircraftman First Class Eric McDonald
Aircraftman First Class E.J. Musker

The 1933 Handley Page Heyford was an all-metal biplane-bomber whose speedy 143 mph (124 knots) earned it the appellation 'Express'. Although withdrawn from first-line service in 1939 the type still gave good value as a crew trainer until 1941, being stable and pleasant to fly. But like all aircraft it needed airspace, and when this was denied it the results could be catastrophic; as they were for the occupants of No.166 Squadron's K6875 on 22 July 1937.

The aircraft was being operated by Sergeant Pilot Newton Baker and his crew, the six airmen having been dispatched from RAF Boscombe Down in order to carry out a night navigational exercise while returning to RAF Leconfield, their home station, near Hull. In the course of the flight, however, they became lost, strayed thirteen miles off track, and crashed into the high ground of Broadlee Bank Tor, Edale, dying to a man.

The aircraft had been seen to cross Rushup Edge and fly on up the heavily clouded Edale Valley towards Kinder at not much more than a thousand feet above the valley bottom, a perilously low altitude for that region; further, it was a cloud-darkened night with the summits in mist and with frequent rain showers cutting down visibility still more. Providentially, in view of what was to happen, it was clear that the crew had no idea that they were in any danger, for as investigator Squadron Leader Hugh Wake found, 'having interviewed the most reliable witnesses … the engines were running normally at the time of the accident. It [the aeroplane] did not circle round or fire any lights, and was not in trouble.'

On the fateful night itself the outcome had not been long delayed, for, as if inevitably, the moment came when the starboard wing clipped the shoulder of the 1,700-feet-above-sea-level Broadlee Bank Tor, yawing the Heyford fierily into the ground. Those who had watched in trepidation swiftly came together into extempore rescue parties and laboured up the zigzag path to the site, only to discover that the aircraft had smashed through and levelled fifty feet of a drystone wall, and that the crew were beyond all aid. 'The summit is in thick mist', Mr H.W. Porter of the Nag's Head Inn told the authorities on the phone, 'and the wreckage is still burning. We found two bodies near the aircraft, and four inside it, but nobody could have lived in that blaze.'

The court of inquiry had little to do. As Squadron Leader Wake had ascertained, the aircraft had shown no sign of being lost, and imaginative early newspaper reports – and subsequent accounts derived from them – notwithstanding, had neither circled, nor sought to determine its position with flares. It was clear then, that the crew had not been in the least perturbed; that quite unaware of the fact that they were thirteen miles off track and therefore flying below the level of high ground, they had simply been going about their in-flight duties, chatting idly, no doubt, while waiting out the lapse time to the next turning point, the unwonted, catastrophic impact taking them totally – and blessedly – unawares.

The accident had clearly been avoidable, and the finding of the court of inquiry was correspondingly brief: navigational error. The court further observed that the aircraft had also been flying at such an altitude that it allowed of no compensation for the sort of navigational error that had, in fact, occurred. Both cause and effect being clear cut, nothing else needed saying.

Nevertheless, shortly after the court had delivered its findings, Squadron Leader Wake wrote a personal letter to Sergeant Jim Barker's widow, Mrs Muriel Barker, a letter relied upon throughout this narrative by the courtesy of Mr James Watson, of Tunbridge Wells, a relative of Sergeant Barker. In his letter Squadron Leader Wake expressed the fellow feeling that all members of the inquiry would have felt: 'I blame no one for the accident which was due solely to the aircraft being slightly off its course and over high ground. Had it been on its course it would have been clear of the hills. This slight error could easily occur in conditions of low cloud, and, as we know well, happens frequently to all of us.' [How true!]

It is not known if Squadron Leader Wake wrote a similar letter to all the bereaved families, but one has the feeling that he singled out Mrs Barker with a special consolatory purpose. For while it has to be admitted that the disposition of crew tasks on this particular flight has not yet been positively re-established, the function of two of the three pilots on board was clear: Sergeants Baker and McMillan were operating as first and second-pilot respectively. Of the non-senior NCO crew members, Aircraftman First Class Harold Gray was the wireless operator, and it is a fair assumption that Aircraftmen First Class Eric McDonald and Musker were either gunners or mechanics. Which leaves qualified pilot Sergeant Jim Barker to be acting as navigator. And although this has to be somewhat speculative, the crew disposition would have been common knowledge on the squadron – and most certainly in married quarters – at the time. Therefore one notes the gentleness with which Squadron Leader Wake reiterates that the error was slight, and one which not only could happen to any of them, but one which 'frequently happens to all of us'.

Nor was he being unduly kind, for, in truth, thirteen miles is nothing in the context of such a night navigational flight. Nor would it have been of concern had the aircraft been south of its track, and over low ground; the tragedy being that it was to the north of track, and over the High Peakland hills. In time to come, and not a little as an outcome of such accidents, a safety-height formula would be established which would help obviate such collisions with high ground; but as the war clouds thickened, and flights over the high moorlands intensified, this beneficence to aviators still lay at a regrettably long remove.

Setting aside both responsibility and tragedy, even the composition of this early crew is of interest, for at that time aircrew categories were not as well established as they would later become, and airmen fliers were essentially ground tradesmen and only part-time fliers. Indeed even the captain, Sergeant Baker, a pilot of some eleven years' standing, had only recently returned to flying duties after five years back in his ground trade.

Regarding the crash site of the Heyford, in 2005 Mr Robert Allen Atkin, of Lady Booth Farm, Edale, described how he helped bring down the wreckage from the scene. 'At the time,' he explained, 'Maurice Oaks had a Fordson Standard tractor, but he couldn't get all the way up with it, so we took a pair of horses and dragged the wreckage down to him.'

Certainly, by 2006 all that was left was a rock-encircled pool of minor fragments just north of the wall the aircraft had crashed through before coming to rest. Nothing else, bar, perhaps, a forlorn linen poppy.

Above: looking towards Mam Tor from the terminal point, showing the drystone wall

Right: the data plate from one of the Heyford's Rolls-Royce Kestrel engines, courtesy of Mr James Watson

## Handley Page Heyford K4874, Dingle Farm, Oldham

SD 94939 08465 226m
No.102 Squadron, RAF Finningley (near Doncaster), No.3 Group, Bomber Command
12 December 1936

Occupants: four crew, three injured:
Flight Lieutenant Charles Patrick Villiers, pilot
Observer, presently unidentified, uninjured
Leading Aircraftman John Mackan, wireless operator
Leading Aircraftman Donald J.M. Keys, air gunner

On Saturday 12 December 1936, a markedly foggy day, seven Handley Page Heyford bombers of No.102 (Ceylon) Squadron, having completed a detachment to Ulster, were detailed to return in formation to their home station of RAF Finningley, near Doncaster, in Yorkshire. Prior to their departure from RAF Aldergrove (subsequently Belfast International) they were updated on the weather pattern in the mainland, where widespread fog and ice had led to chaotic conditions which were now exacerbated by snow; such a conjunction of fog and snow storms being indicative of very significant wind changes aloft.

The detachment leader, Squadron Leader Attwood, planned to return in a loose Vic formation – the Heyford being renowned for its stability in formation – initially aiming for the shortest sea crossing, of 115 miles to Barrow, then steering directly for Finningley, some 110 miles further on. Nevertheless, and particularly in view of the weather, each pilot and observer (navigator) would have produced a flight plan for their own aircraft against the not unlikely event that they became detached from the formation.

Heyfords, eminently suitable for formation flying, by courtesy of Handley Page

By all accounts, the plan went well as far as the landfall. After that, however, the weather seems to have been even worse than anticipated, and things began to go awry. The full story of the other six machines is recounted in the Central volume of this series (pp. 63-6), but some time later people on the ground at Moorside, to the north of Oldham, became aware that an aircraft – Heyford K4874, it would transpire, piloted by Flight Lieutenant Charles Villiers – was circling in the clouds above them. The engine roar reverberated downwards for a good thirty minutes, during which time it became evident that the pilot was unable to find a break in the clouds wide enough to show him the ground. It would also have indicated to the initiated, that, having become uncertain of his position, the pilot was not about to take the chance of descending blind. It is likely too, in view of the general weather pattern, that his aircraft was collecting a substantial amount of profile-spoiling ice on its lifting surfaces. The time came, therefore, when Flight Lieutenant Villiers gave the order to abandon, his three crew members taking to their parachutes in a disciplined fashion.

Deservedly, the abandonment itself went well. Just the same, Leading Aircraftman John Mackan, the wireless operator, landed on a mill roof, and having divested himself of his parachute the better to slide further down, fell through a skylight and had to be hospitalised with a badly cut hand. For his part, Flight Lieutenant Villiers alighted on the roof of a cottage; and then fell off, breaking his leg. Another crew member, Leading Aircraftman Donald J.M. Keys, also had to be hospitalised with head injuries. The observer, however, presently unidentified, came to earth safely in the middle of a football field.

Their abandoned Heyford, left to its own devices, lost height and crashed only yards from Dingle Farm, near Besom Hill Reservoir, impacting heavily and burning out. Press photographs of the burnt-out machine are graphic, but the fair prints have been disposed of and the extant copies are too blurred to usefully reproduce. Significantly, the aircraft, while only twelve miles off track, was forty miles short of Finningley when it crashed.

The whole incident represented a debacle of the first order; but it was a setback from which lessons could be learnt, and one which spurred on the development of de-icing systems on large aircraft. Nor did it adversely affect the future of Flight Lieutenant Villiers, who emerged from the Second World War as a Wing Commander.

In late 2005, rather remarkably, there was still a local awareness of the accident; accordingly Mr Walter Taylor, of Button Hole, was able to point out the site where the aircraft had impacted and burnt out. 'Dad and I', he explained, standing at the impact site only yards from the heaped stones which alone marked the erstwhile Dingle Farm, 'knew the place well, for being coal merchants we delivered here every day.' He paused, and indicated the spread of the town beyond. 'At that time there were scores upon scores of mill chimneys belching smoke in Oldham alone, so our fogs were actually smogs, even cutting out the daylight on occasion. And visibility was particularly bad that day. This large aeroplane had been circling for some time before it crashed, but with Dad knowing his way so well, he was able to run directly from Button Hole to where it had come down, despite the fog. Fortunately the plane had missed the farmhouse and piled up into this drystone wall. But it soon became clear to Dad that the crew had not been on board, and that there was nothing he could do. I believe he got some maps from it, however, and something else, although the police took that away [local belief had it that this was the aircraft's Very signal pistol]. There was little enough left of the plane, though. And eventually that was dragged away. Now even the farm's gone.'

Nor was there anything to see at the site; just the same, a public footpath passed within yards of the impact point, so that its proximity to the tumbled farm, itself a token of days gone by, might well be worth a ponder or two.

2005. Mr Walter Taylor at the (tumbled) drystone-wall impact site. The ruins of Dingle Farm are to the left, out of shot. Beyond are some of the few remaining Oldham mills

## Hawker Hind, Higher Haugh, near Greasbrough, Rotherham

SK 42057 97484 109m
Royal Auxiliary Air Force
18 January 1939

On 19 January 1939, the *Sheffield Star* carried the report of a Hawker Hind being forced down by bad weather at Stubbin, Higher Haugh, near Greasbrough, on land owned at the time by farmer Mr Hobson. The field was adequately sized, and level enough, it seemed, but having been newly sown, was soft, so that although the aircraft was undamaged, it could not be safely flown off. The *Sheffield Star* further reported that RAF personnel attended the machine, setting NCO guards at the gate to the field.

In late 2005 the farm formerly owned by Mr Hobson was still in operation, although the incumbent knew nothing of the incident. The site pictured, therefore, is the best that could be derived from the information to hand, for although many acres have been swallowed up by housing, this proposed itself as the most likely of the original Stubbin fields to be chosen for a precautionary landing. A landing, moreover, which proved successful; at least, as far as the touchdown was concerned.

The field at Stubbin

## Lockheed Hudson AM531, Deepcar, Soughley Bridge, north-east of Stocksbridge

SK 29103 98274 146m touchdown area
SK 29228 98285 138m terminal area in ravine
No.6 (Coastal) Operational Training Unit (OTU),
RAF Thornaby (south of Stockton on Tees), No.17
Group, Coastal Command
4 November 1942

Crew: three, all injured:
Flying Officer William Hampson, OTU staff pilot, superficial injury
Pilot Officer G.M.I. Tweedie, staff navigator/bomb aimer, hand injury
Flight Lieutenant Leslie Roy Aust, wireless operator/air gunner, leg injury

By November 1942, No.6 Operational Training Unit, specialising in training general-reconnaissance crews for Coastal Command, had largely replaced its Hudsons with Wellingtons. But clearly not all, for in the early evening of 4 November 1942, it was a Hudson – AM531 – that Flying Officer William Hampson was flying on a ferry leg from St Eval, in Cornwall, to Thornaby, in Yorkshire, intending to make an interim stop at Manchester's Ringway. While heading for Manchester, however, his wireless operator, Flight Lieutenant Roy Aust, found himself unable to obtain radio-navigational assistance, as a consequence of which they got lost in low cloud and poor visibility. Fortunately, and notwithstanding that it was dusk, Flying Officer Hampson saw the ground through the fog-exacerbated gloom, and having circled to set up a pattern, decided upon making a precautionary landing. In accordance with contemporary practice he made a wheels-up approach, choosing, as it happened, the plateau-like summit of one of the region's enormously extensive slag heaps. The site which had so opportunely presented itself was also well suited to the purpose; only, having touched down safely, Flying Officer Hampson's aircraft hit an obstruction, then slewed off into a deep gully, suffering so much damage in the process that it had to be scrapped. The three occupants, conversely, survived the tumble with relatively minor injuries.

The court of inquiry found that the cause of the crash lay in the failure to obtain navigational assistance by using the aircraft's wireless-telegraphy (morse) equipment. It also commented upon what it termed 'the reluctance of the pilot to ask for control assistance'; meaning that, having failed to make contact with any airfield, or direction-finding, facility, the crew should have switched to

Channel D on the high-frequency voice radio and called upon 'Darky', the emergency homing service which utilised the shortcomings of this limited-range equipment. The court laid emphasis, however, on the fact that the signals staff at the departure airfield had not supplied the crew with the correct frequencies-for-the-day for their main set, wartime signals-security practice necessitating periodic frequency changes; indeed the higher-echelon signals staff at No.17 Group considered that such dereliction of duty by their warrant officer and his corporal at St Eval merited disciplinary action.

The Form 1180 crash report summary used as source material here does not record whether this disciplinary action was ever taken, but the fact that the accident was, even in part, attributed to a failure by ground-staff personnel makes this one of very few incidents covered in this Peakland series to be so ascribed. This is a fact well worth emphasising, for although pilots are taught from their fledgling days to trust their instruments, this is never a blind faith; and yet daily experience swiftly, and very properly, teaches all aircrew to place implicit trust in the personnel on the ground, whether administrative, operations or technical.

It is interesting, too, to reflect upon the supportive comments of RAF Thornaby's station commander regarding Flying Officer Hampson's actions having become lost: 'Pilot', he wrote, 'found [a] gap in [the] fog at dusk, and rightly in the circumstances, crash landed,' the benignity standing in bright contrast to the tenor of comment in most RAF investigative reports.

In 2005 Mr Roy Ashby, of Wakefield, recalled that he had been a seven-year-old at the time. 'On this particular evening,' he said, 'I suddenly became aware of an aircraft circling very low over our house. It was already dark, but the plane seemed to be looking for somewhere to put down. Then, suddenly, it was no longer there! Only when my father, who was an ARP warden [air-raid precautions: popularly, air-raid warden], came back from his duty he told us that the circling aircraft had crashed in the vicinity, but that the fog had thickened so much that he and his associates had been unable to find it. Others had been better positioned, however, and we soon learnt that it had been a Hudson, and that it had crashed on a giant slag heap nearby, and fallen into a gully, out of sight.' He paused. 'What I couldn't quite reconcile, for years afterwards, was that within thirty-six hours there was no trace of it. Indeed, what with wartime censorship, very few people knew that a bomber had come down at all, and later many would scoff at the very idea. Luckily, in August 2001, when I finally got down to researching what had happened, I encountered Mr Bert Fisher, at that time a very sprightly, and very, very lucid, 93 years of age; and the perfect source.'

The substance of Mr Fisher's account, which follows, is given with Mr Ashby's permission.

On the evening in question, it seems, back in 1942, railwayman Mr Bert Fisher had been about his track-laying duty, but with an additional 'duration-of-hostilities' function of 'bomb-watch'; his being the responsibility for assuring the succeeding shift that the track along his assigned stretch had suffered no bomb damage during his term of duty. At just gone six on this particular evening, as he and a colleague were walking the track, with night falling ever more rapidly, an aircraft flew low overhead in the direction of Sheffield, only to return a short while later. It then circled, until finally they realised that it intended to land on the flat surface of the slag heap. Divining that the pilot could not see the various obstructions in his way – the brickworks' chimneys and a line of high-voltage-carrying pylons – nor, with the mist welling up from the River Porter to intensify the blackout, appreciate how steeply the plateau's sides fell to the river, Mr Fisher recognised how perilous a setdown must be, and frantically waved his lantern in warning. But even as he did so he heard the pilot close the throttles, and as the engine note died away, saw the aircraft sink, wheels up, onto the surface.

Missing all obstructions by a lucky fortuity, the actual touchdown on the partly levelled slag was unexceptional; only then the starboard wingtip struck a bank, slewing the aircraft and sending it backwards over the edge into the ravine. At this, having dispatched his colleague to summon help, Mr Fisher launched himself over the brink, only too well aware that the aircraft might burst into flames and explode at any moment, but discarding such considerations in his drive to succour the men trapped inside.

Mr Bert Fisher, courtesy of Mr Roy Ashby

It was a wing surface that ended his precipitous slide, and in the same instant he saw a man clambering from the wreckage – the pilot, it would transpire. The tailplane, Mr Fisher could see, was lodged in the waterwheel feeder he knew as Rat Dike, while the fuselage had broken apart so that the dinghy which had spilled out from its stowage in the main door had not only inflated, but with a fine irony, was now sitting just yards from the river locally known as the Little Don.

The pilot, although badly shocked, begged the help of this so-timely deliverer in extricating the two other crew members; and Mr Fisher proved equal to the task, finding that both men had what, at the time, appeared to be relatively serious injuries, one to his leg, the other to a hand. Settling somewhat, the pilot asked where he was, and on being told, explained that he had been aiming for Manchester's Ringway aerodrome, but that he had become lost. Surprisingly, he had not only seen Mr Fisher's warning signals, but had assimilated what they meant. Only, having throttled back and reduced to minimum speed preparatory to actually touching down, he had deemed it best not to attempt to open up and go around again at that late stage. Indeed, considering the terrain beyond the slag heap, not least the nearby Wharncliffe Crags, it seems probable that any such last-moment attempt would have been catastrophic in the extreme.

The RAF recovery team swiftly categorised the aircraft as a total write-off, so that by next day, when Mr Ashby arrived at the scene, the wreckage had already been tractored up from the depths, to be trailered away only hours later by Queen Mary low-loaders. Following which the incident was closed, and duly passed from the ken of most.

Of the Hudson's crew, both the pilot and the navigator survived the war, Flying Officer Hampson leaving the RAF as a flight lieutenant, Pilot Officer Tweedie as a squadron leader. Regarding Flight Lieutenant Leslie Aust, the wireless operator/air gunner, it is possible that he had anticipated dropping off at Manchester in order to get married. If that were the case, then it is not known whether his injury delayed the ceremony. In the course of time, however, he returned to flying duties, retrained on Liberators at St Eval, engaged in Coastal Command operations with No.224 Squadron, and was killed in action on 7 June 1944.

A point which continued to intrigue Mr Fisher was that before leaving the crash scene, Flying Officer Hampson had besought him to retrieve a black box from the wreckage, urging that he should handle it with all care, and not subject it to any further shocks. Undoubtedly this would have been the box containing the frequency-controlling – and therefore, secret – crystals for the radio/telephony (voice) set; or conceivably, set-frequency coils for any 1082/83 W/T equipment. The box, Mr Fisher remembered, was padded, and stencilled with 'Handle like eggs'; although one wonders, recalling wartime austerity, whether the time-honoured RAF stencil might not have been amended for the duration to read 'Handle like egg'.

Wreckage, evidently, had been left in a trail from the touchdown point to where the aircraft had gone over the edge, and even in the gully much was hung on the scatter of birches; all very enticing to young eyes. For Mr Ashby recalled that the local policeman had visited the school to urge the return of any souvenirs. Additionally, a Mrs Sylvia Steers, of Stockbridge, confessed to having made rings from the Perspex taken from the site, other opportunist devotees of this quaint, homespun industry being the Italian prisoners of war from the camp nearby.

In early 2006, it was clear that the crash site had undergone a major transformation. At the time of the crash the slag heap was estimated at nearly three-quarters of a mile long, and half a mile wide: ample space in which to put down a Hudson. Since then the access roads to the A616(T) had carved away much of the summit; additionally, what had then been a barren slag-soil plateau had begun to thrive, with pathways threading through trees, shrubs and brambles. Just the same, a descent of the steep sides falling down to the masonry-sided and long-defunct Rat Dike still tended towards the precipitous, as in 1942, although there were many more trees to give purchase than when Mr Fisher made his selfless descent.

The slag-heap touchdown area, with the pylons which hazarded the Hudson

And beyond the Dike, the sparkling River Porter – the little Don – as if unconscious that the sylvan slopes it threaded had sprung from nothing more than slag heaps, made a picture worthy of much more salubrious surroundings. Nothing remained, however, at least upon the surface, of the Hudson that had so ingloriously finished up its transatlantic journeyings on the spot, so very long ago.

## Lockheed Hudson (spurious), Edale Moor

**SK 10100 87800** 610m

At least one enthusiast list holds that a Lockheed Hudson came down just 'fifty yards from Anson N9853 on Edale Moor', and that the RAF 'dragged the wreckage away over the snow'. As late as mid-2006, however, nothing had been found to substantiate even this much, neither in the course of site visits, nor through archive research and discussion with rangers and veteran researchers.

## Lockheed Hudson (probably spurious), Blindstones (south of Chew Reservoir)

**SK 03800 01500**

Similar enthusiast lists to the above hold that a Hudson came down at Blindstones, and that wreckage existed for some time, but was removed. As with the previous case, by mid-2006 nothing had been found to support this contention.

## Hawker Hunter TMk.7 G-BTYL (formerly XL595), Bruston Croft Ridge, Broomhead Moor

**SK 20873 94337** 476m
Cubitt Aviation
11 June 1993

Pilot: killed:
Mr Wallace Cubitt

The Hunter being so effective a fighter, and such a joy to fly, it was hardly surprising that the RAF retained many in both operational and training roles long after the type was retired from first-line service at home. It is equally unsurprising that several of those released from the Service subsequently passed into civilian hands, among these being XL595, which, purchased by Cubitt Aviation, and re-registered as G-BTYL, fatally crashed on 11 June 1993.

Limitations imposed by the Ministry upon the operation of this aircraft by the owner, Mr Wallace Cubitt, included the stipulations that it was not to be flown above 10,000 feet or in anything but good weather. The 10,000-feet restriction reflected the fact that, only having climbed past 10,000-feet cabin altitude, does the human body begin to require a supplementary supply of oxygen. In view of the height restriction then, it hardly seems likely that Mr Cubitt would have gone to the extra expense and trouble of keeping the effectively-redundant oxygen system topped up and ready for use. Again, not being permitted to fly the Hunter above 10,000 feet meant that all its greyhound-like performance had to be gallingly leashed in. All of which meant that there were heavy, officially-imposed, restraints upon Mr Cubitt as he prepared to depart from RAF Coltishall to fly his aircraft to Preston's Warton airfield, where the fortieth anniversary of the Hunter was being celebrated.

He had been especially invited, and as Mrs Cubitt remembered, when she spoke to the author, was very keen to make the flight. However, on repairing to the met office at 0945 hours, he found that heavy build-ups of turbulent cloud precluded the filing of a clear-weather flight plan. Disappointed, Mr Cubitt kept checking periodically, until 1350 hours when he made a final visit. On being told that the weather conditions had still not improved, he nodded, and clearly dismayed, muttered, 'I'll have to think about it.' Accordingly, having thought about it, and without doubt considering that the actual conditions were such that he stood a good chance of finding gaps enough to enable him to complete the flight in the clear, he made his very proper decision, and got airborne at 1431 hours. Only not long afterwards his aircraft dived into Bruston Croft Moor at very high speed, burying itself in a deep, peaty crater.

Attempts were made at salvage and recovery, but in the end Mr Cubitt's body was left interred with his machine. In part because of this, and in the absence of any radio report regarding mechanical malfunction, determining the cause of the accident had to be somewhat speculative.

One line taken was that Mr Cubitt had found that the weather conditions did not, after all, lend themselves to a clear-weather penetration; that he had entered cloud, had been obliged to resort to flight by reference to instruments alone, and either from disorientation or from the effects of turbulence, had lost control; after which the Hunter, being such an eager machine, would have lost height with extreme rapidity. On the other hand, although Mr Cubitt had flown only eight hours in the Hunter, the investigation recorded that he had 5,600 hours overall, an experience level which speaks for his probable competence in instrument flying; except that his currency – that so-vital factor where instrument flying is concerned! – was not specified.

Another line pursued was that, in seeking to find clear weather, Mr Cubitt had climbed above the limiting 10,000 feet to an altitude where he could pick his way between the tops of build-ups. Doing so, however, would have been fraught, for by 25,000 feet, without supplementary oxygen or a pressurised cabin, and with the faculties being gradually diminished by lack of oxygen, the average person might expect to lapse into actual unconsciousness.

Of the two, it has to be said that the latter cause, loss of control due to lack of oxygen – hypoxia – seems the more likely.

In late 2006 the crater gave every appearance of remaining a prominent feature of the moor for many years to come, the surrounding area being silvered with tiny fragments of surprisingly thick-gauge metal literally torn apart by the force of the impact. All the more shame, then, that sections of perforated-steel-plate, abandoned by some, presumably latter-day, salvage party, had been left protruding from the steadily gathering water. Poignantly, in July 2006, Mrs Margaret Clancy, the then-incumbent of Garlic House Farm, remembered Mr Cubitt's wife and children being escorted to view the moor in the days following the tragedy, hopefully achieving thereby some sort of closure on their loss.

It might be politic to record that on the return from a 2006 revisit of this site a partly-corroded 75mm tank shell was found only yards from the Duke's Road track. Crash-site researcher Mr John Ownsworth, for the nonce wearing his ordnance-specialist hat, advised that it is likely to have been part of the French First World War stock utilised by the British Army during the Second World War when the moor was extensively used for military training. Just one example of the vast amount of still-lethal ordnance that can, even after all this time, hazard the unwary – or too inquisitive – walker on these moors. Indeed, what with poorly capped mine shafts and time-capsule munitions – to say nothing of grouse erupting, grenade-like, from the heather underfoot –, how desirable the designated footpaths, thronged though they might be, suddenly seem!

The Hunter crash site in 2006

75mm calibre tank shell, not far from a footpath

## Hawker Hurricanes Mk.2C PZ851, PZ765, PZ854, Tintwistle Knarr, Longdendale Valley

SK 03569 98893 376m
No.11 (Pilots) Advanced Flying Unit, RAF Calveley
(north-west of Crewe), No.21 Group, Flying Training
Command
22 February 1945

Pilots: three, all killed:
Sergeant Ernest Mary Leon Marien, Belgium Air Force, leader (PZ851)
Flight Sergeant Marcel Henry Leon Orban, Belgium Air Force (PZ765)
Sergeant John Victor Robinson, RAF (PZ854)

Thanks largely to the private-initiative forward planning of designer Sidney Camm and the Hawkers Aviation Company, the RAF found itself adequately possessed of Hurricane squadrons when the Second World War broke out. The type was extensively modified as the war progressed, yet even the older marks still gave sterling service to such training establishments as the Advanced Flying Unit at RAF Calveley, a unit which, on 22 February 1945, launched a trio of Hurricanes fated, lamentably, to add nothing to the type's illustrious history.

These three aircraft were flown by pupil pilots in the final stage of their flying training, each having something over 200 hours' flying in total and getting on for twenty on the Hurricane. Their detail that day was to carry out a formation flight, with Sergeant Ernest Marien acting as the leader.

Such a sortie would have followed the pattern of practising various close-formation evolutions, and although by 1945 close formation in 'Vic' had long been found too restrictive for operations, the grouping was essential as a discipline, and also as a method of honing flying skills to the level required for the more flexible tactical formations used on first-line squadrons. Just the same, turns in each direction in 'Vic' would be interspersed with changes into echelon and line astern; and to give relief, a follow-my-leader tail-chase or two, the only exercise which in any way approached the manoeuvres called for by combat flying.

It should also be appreciated that, when flying in close formation, each pilot formating on another will be concentrating solely on maintaining certain known alignments on that other pilot's machine; in line astern, for instance, on seeing rather more of the under surface of its wings, it might be, than of the upper surfaces, while at the same time keeping its tailplane at a given level on his own windshield. Conversely it is the formation leader's job to do the navigation; to look out for other aircraft; to ensure that fuel states and engine readings are regularly monitored; to see that gyroscopic instruments are re-stabilised against any inadvertent formation break-up which leaves individuals alone in cloud; in general, to *lead*, and above all to keep the formation clear of the ground.

After leaving RAF Calveley Sergeant Marien headed his three machines north-eastwards, passing over Manchester and into the Longdendale Valley. But there, although the weather was generally good, the prevailing wind had brought in the industrial haze from Manchester, so that Sergeant Marien suddenly found himself flying in considerably reduced visibility. Indeed, he had been airborne for just twenty minutes, when, having turned the formation onto a northerly heading, possibly intending to clear from the valley, he became aware of ground rising steeply through the haze. Realising that he had inadvertently led his section into a hillside he attempted to pull up and over; except that he had been too low, and instead he and his two hapless followers flew into the rocks at twelve hundred feet above sea level, well below the summit ridge, not bursting into flames, but disintegrating, all three pilots dying instantly from the impact.

The inquiry's deliberations did not have to be lengthy: having taken his formation into conditions of poor visibility, at far too low a level, in a valley hedged about by high terrain, the leader had to bear the blame. Certainly none could devolve upon his numbers two and three, for their only responsibility had been to tuck in close and trust to their leader. But back at base their flight commander was duly disciplined – because two of the pilots involved had failed to sign the flying order book before departure!

A threefold tragedy. But how especially grievous that two of those trainee pilots had gone to such lengths to join up with the RAF and carry on the fight, escaping from German-Occupied Belgium with all the hazards that entailed. So what a tragedy in itself, that all those high patriotic hopes should be so futilely dashed upon an English scree slope!

In 2005 Mr Bob Sie, of Doveholes, remembered the scene the day after the crash, when he was accompanying his father, a quarryman lorry driver. 'The wreckage was widespread on the slope,' he said, 'but well guarded by RAF men who were setting fire to some, and preparing to bring other stuff down.' In similar vein, in July 2006, Mr George Sherratt, formerly of Whitfield Barn Farm, Glossop, recalled, 'The day after the crash my friend, Ken Bancroft, who used to visit all the local crashes, went up there to see what was what and to get some souvenirs, only to be turned away by the police. But for ages there were what looked like three shell holes in the hillside, one above the other.'

Mr Wright Cooper, of Townend Farm, 'See them? I thought they'd take my head off!'

The most intimately involved witness, however, was Mr Wright Cooper, of Townhead Farm, Tintwistle. In July 2006, he still had good reason to remember that day. 'I was working on the slopes, spreading manure: we'd drop it off in piles, then spread it: a silly method, really; instead of spreading it straight off the wagon. Anyway, it was a very misty day, when suddenly these three Hurricanes appeared from the Broadbottom direction, and they were so low and

Section line astern formation

close that I thought they were going to take my head off. They didn't seem to be in formation, one was high, while the lowest one actually went under the power lines – there were big pylons on that side of the valley at the time, though they've been repositioned since. I knew full well what the planes were heading into, so I mouthed, "You've had it." And just an instant later I heard this triple thump through the mist.' He paused. 'I rushed up there, and found that the pilot of the lowest one was still in his seat; but clearly dead. The one immediately above him had struck in much the same way, nose first. But the highest one must have seen the hill, for he'd pulled up and was pretty well flat on the slope.' He paused again. 'What stayed with me was that although the propellers were smashed, and virtually everything else, the engines were complete, and I remember thinking how well made they must have been. There was no fire – for what it was worth.'

Seeing the three Hurricanes coming at him head on, Mr Cooper's impression had been that they were not formating; that is, not flying in the so-familiar 'Vic'. In fact, it is evident that Sergeant Marien had put his trio into 'section line astern' formation. This meant that his number two would have been sitting directly behind, and just below, Sergeant Marien's tail; that his number three would have been holding a similar station on the number two: the number two then, must have passed above the power lines by as narrow a margin as the 'lowest one', the number three, had passed below them! The two followers, accordingly, would have been intent on holding station, and would never have seen the hillside looming up. Sergeant Marien, on the other hand, was afforded just sufficient time to haul back on the stick. But not an instant more …

The crash site of Hurricanes Mk.2C PZ851, PZ765 and PZ854 in 2006, looking south-eastwards. Inset: the few scraps of debris remaining

It would seem that those airmen subsequently seen clearing the site did a good job, and that the passage of time, and more-persistent souvenir collectors, finished off the task, for there was little enough left of the three aircraft in 2006, merely a few grey scraps of metal enclosed within a circle of rocks amid a steeply sloping hillside full of tumbled boulders, heather, and dark-hued scree.

### Hawker Hurricane, Hoarstone Edge, above Dovestone Reservoir

SE 01316 01712 439m

In March 1978, when researcher Mr John Ownsworth undertook a search at this known Hurricane site, he found 'a bolt with a bearing, and some aluminium scraps'. Beyond that, nothing more is known of the background to this crash, which is recorded here for posterity.

Left: Hurricane site, Hoarstone Edge

### Hawker Hurricane (probably spurious), Ravenstone Brow, Diggle

SE 02313 07800 248m

Hurricane (probably spurious), Diggle

An enthusiast list has a Hurricane coming down at this location, but nothing else is known of the incident. In 2006 no sign of debris was seen at the site, on a steep hillside above Diggle Reservoir, and just outside the warning markers of the rifle-firing range; and not even the longest-term farming families had ever heard of an aircraft coming down here. The report, then, seems almost certainly spurious, but is included against something more tangible coming to light in the future. What the upland approach from the Running Hill Head track does compensate with, however, is a panoramic view of the whole Tame Valley.

### Bell 206B Jet Ranger Helicopter G-ODIL, William Clough, Kinder

SK 06655 89697 533m
Yorkshire Helicopters
24 October 1997

Pilot: uninjured: newspapers, both local and national, asked not to divulge the pilot's identity, chose to honour the request; neither is it Air Accident Investigation Branch policy to publish names.

Helicopters have been widely employed in conservation and restoration work in the Peak District, one of their major tasks being to airlift stone slabs from redundant mills to be laid as paving in the style of the medieval 'causey paths' over the most boot-eroded sections of the area's peaty tracks. Among other tasks have been the airlifting of fencing materials; of heather tops from lower moors for reseeding denuded moorland; and of water for fighting fires. Hiring helicopters, although expensive, has proved to make economic sense, one of the many advantages being that the moors do not suffer the damage caused by surface vehicles. Indeed the ground was barely marked when Jet Ranger G-ODIL suffered a dynamic-rollover upset – effectively, tipping itself over – in the course of lifting stone from the shoulder of Ashop Head, at the summit of Kinder's William Clough.

A first load, at an estimated weight of one thousand pounds, had been successfully lifted. However, the steep and restricted nature of the 1,750-feet-above-sea-level site had made it difficult to turn into wind, so that, without the assistance of the full wind speed, the helicopter had required its maximum torque to lift off, and then move forwards from the hover. Notwithstanding this, the second load proffered was even heavier; only then the pilot was quite unable to accomplish the transition to forward flight. He tried to set the load down again, but as a skid made contact with the ground a rolling motion was imparted and the helicopter, with its ability to respond to corrective

Jet Ranger G-ODIL, above William Clough, photograph by courtesy of Area Ranger Gordon Miller.

Fragments from G-ODIL, in 2006, held in the Ranger's office at Bowden Bridge, Hayfield

lateral control now diminished, tipped onto its side. The pilot was unhurt, but the machine sustained extensive damage and was eventually airlifted to the A57 at Doctor's Gate.

Although the aircraft was severely damaged it was not that badly fragmented and in 2006 nothing remained, certainly on the surface of the site, the few scraps of debris left behind after the clear-up operation having been taken to the Hayfield Ranger's station near Bowden Bridge, where they were still to be seen.

## Avro Lancaster BMk.1 PA411, Tintwistle Knarr (north of Glossop)

SK 03570 99254 438m
No.230 Operational Conversion Unit (OCU), RAF Lindholme (north-east of Doncaster), No.1 Group, Bomber Command
21 December 1948

Lancaster PA411

Crew: all killed:
Flight Lieutenant Thomas Iowerth Johnson, pilot, OCU instructor
Flight Sergeant Jack Sherwood Thompson, pilot
Flight Lieutenant Peter Maskell, navigator
Flight Sergeant Robert Smith, air signaller, OCU instructor
Sergeant William Love, air signaller
Flight Sergeant David Harris, flight-engineer, OCU instructor
Flight Sergeant Vincent Graham, flight-engineer

The function of the Operational Conversion Unit (The Operational *Training* Unit throughout the Second World War) was to bring together members of the respective aircrew categories and teach them to operate the machines they would fly on first-line squadrons. Some crew members might have newly gained their wings, or brevets, others might be experienced aircrew changing types or even roles. So on 20 December 1948, when Flight Lieutenant Thomas Johnson, a staff instructor on No.230 Operational Conversion Unit, located at RAF Lindholme, got airborne with his largely-pupil crew, three of them were being 'screened' in their respective specialisations by staff instructors overlooking their operation.

The sortie in hand was night-familiarisation, which suggests that the crew had already completed a fair part of the syllabus. A typical pattern for the familiarisation would have been to clear the circuit and climb away into uncluttered airspace. Once away from the airfield the trainee crew could then begin to assimilate any differences between day and night handling; not least getting used to the switches and dials as illuminated by the aircraft's lighting alone, and almost certainly learning to deal with engine failures by stopping various engines in order to familiarise all aboard with the problems posed by asymmetric flight at night.

Having sufficiently exercised each crew member in his own province, Flight Lieutenant Johnson would then have directed a return to the airfield to join the circuit and allow the trainee pilot to get to grips with night-time landings and take-offs. Since getting airborne, however, Lancaster PA411 had been perambulating around the sky as the wind and the various manoeuvres took it, the pilots concentrating on the handling and leaving the navigator to keep track of where they actually were. Except that at some stage during the homing a 'very strong radio signal' (according to the accident report) convinced the flying pilot that he was actually overhead Lindholme. At which – with the navigator offering nothing contradictory – he commenced his descent.

The pilot would have told the tower of this 'strong radio signal', but just where it emanated from is not specified. Certainly it was not from an approach beam, for the orientation of the crash site matches up with none of Lindholme's runways. It was most likely, therefore, a homing signal derived from the aircraft's direction-finding loop aerial. Unfortunately, unappreciated by any on board as they were now over thick cloud, and owing to the combination of the arbitrary patterns flown and an insidious drifting with the wind, they were nowhere near overhead Lindholme but forty miles to the west of it; and not that many feet above the Peak District highlands. So it was that their confident descent through cloud was abruptly terminated by the obdurate presence of Tintwistle Knarr, the aircraft bursting into flames on impact, disintegrating, and throwing clear some members of the crew, none of whom survived for any length of time.

Lancaster PA411 on Tintwistle Knarr, photo by courtesy of Mrs Margaret Buxton-Doyle, vice her father, Mr Harry Buxton, *Glossop Chronicle*

Tailplane, with Mr Max Webberley, editor of the *Glossop Chronicle*, courtesy of Mrs Margaret Buxton-Doyle

First on the scene were five members of the Bagshaw family of Old Road, Tintwistle, who had witnessed the explosion. Mr John Bagshaw told the *Glossop Chronicle* how he and his four sons (Jack, Basil, Neville, and Ernest) had accomplished a thirty-minute climb to the site, 'with no moon, and … no lantern', but guided by the fires. The newspaper account described in harrowing detail what the Bagshaws had found there; suffice to say here that it was evident to them that nothing could have been done for any of the crew.

Thanks to prompt alerting, not least by Councillor I. Hardy, chairman of the District Council, the rescue services arrived at the scene in good time, after which the laborious undertaking of bringing the bodies down to the Hollingworth mortuary got under way.

This loss, tragic though it was in human terms, would have been a double blow to the unit, for the captain of the aircraft, Flight Lieutenant Johnson, although not at the controls at the time of the crash, but overseeing his pupil, was a pilot whose level of experience had risen to some 1,700 hours; a level which should have equipped him with command skills enough to keep him attentive to the wider picture. Notwithstanding that in all instruction, and in flying instruction in particular, there is a fine line to be observed between stultifying the development of the student – and prospective captain, in this case – by over-monitoring, and standing too far back.

So it was that the court of inquiry had to lodge charges of poor airmanship against Flight Lieutenant Johnson; firstly, for not double-checking on the navigator's performance, and secondly, for allowing the trainee pilot to descend through cloud without having definitely established their position himself.

The only positive recommendation that could be made, retrospective perforce, was that, in the future, navigators on the unit must determine their position at fifteen-minute intervals whenever engaged in such free-ranging exercises.

Mr Wright Cooper, of Tintwistle's Townhead Farm, immediately below the Knarr, did not actually visit this crash site at the time: jaundiced it might well be (although he did not say so), after his gruesome discoveries as first arrival at both the nearby P-38 and triple-Hurricane crashes. 'I was out snaring rabbits,' he explained in 2006, 'on another part of the moor. But when I saw all the lights I guessed what must have happened. Only, even from that distance I could see other people there. So it was clear that whatever could be done, had been.' Researcher Mr Arnold Willerton, of Hyde, for his part, harboured a poignant memory of the aftermath of the tragedy. 'The day afterwards,' he remembered, likewise speaking in 2006, 'as we left Mottram, we could see the wreckage sparkling all across the face of Tintwistle Knarr.'

Over the years, however, and despite the remote location of the crash site, high above the Rhodeswood Reservoir, most of the wreckage has disappeared, much disposed of by an enterprising local scrap dealer, in part utilising, it is held, a Reliant Robin three-wheeler! Certainly in July 2006 the remains comprised just a few heavy components high in a stony gully on the south-western flank of brooding Tintwistle Knarr.

The crash site in 2006, looking towards Tintwistle Knarr summit

### Avro Lancaster BMk.10 KB993, James's Thorn, Shelf Moor

SK 07928 94781 542m
No.408 Squadron, Royal Canadian Air Force, RAF Linton-on-Ouse (north-west of York), No.6 Group, Bomber Command
18 May 1945

Crew: six, all killed:
Flying Officer Anthony Arthur Clifford, RCAF, pilot
Flying Officer David Fehrman, RCAF, bomb aimer
Pilot Officer Kenneth McIver, RCAF, flight engineer
Warrant Officer Michael Cecil Cameron, RCAF, wireless operator
Flight Sergeant Clarence Halvorson, RCAF, air gunner
Flight Sergeant Leslie Claude Hellerson, RCAF, air gunner

Having begun in 1941, Lancaster production continued throughout the Second World War with the Avro Company making full use of the capacity of other manufacturers and sub-contractors. Despite this, demand was so high that in 1942 the Victory Aircraft Company was set to producing Packard-built, Merlin-engined Lancasters in Canada, the first of 430 being received in August 1943. Having been flown over the Atlantic, these aircraft, designated Lancaster BMk.10s, were then operationally equipped and allocated to their respective squadrons. One BMk.10, however, Lancaster KB993, was to be tragically lost, not on operations, but on a local detail; and lost, moreover, just ten days after the cessation of hostilities in the European Theatre.

On the night of 18 May 1945, Flying Officer Anthony Clifford, of the Royal Canadian Air Force, was tasked to carry out a detail of circuits and local-area flying from RAF Linton-on-Ouse, near York. The squadron had just been given notice of its return to Canada so this detail would have been seen as a chance to relax and to enjoy flying in a way that had scarcely been possible since any of those on board had embarked upon aircrew training; it would also afford them a chance to see what the newly-emergent Britain really looked like at night, although the blackout restrictions had, in fact, been gradually relaxing over the past twelve months.

Because the detail was to involve only local flying, albeit at night, Flying Officer Clifford clearly did not feel it necessary to take his navigator along, for he got airborne with just five of his regular crew. Just the same, as air gunners were hardly required on a peacetime circuit detail, their presence gives credibility to the notion that the forthcoming sortie was regarded as a well-deserved pleasure flight.

Once airborne Flying Officer Clifford soon cleared the circuit, and it might be said, proceeded to stretch the meaning of 'local area' a little more than might be regarded as acceptable, for when next seen his aircraft was circling Glossop, forty-six miles to the south-west of its Yorkshire base.

It was later established that, shortly after this sighting, and while climbing in cloud, the Lancaster was flown into the shoulder of the 1,900 feet-above-sea-level James's Thorn, striking at 1,800 feet and bursting into an inferno of flames, a combination which killed most of the crew instantly, with a sole occupant, very seriously injured, surviving only briefly.

One might well wonder that Flying Officer Clifford should steer anywhere near James's Thorn, at night, and at such a low altitude. But if, as seems likely, he had become uncertain of his position – being more confused, perhaps, than aided by the unaccustomed, horizon-filling vastness of Manchester's lights – he would have been able to fix himself by craning down from left-hand orbits over Glossop. After which, being more accustomed to having a navigator at his shoulder, he would have had to estimate a line on the map north-east to Linton-on-Ouse. Yet if such a course is actually plotted, allowing for the aircraft to have rolled out from overhead Glossop, then James's Thorn does indeed lie on the track to Linton. So it must have seemed to Flying Officer Clifford that he had things well under control once more as he stopped his turn and climbed away north-eastwards. As indeed he might have had, if only he had searched out the contours as accurately as he had the track, and realised just how little distance he had in hand to climb to any sort of safety height at all.

Neither the inquiry nor senior authority were able to condone Flying Officer Clifford's action in taking his aircraft so far from base while on a specifically 'local-area' clearance. Where the surviving members of the squadron were concerned, and particularly those of Flying Officer Clifford's regular crew who had not been on board, the tragedy must have sadly dampened the anticipation of their return to Canada. Yet inexorably, the move went ahead on schedule, just a matter of days after the remains of those unfortunates of the squadron had been laboriously stretchered down to the Doctor's Gate track, and thence to a road.

By 2006 the spine of James's Thorn, high above Doctor's Gate, had become a relatively popular footpath; which made it surprising that quite so much debris remained. Especially as, in 1995, a memorial column was air-lifted into place by a Sea-King helicopter in an operation organised by two enthusiasts, identified by the *Glossop Chronicle* as Mr Paul Brook and Mr Steve Lewis, both described as gardeners for the New Mills Council. Then, on 22 May 1995, a month or so later, a ceremony was held on the site with some participants being helicoptered in. Foremost among these was Mrs Marion Clifford, the 91-year old mother of Flying Officer Clifford; she and other relatives being picturesquely supported by pipes and drums from the Clan Urquhart Highlanders. The monument, movingly, pays tribute, not only to the Lancaster crew, but to other Allied airmen who died close by, for the combined plaque indicates too the location of the American cargo aircraft, Skytrain 42-108982, which crashed just a matter of yards to the east only two months after the destruction of Lancaster KB993.

Since 1995 then, the monument, if set back somewhat non-committally from the fire-ravaged fragments of the Lancaster, faithfully overlooks the valley out of which the newly-orientated Canadian captain had begun his climb with such resurgent confidence.

Left: debris in 2006, showing the monument

## Avro Lancaster (spurious), Wessenden Head, east of Wessenden Head Reservoir

SE 16542 13643 164m

This reputed site, just yards off the A635, appears on some enthusiast lists, but is almost certainly spurious. Certainly nothing was found during an early-2006 visit, and no archive or anecdotal evidence has come to light regarding any such incident.

Lancaster site (spurious)

## De Havilland DH85 Leopard Moth AV986, Rushup Edge summit

SK 11230 83450 540m Lord's Seat
No.14 Ferry-Pilots Pool, RAF Ringway (Manchester), Air
Transport Auxiliary, RAF Maintenance Command
30 August 1941

Pilot: uninjured:
First Officer Bernard Short, Air Transport Auxiliary

The Leopard Moth was one of a series of very successful light aircraft produced by de Havillands during the later inter-war years. With the outbreak of the Second World War many were commandeered by the Services for use as communications aircraft, with several passing to the Air Transport Auxiliary fleet.

This organisation, a force of mainly civilian pilots, men and women alike, used Moths for short-distance taxi work. Of those Moths commandeered, some, belonging to rich owners, were fitted out luxuriously and had been regularly cared for, others were meagrely furnished, while some had been unashamedly neglected. But all had to be brought to a standard acceptable to the Service, a job which devolved upon such RAF maintenance units as that at Ringway, Manchester. Also impressed into service were those newly produced aircraft which had not yet been delivered by de Havillands to their prospective civilian owners.

On 30 August 1941, the task of delivering one of these brand-new Moths to an anti-aircraft liaison unit fell to First Officer Bernard Short, an Air Transport Auxiliary pilot, and a member of the pool of ferry pilots stationed at Ringway.

In good summer weather Flying Officer Short duly got airborne at 1100 hours. However, as his report to the subsequent RAF court of inquiry testified, just under fifteen minutes into the flight his Moth's engine began to cause him concern. He therefore made a precautionary landing, touching down above Edale near the very summit of the high-level spine of Rushup Edge, where the tumulus of Lord's Seat stands at 1,800 feet above sea level.

Carrying out the repair to the engine evidently took Flying Officer Short only a matter of minutes, for by 1130 hours, again according to his report, he was ready to depart once more. The inquiry does not seem to have established whether he had to stop his suspect engine – and subsequently manage an unaided propeller-swing to restart. But getting airborne again clearly posed more problems than he had anticipated. For at a relatively late stage in his take-off run a gust upset his Moth's equilibrium, a wing dropped, the tail struck a drystone wall, and as the machine bounced (as Moths were so wont to do), a wing broke off and the undercarriage collapsed, although First Officer Short sustained no injuries.

Despite being badly damaged the Moth was deemed repairable at depot, and so it was dismantled and ignominiously taken back to Ringway by road. No such ignominy, however, settled upon First Officer Short, who received only mild censure from the RAF court of inquiry which merely criticised his technique in having held the machine down too long on take-off. Accordingly the aircraft was repaired and First Officer Short resumed his ferrying duties.

This was an incident then, which unhappily became an accident, but in which nobody was hurt, and in which even the aircraft was only temporarily lost to the Service. Indeed as a flight-safety occurrence it was so everyday that after the court of inquiry's findings had been approved by higher authority nothing more was heard of it. And very properly so.

Yet what an intriguing incident, especially one to have so untimely become an accident! And what questions any contemplation of the site conjures up! Certainly for many walkers the exposed aspect of Rushup Edge must be reminiscent of the Helvellyn summit ridge in Lakeland where, in 1926, an aviator achieved some degree of fame – or notoriety – by landing on the stony ridge and then successfully taking off again; a feat which someone evidently deemed worthy of commemorating by a stone tablet.

But then the two cases are quite different. The Helvellyn aviator purposefully set out to perform a stunt. First Officer Short's case, conversely, was that his engine was playing up, when good airmanship dictated that it was politic to alight and sort things out.

It is not that easy, however, to follow his reasoning much further; even allowing for the fact that with some 1,100 hours' flying, 300 of which had been on Moths, First Officer Short was considerably more experienced than most pilots of his era; and always discounting, as a possibly anachronistic reflection, that eleven hundred hours has long been viewed as one of those recognised danger points at which any young pilot might begin to exhibit signs of overconfidence. For although sixty years and more have passed, what essential change can there have been in those areas of Rushup Edge where even alighting would be tenable? Let alone getting airborne once again. Indeed the walker might speculate upon which line it were best to take if envisaging accelerating, say, the family car, up to some 40 mph; a speed comparable to the Moth's lift-off requirement.

In contrast, below the ridge on either side, lie green, flat, and uncluttered pastures, each close to a farmhouse or a hamlet, and all lying amid a network of accessing roads and tracks; on the Edale side, even a railway! But First Officer Short's engine was playing up, and he had to take action.

And yet there is a long-held tenet in aviation that the first emergency action is to sit on one's hands; supplementing this being the entreaty, always so devoutly uttered post-incident, '*God! grant me again that last five minutes*'. Minutes which were a mere twitch of the stick away for First Officer Short, when easing to either side would have allowed him to take advantage of any of a myriad eminently suitable locations; except that he chose instead to settle upon the rough, restricted, remote, and rock-hedged ridge of Rushup Edge … But then, what an exploit to regale them with around the bar! Had it not gone so embarrassingly pear-shaped.

To the crash-site enthusiast the summit area can never have held much prospect of souvenirs, for the various components shed during First Officer Short's abortive attempt at a rough-field take-off notwithstanding, the Moth was a very simply constructed aircraft. Additionally the area, while difficult of vehicular access, is relatively close to roads. Certainly several hours of assiduous metal-detecting in early 2006, carried out with the aim of positively determining the terminal impact site, and probing,

The touchdown area on Rushup Edge, looking westerly, from the Lord's Seat tumulus

therefore, both sides of every wall-site on the plateau – walls both extant and defunct – produced nothing even remotely aircraft-related.

First Officer Short's career with the Air Transport Auxiliary, as indicated earlier, progressed satisfactorily after his Rushup Edge mishap. Of course, ATA personnel, by the nature of their jobs, flew a staggering variety of types, so that their log books reflect that in a single day each might have flown light trainers, twin-engined high-performance fighter-bombers, heavy four-engined bombers, and various single-seat fighters. And not only British machines, for as the war progressed so American types proliferated. Further, on leaving the factories many of these aircraft lacked all manner of equipment essential for operational flying, the rest being installed only once the machine had been accepted into service. So it was that ATA pilots, often flying previously unseen, multi-engined, and nominally multi-crewed, machines single-handedly, were also deprived of radio communications and navigational equipment.

Naturally this imposed limitations on the weather conditions under which ferry flights could be tasked. Accordingly regulations demanded that if a flight encountered hazardous meteorological conditions which could not be circumvented, then it should be aborted, the ferry pilot either returning to base or diverting to a suitable airfield to await an acceptable clearance: aircraft were very valuable commodities in all senses of the word.

Such restrictive regulations, of course, also recognised the fact that ferry pilots could never become thoroughly conversant with any specific aircraft. Additionally, with the UK being so small, the average ferry flight was of the order of minutes, rather than as much as an hour. It is not surprising, therefore, that by early 1944, some two and a half years after his Rushup Edge misadventure, the erstwhile First Officer, now Flight Captain, Bernard Short, and despite the busiest-ever flying pattern – wide but essentially shallow – had barely advanced his total to two thousand hours.

And it was with experience of that order behind him that on 24 January 1944, Flight Captain Short and his ATA colleague, Senior Flight Engineer Arthur Bird, were tasked to ferry Halifax heavy-bomber JP182 from RAF Kinloss, on the Moray Firth, near Inverness, on the 425-mile flight down to RAF Kemble, near Cirencester, in Wiltshire.

The route-forecast reflected weather typical of the season, but possibly this deteriorated more rapidly than was anticipated. Certainly by the time Flight Captain Short was over the Lake District, about halfway into the flight, he seems to have become uncertain of his position. Only, in the course of attempting to clear cloud and fix himself, he flew westwards up the cul-de-sac valley of Coledale, near Keswick, and in blizzard conditions impacted below the summit of what is variously known as Eel Crag or Crag Hill. Both men died instantly, the machine exploding and burning and sending forth a wind-ripped pyre to briefly flare amid the snow flurries as if in testimony to the passing of this ill-starred but so evidently zealous pilot.

Coledale, showing the cloud-shrouded summit of Crag Hill

### Halifax Mk.2 JP182, Lake District

NY 19303 20390 817m impact point
NY 19563 20584 563m sheepfold debris
NY 19548 20618 547m debris in hollows

Left: 2006. Pooled debris from Halifax JP182 below Scott Crag

Right: mist-shrouded Coledale from the impact point; with debris

### Westland Lysander Mk.3A V9403, Slate Pit Moss, north of Chew Reservoir

SE 04081 03254 520m
No.6 Anti-Aircraft Co-operation Unit, RAF Ringway
(Manchester), No.70 Group, RAF Army Co-operation
Command
19 August 1941

Crew: both injured, one mortally:
Pilot Officer Frederick W. Hoddinott, pilot, injured
Leading Aircraftman Alan Masheder Chadwick, wireless operator, died of his injuries

The Westland Lysander was a rugged workhorse of a machine, slow-flying, and, being capable of short landings and take-offs, often employed in clandestine operations in occupied Europe. However, it had been designed for, and was mainly engaged in, Army co-operation tasks, which, carried out by units of the RAF's Army Co-operation Command, included exercising the personnel of the ground-defence organisation; the crews manning guns, searchlights, sound-locators, listening posts, some radar installations, and even barrage-balloon sites.

So it was in furtherance of this task that, in the early hours of 19 August 1941, Pilot Officer

Frederick Hoddinott and his wireless operator, Leading Aircraftman Alan Chadwick, got airborne from Manchester's Ringway airfield. They were to fly a two-hour detail during which they were to liaise with the guns and searchlights covering the Rhyl sector. However, Pilot Officer Hoddinott was not permitted to fly directly to Rhyl, but was initially obliged to fly a south-westerly dog-leg around the Liverpool anti-aircraft balloon and gun defences; this would have taken him all the way down to Chester, before allowing him to turn for Rhyl. His compass-setting procedure after take-off, on the other hand, would have been much more a matter of routine.

First, he would have set his magnetic compass to the pre-calculated heading for the initial leg, then turned the aircraft onto that course. But magnetic compasses are prone to swinging about when aircraft bump around the sky, and so he would have turned to his complementary Directional-Gyro Indicator (DG), a 1930s-designed gyroscopically stabilised heading-indicator that, among its other advantages over the compass, would not hunt about in turbulence. Having matched this DG to the compass he would thereafter use it as his primary heading reference, resetting it periodically, and every time he settled onto any new leg.

It is a fundamental precept in aviation that the flier should always trust his instruments over his spatial instincts; but this is not to advocate a slavishly blind trust, for few aircraft instruments are as trustworthy as they might be, so that while directional aids harbour a multitude of inherent errors, others can only too easily be fed in by the user.

Any walkers will appreciate this, who, having set the required heading on their Silva-style compass, have then found themselves momentarily lining up the white end of the needle (instead of the red end) with the broad, red North arrow; so that had they not turned themselves about they would have been travelling in the opposite direction to that intended. Accordingly, because it was just as easy for an aviator to do this, the mnemonic adopted was, 'Red on Red, full ahead': align the red needle with the red datum, and you were going in the correct direction. But inadvertently align the blue needle (white on the Silva) with the red datum, and you were off in the reverse direction: 'Red on Blue, this you'll rue'.

But compass errors aside it was also possible to mis-set the directional-gyro, either by not ensuring that its gyroscope was fully stabilised before making the adjustment, or by failing to synchronise it correctly; no sinecure given indifferent cockpit lighting.

An incidental way of checking on such gross errors was to get a directional bearing by wireless-telegraphy soon after take-off, which, although primarily aimed at proving the communications set, also proved the track being flown. In this instance, however, it seems probable that the machine's radio had been unserviceable from the outset. As it was, Pilot Officer Hoddinott duly set off on his initial leg, finding himself in cloud in a very short time. Except that, some fifteen minutes along the leg, coming up to his first turn, he discovered a discrepancy between DG and compass of some one hundred and eighty degrees! Which meant that he might well have been flying on a reciprocal course, heading north-easterly, instead of south-westerly.

This would have been a mind-numbing revelation, and one very difficult to readily assimilate, especially at night, in cloud, with a radio that was providing no assistance, and when flying at low level. For his altimeter was reading only 2,500 feet, and somewhere close by, out there in the cloud-filled night, the balloon-barrage defences – don't even think about the guns! – would be straining skywards on their cables, their sole purpose being to deter just such low-flying intruders as he had now become.

Hastily, Pilot Officer Hoddinott reassessed the situation, and (incorrectly) decided that his aircraft's directional-gyro must have been as faulty as its radio seemed to be. Reverting to his magnetic compass he turned south, and after a while, reasoning that he was now approaching the Cheshire Plain – an area, in general, less than three hundred feet above sea level – he began to descend in order to break clear of cloud;. only, just as his altimeter passed through 1,900 feet, so his aircraft abruptly flew into the ground. Both he and his wireless operator lost consciousness, eventually coming around to find themselves providentially alive, albeit injured to some degree, but helplessly trapped amidst the wreckage.

As dawn broke Pilot Officer Hoddinott realised that he was in a truly unenviable position. Instead of the lowland Cheshire Plain, he had clearly come down on some high-level moor. Further, if he

The former Pilot Officer Fred Hoddinott, at a book launch in the 1980s. Courtesy of Ranger Peter Jackson

had indeed flown the wrong way, then a search of the area he actually found himself in was most unlikely; and in the event, although he had crashed only seventeen miles north-east of Ringway, few search aircraft came that way. True, one circled tantalisingly over what Pilot Officer Hoddinott would later learn was the wreckage of a Swordfish which had crashed three miles to the east some eighteen months before [Swordfish P4223, p. 135 this volume]. But although this search aircraft never suspected their presence its very concentration on the Swordfish debris further diverted the search effort; always a hazard when wreckage has been left exposed. Indeed the two men aboard the Lysander were to remain trapped throughout a second night before a Water Board worker at nearby Chew Reservoir happened to notice an unusual protuberance and set out across what, in 2006, was still a pathless and largely trackless moor, to investigate.

In the interim the situation of the survivors had been harrowing. With the initial shock of the crash receding, each had become conscious of his plight. For Pilot Officer Hoddinott, who could release only one leg from beneath the engine, thirst had outweighed his pain. But wireless operator Leading Aircraftman Alan Chadwick, with only debris in his field of vision, and with both legs painfully trapped, had quickly become despondent, his morale plummeting. But worse was to befall him. For although his injuries had not been that serious in themselves, the sudden cessation of pressure when the wreckage was finally lifted from him left him open to the since well-documented 'crush syndrome', in which tissue damage and the release of toxins combine to produce a potentially fatal condition. In fact, Leading Aircraftman Alan Chadwick was to linger for five more days.

During his time on the moor Pilot Officer Hoddinott had been afforded plenty of time to reflect on what had gone wrong, except that he had now (equally erroneously) settled the blame upon a faulty altimeter. He was well aware that a pressure altimeter, like a compass, suffers from inherent errors. As it was, it would take a map to persuade Pilot Officer Hoddinott that Slate Pit Moss was indeed at 1,700 feet above sea level. Despite which, when interviewed forty years later by author Ron Collier, he still persisted in believing that his instruments – whether compass, DG, or altimeter – had been faulty.

Pilot Officer Hoddinott's flight on a near-reciprocal heading has been likened, by some, to that of America's 'Wrong-way' Corrigan, who crossed the Atlantic in 1938 having ostensibly flown the reciprocal; but that had simply been Corrigan's ploy after being refused permission to make the flight; the point being that the error was so commonplace that the outraged authorities, with public adulation against them, were able to save face and accept his claim. In reality, the Lysander epic had more in common with the British Hermes airliner which, in 1951, flew 900 miles astray over the Sahara and crashed, out of fuel, after its compass-system had been incorrectly set by a crew member.

In the Lysander's case the inquiry was to note that, although relatively experienced, having logged some one thousand hours' flying, Pilot Officer Hoddinott had flown only two hours at night on Lysanders, when familiarity with such 'switchery' as the setting of compasses and DGs was critical. It therefore found the cause to have been twofold. Firstly, that the aircraft had become airborne without the serviceability of its wireless being established; additionally noting that having no W/T would have significantly reduced its usefulness once at Rhyl. Secondly, and most significantly, that the aircraft had been flown on a reciprocal course.

Pilot Officer Hoddinott must have grieved a great deal during the many months of his convalescence, yet among the most poignant memories of the ordeal that he was to carry into his future flying would have been the plaintive reproach from his erstwhile crewman, the pain-racked voice coming forwards to him from the wreckage at his rear, 'But I thought you were a good pilot.'

In 2006 the crash site, although located on a particularly featureless stretch of moor, was marked by what must

Lysander V9403, in 2006; the sparse, inevitably evanescent remains.

inevitably be merely evanescent traces of the Lysander. Notwithstanding which, a sprinkling of wooden splinters and some metal oddments had managed to survive, thinly splayed though they were across a patch of grass-starved peat.

## Westland Lysander P9119, Festival Road, Wath Upon Dearne, near Rotherham

SE 43577 00297 58m
No.4 Squadron, RAF Clifton (York), No.71 Group, Army Co-operation Command
16 January 1941

Pilot: solo, uninjured:
Pilot Officer Algernon Christopher Chaldecott, formerly Second Lieutenant, Royal Engineers (TA)

After the outbreak of war in September 1939, No.4 Squadron, with its cantilever-winged Lysander army co-operation monoplanes, was deployed to France as part of the British Expeditionary Force. Operated as fighting machines in their own right, however, the Lysanders were totally outclassed by the enemy fighters, so that in a thirteen-day period in May 1940 the squadron lost eleven of its aircraft. [The RAF as a whole lost 118 of the 174 Lysanders sent across the Channel!] Back in England, with invasion imminent, the squadron was set to coastal-patrol duties, so that it was not until the end of 1940, as the perceived threat receded, that they were returned to full-time army co-operation tasks and target-tug duties.

The Lysander may have been outclassed by the German first-line fighters, but among its design characteristics was a short-field landing-and-take-off capability enhanced by a sophisticated system of automatically-operating slots and variable-camber flaps: it could be airborne well within 100 yards and could land in a far shorter space. Only to perform in that way demanded a carefully organised approach.

No.4 Squadron's motto was *futurem videre* – to see into the future – but on 16 January 1941 it would not have needed a crystal ball to save the day for the squadron's Pilot Officer Algernon Chaldecott, just rather more attention to what he was about. Or so his commanding officer would record.

Until 7 March 1940, Pilot Officer Chaldecott had been a second lieutenant in the Royal Engineers (Territorial Army). Since transferring to the Royal Air Force, however, he had flown just under three hundred flying hours, of which over two hundred had been on Lysanders. On the day in question, he was sent to search for an aircraft which had gone missing between Grantham and Northampton, but at some stage on the seventy-mile return flight, he ran into bad weather. Unable to re-establish his position, he finally accepted that he was lost, and with fuel running short, decided that it would be politic to make a precautionary landing.

By good fortune he saw an open area immediately ahead of him, the snow-covered playing fields, as it happened, of the Wath Upon Dearne Grammar School, near Rotherham; and some thirty miles to the south-west of his home station. In its entirety the space was more than adequate for landing a Lysander, but Pilot Officer Chaldecott failed to appreciate that he had elected to make his approach onto a downslope, the result being that, as he held off, feeling for the ground, so it was falling away beneath him. Touching down, as a further consequence, far too far into the field, and presumably having left too little space in which to safely go around again, he could do nothing but rudder the machine towards a gap in a wall he found running across his front. In the event, he was late in being able to employ his pneumatically-powered wheelbrakes, so that with the aircraft's speed barely diminished, one wing struck the edge of the gap, and then a tree, slewing the Lysander to a violent halt.

Shaken, Pilot Officer Chaldecott shucked off his harness, and clambered the fourteen feet down from his cockpit to the ground. Then, shocked, but otherwise unhurt, he left the lopsided wreck where it lay and made his way towards some nearby houses with the evident aim of seeking succour, seemingly unaware of the rapidly nearing figures running towards him.

In 2006 Mr Maurice Hobson, of Rawmarsh, recalled the setdown as it had appeared to him as a schoolboy back in 1941. 'We'd walked from school', he explained, 'up what is now Festival Road, but then was just a path past the Grammar School playing fields, and were some way along Sandygate when we heard the sound of this plane's engine. We looked back, and saw it touching down. The playing fields were the biggest space around, but they clearly weren't long enough, for the plane ran on into a paling fence, and then into a stone wall. But the pilot seemed to have headed for a gap where people had climbed it, for the plane's nose went through the gap. One wing struck the wall, though, and then a tree after that, and broke off. Of course, we ran back at once. And I have this mental picture of a man suddenly appearing from the caretaker's house beside the Grammar School. He'd clearly been shaving, for he was in his white vest – and army trousers, I seem to recall – and had a face full of lather. Just the same, he beat us to the spot. There was no explosion, and no fire, but I can still conjure up the smell of electrical burning from the wires where the wing had been torn off.'

Mr Geoff Anderson, witness

Mr Geoff Anderson, still resident in Wath Upon Dearne in 2006, was rather closer to the action, it transpired, and accomplished in the wartime art of aircraft recognition. 'It was a Lysander,' he said at once. Then paused. 'All these years', he said wonderingly, 'and nobody's ever asked me about it before! Yet when I've mentioned an aeroplane putting down hereabouts people've looked at me gone out.'

He thought back. 'I would have been eleven, so it would have been in 1941. Being wartime we used to go home at dinner time so on this occasion we looked around to see this Lysander descending into the playing fields. He touched down well into the field, but then seemed to keep going, bouncing quite a bit, with his wings rocking. He didn't seem able to stop. Then he went through a thin wooden fence – and yes, there was a wall, of course, and a gap in it: I'd forgotten that! Then one wing caught this tree – the only tree around – and the plane slewed about and stopped. The pilot got out, I remember, and couldn't have been more than shaken, for we saw him making his own way over to the houses in Fitzwilliam Street where he was taken in at Frank Wade, the builder's, and looked after.' Mr Anderson reflected again. 'I never saw any guards, so I suppose, after a while, we just carried on home for dinner.'

Mrs Sheila Thompson, destined to become a teacher at the Grammar School, in 2006 a local artist and still living in what had been Mr Frank Wade's house, also recalled the crash. 'I remember', she smiled, 'that both Cliff and Frank Wade ran out into what was then just a cornfield, thinking they'd be grappling with a German.'

The RAF court of inquiry was not impressed by Pilot Officer Chaldecott's handling of the incident. In detail, his commanding officer castigated him for 'carelessness, for failing to watch the weather, for not having obtained a met forecast, and for having failed to keep a navigational log'; but, above all, for not appreciating that he had chosen to land his valuable machine downslope on a snow-covered surface. The Air Officer Commanding No.71 Group, however, no doubt knowing that the ex-soldier would have been feeling badly enough even before being 'torn off a strip' by his squadron commander (to say nothing of the ribbing his fellow pilots would have subjected their pet 'brown-job' to), decreed that the matter need be taken no further.

Mr Hobson brought the story up to date. 'In 1951 – Festival of Britain year – Festival Road was built along what had been just a footpath,' he said. 'Then, in about 2005 the Grammar School was demolished. But even by then the Wath Comprehensive School had been built across the space that was available for his landing run.'

The task of identifying the particular Pilot Officer Chaldecott concerned, and then tracing his future career, was eased by information independently furnished by air historian Mr Malcolm Barrass and author Mr David W. Earl from their *Air Force List* and *London Gazette* sources. From which it seems that, after the crash at Wath, Pilot Officer Algernon Chaldecott then applied himself to the task in a way that could only have pleased his commanding officer, for with this shaky downhill start behind him, things took what was to be a prolonged upturn.

Second Lieutenant Chaldecott had been commissioned into the Royal Engineers on 29 November

1938, and on 7 March 1940, as recorded earlier, he had been accepted into the RAF as a duration-of-hostilities acting pilot officer (on probation). Now, just two months after the crash, he was promoted to flying officer, being gazetted on 7 March 1941. Another promotion followed, but the second braid of his flight lieutenancy could hardly have lost its rawness before the two were eased apart by the thin ring lifting him to the senior-officer status of squadron leader; for just a year later, on 7 March 1942, he was promoted yet again, to wing commander – if only the temporary rank, and almost certainly without a regular wing commander's pay! No mean progression, just the same, for an erstwhile pongo! Yet even better was to come, for, surviving as he had proved he could on the playing fields of Wath, he flew on, and with equal success, survived the war itself.

Mr Maurice Hobson indicates the line of the wall struck by the aircraft; the railings parallel the former path, long-since Festival Road.

## Miles Magister Mk.1 N5418, Upper House Farm, Cowms Moor, Woodlands Valley

SK 12499 90076 401m
No.145 Squadron, RAF Catterick (Yorkshire), No.11 Group, Fighter Command
28 July 1941

Pilot: solo, uninjured:
Sergeant Pilot W.J. Johnson

On 28 July 1941, in the course of Spitfire-equipped No.145 Squadron's move from RAF Merston, near Chichester, in Sussex, to RAF Catterick, in Yorkshire, Sergeant W.J. Johnson was detailed to ferry the squadron's Magister runabout. On route he ran into bad weather while transiting a valley bordered by high terrain and elected to carry out a precautionary landing. The touchdown was made on Cowms Moor, in the Woodlands Valley, in a field belonging to Upper House Farm, but the aircraft was damaged when a wheel ran into a hole on rough ground. Sergeant Pilot Johnson was not held to blame, however, and no disciplinary action was taken.

   In late 2005 the valley was canvassed for information, but nobody was found who knew of the incident, not even Mr Maurice Cotterell, of Hayridge Farm, resident in the wartime years at the adjacent Gillott Hey Farm; nor, as might be expected, was any trace to be found at the site.

Magister N5418; the touchdown area on Cowms Moor

## Miles Master Mk.3 W8474, Warhill, Mottram in Longdendale

SJ 99773 95325 221m
No.16 (Polish) Service Flying Training School, RAF Newton (Nottingham),
No.21 Group, Flying Training Command
19 July 1942

Pilot: killed:
Pupil Pilot Leading Aircraftman Józef Gawkowski, Polish Air Force under RAF Command

The Miles Master was an advanced trainer whose performance and handling characteristics were such that pilots passing from it to first-line types like the Spitfire had little trouble with the transition. Undoubtedly it gave a sense of unbounded freedom to those pupils newly unleashed from the lower-performance Tiger Moths. But it also tested their powers of self-discipline.

   As a pupil pilot stationed at the Polish Flying Training School at RAF Newton, near Nottingham, Leading Aircraftman Józef Gawkowski was briefed for general training in the local area. Some time later, however, his aircraft was seen flying near Glossop, over fifty miles from base, and at best a very liberal interpretation of 'local'. But it was also flying at such a level that the pilot could be seen waving from the cockpit. Next it was to be flown even lower along the Longdendale Valley, skimming the reservoirs and circling points of interest as it went, until eventually, no doubt as the pilot spotted the singular hilltop church at Mottram, it turned that way.

One of those to watch the Master as it approached was thirteen-year-old Arnold Willerton, a keen aircraft spotter – and dedicated bicycle visitor to recent crash sites! – whose attention had already been drawn to Longdendale by a twin-engined aircraft performing evolutions near Tintwistle. When the blunt-nosed Master appeared he recognised it for a radial-engined Mark Three, and watched as it proceeded to set up a right-hand pattern, consistently circling the Mottram church and village at a very low level.

On occasion, as he remembered in 2005, it would break off and head towards Broadbottom and Hague, but would then come back and resume its circling. Only on its final return, having embarked on its third circuit, he saw it rear up. 'I have the picture of it in my mind to this day,' he said. 'I got the impression that the pilot had suddenly seen the power cables, and the pylons, and pulled up, only to stall. For a moment later the aircraft flipped onto its nose, and then began a flat turn. Until suddenly it disappeared, when there was a bang, and then a great plume of black smoke.'

Clearly Leading Aircraftman Gawkowski, his attention on a hoped-for audience, had inadvertently descended in his turns, and having then realised how close the pylons were, had too harshly pulled up; straight into a 'g' stall, from which he had flicked. But having left himself no airspace in which to recover, his machine had fallen away into an incipient spin, bringing down a live cable with its wingtip as it plunged into a deep gully. Impacting above the stream bed it had then exploded, killing Leading Aircraftman Gawkowski, and burning itself out. By an immense stroke of good fortune, however, the crashing aircraft had caused no casualties among the villagers, and with the gully containing the explosion, no village property was damaged.

The court of inquiry was unequivocal in its condemnation of this flagrant breach of discipline. It found that Leading Aircraftman Gawkowski had disobeyed his orders in proceeding beyond the bounds of the designated local flying area – bounds which he would have been well aware of – and again in flouting all the rules forbidding unauthorised low flying; that while banking steeply he had 'stalled his aircraft which went into a spin and crashed to the ground'. As the Air Officer Commanding commented, rather wearily, one imagines, 'Yet another case of the pilot disobeying his instructions'. What went without saying was that one very valuable advanced trainer, and one even more valuable, potentially operational, pilot had been senselessly lost to the war effort. In 2006, Mrs Zosia Martin, formerly Leading Aircraftwoman

Leading Aircraftwoman
Zosia Kowalczyk

The shale lip of the gully crash site, looking towards Mottram's church tower

Mr Alan Jones and the fruit of his thirty-year campaign: the medium-relief cast is taken from his painting of the scene

Kowalczyk, then a WAAF (Polish) cook at RAF Newton, recalled the feeling on the station as long as two years after the event. 'We girls said, "How sad!" But our Corporal Milhaski said it had been a *"Marnowane zycie"* [a wasted life].'

Some sixty years later, the century having turned, it was actually proposed that in addition to a plaque being positioned in the village church to commemorate the incident, a Polish flag should be flown from the church tower on the anniversary of the event. As it was, less roseate views of the incident prevailed. In March 2006, however, a tasteful memorial was placed at the entrance to the cemetery, and overlooking the crash site, to the memory of – as the inscription's drafter saw it – 'this dashing young pilot'. The memorial itself was the fruition of thirty years of heartfelt campaigning by Mr Alan Jones, the locally-born air-crash researcher and a talented artist whose painting of the event is reproduced on the plaque in medium-relief.

Regarding Leading Aircraftman Gawkowski's route to flying with the Polish Air Force under RAF Command, he had joined the Polish Air Force School at Krosno in August 1938. Then, in mid-September 1939, when Russian forces unexpectedly pincered into Poland from the east, three weeks after the German invasion from the west, he had crossed the border into then-neutral Romania. To a certain extent this move, made under orders from the Polish government, had been pre-arranged, and after a purely nominal period of internment, he, in common with the vast number of Polish servicemen similarly extracted, was taken to France and inducted into the French forces. Practically coincident with their arrival, however, France capitulated, but even after the official surrender a British naval operation took off many thousands of personnel, Poles among them, from the west coast.

So it was, that after an odyssey shared by most Poles arriving in Britain, Leading Aircraftman Gawkowski was to come so very close to achieving his ambition of fighting, if not directly for Poland, then certainly against Poland's enemies.

Leading Aircraftman Gawkowski is buried at the Polish Forces Cemetery at Newark, Nottinghamshire, among the rows of his countrymen who actually flew operationally, and with such distinction, in the squadrons of the Polish Air Force under RAF Command. Poles who died in action against the enemy in the cause of a freedom their own land had already lost. Poles whose double tragedy was to be that all their endeavours, all their sustained courage – courage culminating for those at Newark in the ultimate sacrifice – was to benefit their native Poland by not so much as one iota.

2003, and erstwhile Polish airman Stefan Martin (Kowalski) collects soil at Newark Cemetery for a memorial in Poland

Harking back to the Mottram crash, Mr Alan Jones, who had watched as the Master overflew his house, and later saw the coiling black smoke, also remembered that while the main bulk of the wreckage remained just above the brook, the detached engine had rolled some way downstream. Indeed in later years he was to retrieve aircraft fragments from the bank. Souvenir-hunting Arnold Willerton, for his part, remembered that he had had his eyes set on 'liberating', as he put it, the identification plate from the Pratt & Whitney engine, and was chagrined to find that someone had beaten him to it.

At the crash site in 2006, one bank of the gully was still shale-surfaced, the other wooded. But diligent searching yielded not a trace of aircraft debris. Of course, the Master was basically of plywood construction and the fire consumed much, while salvage crews and – evidently not least – souvenir hunters took most of what remained.

Yet for all the trauma of the actual day of the crash, and speaking volumes for the resilience of youth, the image that returns most often to Arnold Willerton's mind, recalled as a vignette, is that as he joined the smoke-wreathed crowd already gathered at the fatal gully's edge, a hare started up – and a woman threw her handbag after it.

How ironic that her action too, like that of Pupil Pilot Leading Aircraftman Gawkowski, should have been one of such utter futility!

## Miles Master Mk.3 W8506, Hepworth, Penistone, near the Victoria Inn

SE 17999 05289 339m touchdown
SE 18054 05305 339m terminal run onto rough ground
No.16 (Polish) Service Flying Training School, RAF Newton (Nottingham), No.21 Group, Flying Training Command
21 March 1943

Pilot: solo, injured:
Pupil Pilot Leading Aircraftman Henryk Kowalski, Polish Air Force under British Command

On 21 March 1943, Polish trainee pilot Leading Aircraftman Henryk Kowalski, an advanced pupil with just under two hundred hours of flying experience, was briefed for what appears to have been a pupil-led solo formation detail from RAF Newton. The formation duly got airborne at 1535 hours but encountered low visibility conditions, so that in the course of the sortie Leading Aircraftman Kowalski was unable to hold station and became unsighted from the formation. Cast upon his own resources he soon realised that he was hopelessly lost, despite which he continued to search about, until, having been airborne for just over two hours and with fuel running short, he decided to put the aircraft down. Accordingly, at 1740 hours, he made a forced landing in a field adjacent to, and to the rear of, the Victoria Inn at Hepworth, Yorkshire, some fifty miles from his base.

The forced landing did not go well, and Leading Aircraftman Kowalski was injured when the aircraft tipped up on rough ground, although to what degree is not recorded. The aircraft, however, was so badly damaged that it had to be written off.

The subsequent enquiry concentrated upon the command and control of the formation, the squadron commander rather lamely submitting that in future only instructors should lead formations when the weather was in any doubt, leaving RAF Newton's officer commanding to note tersely, 'I agree.'

In 2005 Mr Phillip Tinker, of Spring Head Farm, Upper Cumberworth, not only recalled the incident but was able to indicate the landing site. 'I saw it from where I was working,' he explained. 'The Master came curving in, then ran the length of the field, but ended by tipping nose down and tail up. I don't know what state the pilot was in, or what happened to him then. But the RAF soon arrived and took over, only they couldn't repair the plane, so next day Leslie Alsop pulled it out to the road using his Fordson and it was loaded onto a Queen Mary and driven off.'

Even in mid-2006 the field in which Leading Aircraftman Kowalski chose to set down still seemed estimable for the purpose, so it could be that he simply came in a few knots too fast, or touched down a little too far into the field. As is so often the case with constantly worked farmland, and particularly as the incident was so trifling, a visual search showed up nothing related to the incident.

Mr Phillip Tinker,
witness

The rough area which upended Master W8506.
The Victoria Inn is to the right

## Gloster Meteor FMk.4 RA487, Hagg Side, Ladybower

**SK 16610 89087** 320m

No.66 Squadron, RAF Linton-on-Ouse (north-west
of York), No.12 Group, Fighter Command
8 December 1950

Pilot: uninjured, successfully baled out:
Sergeant Joseph Harrington

After the Second World War the Meteor formed the mainstay of Britain's fighter force until replaced by the new generation of swept-wing jet fighters, notably the Sabre, which No.66 Fighter Squadron, among others, were to receive in 1953. But in 1949, when the squadron was still Meteor-equipped, they were joined by Sergeant Joseph Harrington who had re-enlisted in the RAF after a year's absence following late-wartime service on Lancasters and Lincolns. Having quickly settled into this jet-fighter environment, Sergeant Harrington had already become a member of the squadron's Meteor formation team when, towards midnight on 7 December 1950, he was dispatched on a triangular cross-country exercise.

The first leg of his route, to Manchester, was uneventful. Shortly after turning onto an easterly heading for his second leg, however, he realised that his communications radio, the state of the art, four-stud, Very High Frequency set, had totally failed. Accordingly he decided to adhere to his navigation plan, to turn north for base at his estimated time of arrival for the final turning point, and then commence his descent. However, when the time came for the turn, and very conscious of the safety height along the leg, he found himself above a substantial, if occasionally broken, cloud layer.

Reassessing the situation in view of the cloud, with fuel running relatively low, and loath to let down before more accurately determining his position, Sergeant Harrington switched his 'Identification Friend or Foe' equipment to 'Emergency', knowing that this would show up as a distinct 'Help me!' signal on the fighter-control radar screens. He might also have considered flying the arcane emergency procedure known as 'radar triangles', in this case to the left, hoping that the radars would recognise such peregrinations as indicating 'My radio has totally failed, prithee send up a shepherd aircraft to see me home'. But optimism has its bounds for anyone, and with his fuel state increasingly in mind, Sergeant Harrington decided to take advantage of a fortuitous cloud break and investigate the possibility of a forced landing.

Edging down through the gap, maintaining what visual contact he could, he actually succeeded in picking out a straight stretch of road through the darkness. In fact, he even made a tentative pass along it with a touchdown in mind, only to be compelled into a hasty zoom for height as a seemingly sky-tall chimney loomed abeam one wing.

Having ventured so much, however, Sergeant Harrington then did what so many others lost in the region had signally failed to do: deciding that enough was enough, and before his fuel state further cut down his options, he made the balanced decision to leave the aircraft to its own devices.

Not that this was to go without a hitch, for having flown back up to an indicated safe altitude of five thousand feet, and having suitably configured the aircraft, his initial attempt to evacuate was foiled by the forces involved. Indeed, only after laboriously pulling himself back into his seat, and more advantageously trimming the aircraft, was he able to spill himself over the side and thereafter, Fortune herself remaining with him, under the tail. That accomplished, however, his parachute descent was equally successful, and he landed, somewhat shocked and shaken, but otherwise uninjured, in a ploughed field near Castleton. His abandoned aircraft, meanwhile, crashed on the isolated slopes of Hagg Side, high above the Sheffield to Glossop Road.

Station Officer Roe, of the Glossop Fire Service, told the *Glossop Chronicle* how his crew had been forced to leave their fire tender at Rowlee Farm and then Land-Rover their way along tracks to Lockerbrook farm, eventually getting to within 350 yards of the machine, but only locating the wreckage having tortuously scrambled through thick undergrowth. The fire had gone out by the time they reached the site, but all commented upon its having been chance alone which had spared the whole plantation.

Those junior RAF officers enquiring into the loss of the aircraft opined that Sergeant Harrington might have either more accurately planned, or flown, the second leg of the route. Also that he might have realised earlier that he had lost his radio. And no doubt they had something in mind, albeit unstated, regarding what he might have done then. More mature Higher Authority, however, decided that matters need go no further, and it was left to the Station Commander to discuss with Sergeant Harrington the errors the inquiry felt he might have avoided. But clearly the miscreant's cool-headed decision-making was to stand him in good stead, for he subsequently made a career as a captain with Swissair; a premier airline reputedly demanding very nearly the same Teutonic levels of efficiency envisaged by the RAF court of inquiry, only supplying dependable radios, and paying a very great deal more handsomely.

 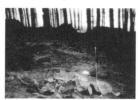

Above left: Swissair Captain (erstwhile Sergeant Pilot) Joseph Harrington, at a book launch in the 1990s. Photo by courtesy of Ranger Peter Jackson

Above right: The crash site of Meteor RA487 in 2006

Ranger Peter Jackson first met former Sergeant Harrington at a Glossop book launch in the 1990s. 'I fly into Manchester in my Swissair jet,' Captain Harrington told him, 'and often get the chance to look down at the area. But this is the first time I've revisited since floating into it on my chute.'

Indeed, Captain Harrington's bale-out was the present author's first introduction to Peakland's air crashes. 'My father's in a Peak District air-crash book,' British Midland air stewardess Anne Harrington confided during a turnround, the conversation having turned to hill-walking, 'but then, of course, he's a captain with a *real* airline ...'

At the crash site a moderate pile of wreckage was still to be found in 2006, pooled within the woods, the only problem having located it being the poor light for photography. Besides, that is, spending five minutes disengaging both legs of one's trousers from a hostile barbed-wire fence.


## Gloster Meteors FMk.8 WA791 and VZ518, Sliddens Moss, south-west of Black Hill

SE 06636 02881 513m initial impact pools
SE 07146 02934 494m final debris pool. The eighth such pool, 450 yards on 088°M
No.66 Squadron, RAF Linton-on-Ouse (north-west of York), No.12 Group, Fighter
Command
12 April 1951

Pilots: both killed:
Flight Lieutenant David Merryweather Leach, formation leader (WA791)
Flying Officer Anthony Hauxwell (VZ518)


It was in the Meteor's heyday as a first-line fighter, on 12 April 1951, that Flight Lieutenant David Leach, of No.66 Squadron, was detailed to exercise four Meteor FMk.8s in practice air-combat manoeuvres at 30,000 feet. This was a standard fighter exercise and would have involved the four dividing into the loosely-formating pairs in which they would hone their tactical skills. In order to get best value out of the exercise the machines had cine-cameras linked to their gun mechanisms so that the likely outcomes of their dummy attacks could be critically assessed after the sortie.

Although routine, and despite strict orders dictating the rules of engagement in such exercises – the nearest thing there was to real aerial combat – risk was inherent. And on this occasion, having led his foursome up through the intermediate-level cloud in a zigzagging, follow-my-leader, 'snake climb', Flight Lieutenant Leach found thick upper cloud baulking his purpose. Accordingly, in view of the unfavourable conditions, he aborted the cine-gun practice and directed his two sections to return to base, heading north-eastwards as independent pairs, each section to utilise the remaining sortie time in carrying out instrument flying and recovery procedures.

A short time later Flight Lieutenant Leach, now leading just Flying Officer Anthony Hauxwell, made a broadcast call that he had sighted Leeds through a gap and that he was commencing descent. In fact, backtracking events, he seems to have seen Stockport, for despite a distance-devouring descent through at least twenty thousand feet of cloud towards Linton, the dive took the pair into the 1,600 feet-above-sea-level Sliddens Moss, still some twenty-one miles short of Leeds. There was no fire, but the impact killed both pilots as their aircraft disintegrated in a 450-yard wing-to-wing spill of wreckage.

That both aircraft should fly into the ground in such a manner might be wondered at, and certainly, while actually practising combat manoeuvres the pair would have flown a loose tactical formation that allowed each to look around and provide cover for the other. However, when descending through such a substantial cloud layer the formating pilot would be tucked in close, his only function being to religiously hold station, leaving the navigation and terrain clearance entirely to his leader.

It is an efficient method of penetrating cloud in company, but one which bears the inherent danger that in the event of a mishap it is very often a case of lose one, lose both. Indeed No.66 Squadron were to experience another such loss three years later, when, having re-equipped with Sabres, another of their pairs spread a wreckage trail between the heights of Kinder Scout and the depths of Black Ashop Moor.

The court of inquiry had no option but to hold the leader to blame. For he had undisputedly led his section down to 1,600 feet, demonstrably below the safety height even had he been where he thought he was (when the safety height would still have been some 2,000 feet), let alone the safety height where he actually was, of 3,800 feet.

In 2006 this appeared to be one crash site where, despite the efforts of the original recovery team, the lapse of time, and the attentions of souvenir hunters, a substantial amount of wreckage seemed likely to remain for many years, not gathered into a particular pool, but still strung out in dual trails across the tufted, still largely trackless, expanse of Sliddens Moss.

Looking along the line of impact towards the Holme Moss television mast

2006, one of the many sections of debris from Meteors WA791 and VZ518

### Gloster Meteor (probably spurious), Dodworth, Church Lane Colliery's spoil heap, Barnsley

SE 31477 06295 151m (spoil heap)
No.211 Flying Training School, RAF
Worksop, No.25 Group, Flying Training
Command

Enthusiast lists hold that a Worksop-based Meteor crashed into Church Lane Colliery's spoil heap in the early 1950s. By 2006 the vast expanse of the Dodworth spoil heap was pleasantly tree-covered, with woodland walks, and even pastures on the summit. Enquiries among ex-miners who had lived in the area throughout the fifties brought universal disavowal that an aeroplane had ever crashed at the pit. Many, conversely, were aware of the 1937 Gladiator crash at Hermit House Farm, a property since made remote from the former Dodworth pit by extensive excavations, not least those made for the M1 Motorway. No verification having been found for any such Meteor crash, it is, therefore, included here merely for the record. It seems likely that Dodworth has been confused with Treeton, a Sheffield location, where Meteor WB108 did indeed crash into a spoil heap in 1954 (See *Peakland Air Crashes: The Central Area, p82*)

## De Havilland Mosquito BMk.16 PF395, Chew Hills, above Dovestone Reservoir

SE 02611 03182 455m impact site
SE 02559 03179 411m debris pool
No.571 Squadron, RAF Oakington (north-west of
Cambridge), No.8 Group, Bomber Command
22 October 1944

Crew: both killed:
Flying Officer Ernest Douglas Scotland, pilot
Sergeant Humphrey Robert Cruse Soan, navigator

The sleek, swift and sure de Havilland Mosquito, the 'all-wood' machine which its crews swore by, caught the public's fancy from the start. In appearance the exemplar of the oft-proven aviation aphorism 'if an aeroplane looks good, it is good', it found many roles for itself after its introduction in late 1941. In all its many guises it impressed, but it was in its design role as a light bomber that it excelled. Its role, in fact, with No.571 Squadron of Bomber Command, in October 1944 an element of the Fast Night-Striking Force (the recently-superseded Light Night-Striking Force in new guise) when Mosquito PF395 was one of the aircraft tasked to bomb a target in Hamburg.

The objective was successfully attacked, but on the way home to RAF Oakington the cockpit coolant-gauge on PF395 showed a temperature rise which told its pilot, Flying Officer Ernest Scotland, that his port engine had suffered a glycol, engine-coolant, leak. Shortly afterwards he reported to others of the flight that he was shutting down the overheating engine.

Being deprived of an engine, especially well on the way home from an operation, was no great matter to the crew. For although the pilot had only sixty or so hours on type, all told he had some 1,600 hours' experience. Besides, the Mosquito was well capable of flying on one engine. Indeed, over the years many would hold that 'Sir' Geoffrey had designed the Mosquito as a single-engined aircraft and only added a second for the sake of appearance; as if in proof of which the prototype is held to have carried out a vertical climb with one engine stopped! For the crew of PF395, therefore, with reasonable weather and just the Cambridgeshire fenlands before them, there should have been no undue problem.

Losing half its power, of course, did mean that PF395 was no longer able to keep company with its fellows, who gradually forged ahead. Only, as they disappeared into the darkness – and one cannot imagine them doing so without the odd jocular remark to the laggard – so too did PF395's best hope vanish. For although the Mosquito was equipped with an engine-driven generator on both power plants, the last transmission received from Flying Officer Scotland was that all his onboard navigational equipment had now become unserviceable.

How chagrined he must have been, and how much more so his now blithely homebound fellow crews would later be, that the suggestion had not been made that one of them should lag in his vicinity, his navigational lights and tell-tale exhaust flares serving as shepherdly guides should the need arise!

And by the well known law that applies equally in aviation as in every other walk of life, that need did arise. For had Flying Officer Scotland remained in company, then regardless of the state of his navigation and communication aids, by simply holding loose station he would have arrived, as all the others did, at their Cambridgeshire base; except that his machine never did arrive.

Notwithstanding the loss of their radio-navigational aids, what caused Flying Officer Scotland and his navigator, Sergeant Humphrey Soan, to go astray at that juncture was almost certainly the substantial sheet of cloud that had moved across the east of the country. For they not only overflew Oakington, but the whole of Cambridgeshire; in fact, they were next seen circling the eastern outskirts of Manchester, 120 miles to the north-west of Oakington, dipping below a ragged cloud base as they desperately sought to fix themselves. The word 'desperately' being used advisedly, because by the time of the sighting they had already been airborne an hour longer than the rest of the raiders, and fuel must have been running short.

The thought must have been in both their minds that, if they could not fix themselves very soon,

The crash site in 2006; looking upwards from the rock-encircled debris pool to the impact site

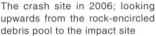

Surface debris at the impact point

the only option left to them would be to bale out and abandon the machine; yet how reluctant any crew would be to follow that course; how pride – or, borrowing a later term, professionalism – would have militated against doing so, when all they needed was a single pinpoint!

Only as they searched, eyes intent without a doubt on the glow even then emanating from the blacked-out, yet still very evident, metropolis to the west, so their circling flight took them ever closer to the east, and to the high ground they had only just overflown. In fact, it could well be that they had finally succeeded in fixing themselves, and that they had already set course away from the area. Except that they flew into a cliff-face with 1,500 feet still indicating on their altimeter, Mosquito PF395 exploding around them, its sleek lines instantaneously fragmenting amid a life-snuffing welter of flames.

At the Chew Hills crash site in 2006 a modest and – measured over a span of ten years – decidedly dwindling amount of wreckage had been pooled in a rock circle at the foot of the cliff-like slope on a shoulder situated high above the Dovestone Reservoir. But the walker should note that this is another site where, having arrived at the reference, a good look around might be required, for it is possible to stand on ledges just feet above the debris and be totally unsighted from it.

The actual impact site is further up the rocky slope from the pooled debris and was still marked by a tiny cache of fragments, with charred wood predominant, although the area for feet around revealed visual evidence, albeit minutiae, of both the impact and the conflagration.


## Airspeed Oxford Mk.1 HN594, Brown Knoll, Edale

SK 08189 85204 558m
No.21 (Pilots) Advanced Flying Unit, RAF Seighford (north-west of Stafford),
No.21 Group, Flying Training Command
28 December 1945

Crew: all injured:
Warrant Officer George Robinson, pilot, pilot-navigation instructor
Flying Officer John E. Dowthwaite, pilot on course
Flying Officer Edward A. Croker, pilot on course


The Second World War had been over for four months and many pilots' eyes were turned to a future in civil aviation. Airlines were expected to favour experience on heavy aircraft, so the chance to transfer to a multi-engined type via the twin-engined Airspeed Oxford trainer would have been warmly regarded. It is not known whether either Flying Officer John Dowthwaite or Flying Officer Edward Croker had such aspirations at that juncture, but they would have been likely candidates, each having logged just under a thousand flying hours.

On 28 December 1945, they were detailed to fly with a staff pilot on a day-navigation test during which they, as course members, would navigate by mapreading, taking turn and turn about. It was a relatively informal exercise, in this case with the instructor, Warrant Officer George Robinson, marking out the legs only once they were in the aircraft, the corollary of which was to be that no record of their intended route was left back at RAF Seighford.

Approaching fifty minutes into the sortie, the pupils changed seats, Flying Officer Dowthwaite handing control to Warrant Officer Robinson during the changeover. The two trainees had just

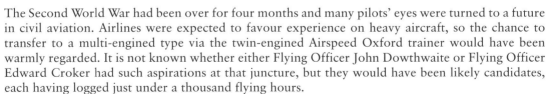

returned from duty tours in fair-weather South Africa and one aim of this course was to re-introduce them to UK flying conditions. So now, as the cloud closing about them tended to blot out the snow-fringed terrain so close below, Flying Officer Croker, slipping into the vacated left-hand seat, mimed his alarm at seeing the ice that had formed on the leading edge of the port wing. But both trainees expressed genuine concern about the proximity of the 2,088-foot spot height of Kinder Scout shown on the topographical chart they were using, well aware that they were only flying at 1,000 feet on the altimeter. Warrant Officer Robinson merely laughed at their apprehensions, assuring them that he knew the area like the back of his hand. Just the same he initiated a climb. However, before Flying Officer Croker could even secure his harness the aircraft struck the ground, bounced, then hit hard, disintegrating and throwing him clear.

Contemporary photograph of the scene, courtesy of Crown Copyright

Providentially, despite the heavy impact, there was no fire, for when Flying Officer Croker hobbled back on what he believed to be broken ankles, he found his fellow aircrew not only seriously injured but sprawled amidst the wreckage.

In view of the poor visibility, and faced with the fact that they had been flying an undeclared route, there seemed little chance of a successful airborne search being launched in the near future, let alone actually finding them. Wrapping the two lightly clothed and badly shocked casualties in parachutes, therefore, Flying Officer Croker set off to seek assistance.

What followed was an epic any walker can only wonder at. For the crash had occurred just below the summit of Brown Knoll. Yet Flying Officer Croker, with his ankles unable to support him for any distance, and so being forced to crawl for much of the way, set off vaguely eastwards, tortuously feeling his way downhill until eventually, after nearly two miles, he came upon the youth hostel, then situated at Upper Booth. This was closed, but a lady living nearby, eventually aroused by his knocking, took him in, and having tended to his immediate needs, made her way along to Edale, and the nearest telephone, where she raised the alarm.

Night was falling, however, and weather conditions had deteriorated so much that a nine-hour ground search for the other survivors proved fruitless. Indeed not until mid-morning next day did an aircraft locate the wreck.

The two airmen forced to overnight on the moor, clad as they were only in battledress and despite the parachute covering, were lucky to survive; indeed Warrant Officer Robinson later had to have a leg amputated. For his part, Flying Officer Croker's ankles turned out to be very badly sprained, rather than broken, so that, in time, with any conceivable aspirations towards civil flying firmly set aside, he went on to play football for Charlton and to become secretary of the Football Association.

For ex-Warrant Officer Robinson the anniversary of the crash became a day set aside for pilgrimage, and in after years, despite his disability, he would unfailingly catch the train to Edale, then make his way up to the crash site; or as the years took their toll, as far up as he was able. On the fortieth anniversary all three men foregathered, when, as Peak Park Ranger Peter Jackson recalled, John Dowthwaite told him feelingly, 'You can't imagine the gratitude I felt as George and I lay there in the wreckage, knowing that, despite his pain, Ted had gone off to do his best for us.'

Former Warrant Officer George Robinson; former Flying Officer Edward Croker; and former Flying Officer John Dowthwaite foregather in the 1980s. Photograph by courtesy of Ranger Peter Jackson

Mr and Mrs Ted and Mary Dalton, of Dethick, but in 1945 farming at Kinder Farm, Chapel-en-le-Frith, had good cause to remember the crash. 'We were newly wed,' Mr Dalton explained in 2005, 'and we'd seen the planes and men

The crash site in 2006, with Brown Knoll summit and its trig column just out of shot to the left

searching for the crash, for they didn't find it for nearly forty-eight hours. But the next Sunday we walked up to Brown Knoll ourselves.'

'We couldn't credit that anyone could have survived in the wreckage we found,' said Mrs Dalton. 'There was a parachute, heavily bloodstained – one of the men had wrapped the others in it, then crawled down to Edale!' She smiled. 'We rolled one of the plane's wheels back with us: it was very naughty, of course.' Her husband grunted. 'It was too big to use for a wheelbarrow, we found. But we also took one of the seats, and that served as a swing for the children for years to come.'

The wreckage, they remembered, was recovered via the remote Shireoaks Farm. 'And then down through thirteen gates before getting to the road,' observed Mr Dalton feelingly.

The crash site still had a moderate amount of wreckage to show in 2006, but being situated in a hollow amid hags and groughs, and being a little way off the main path, tended not to be seen, although it was often temporarily marked by sizeable items of debris raised by walkers.

### Airspeed Oxford Mk.1 LX518, Howden Moor, west of Margery Hill

SK 18025 96697 528m impact point
SK 18043 96738 525m debris tumbled into a gully
No.21 (Pilots) Advanced Flying Unit, RAF Wheaton Aston (south-west of Stafford), No. 21 Group, Flying Training Command
18 October 1943

Pilot: pupil, first night solo on type, killed:
Pilot Officer Dennis Patrick Kyne, Royal New Zealand Air Force

As they entered the advanced phase of their flying training, pupil pilots earmarked for a multi-engined role would be converted to one of the twin-engined trainers; the Oxford, or the Anson. No.21 (Pilots) Advanced Training Unit, then located at RAF Wheaton Aston, just south-west of Stafford, was equipped with Oxfords, and for the initial night solo at this stage of the conversion it was the practice to carry out a short cross-country flight. The triangular course was flown first as a dual familiarisation detail, then as a solo training exercise.

Although integral to pilot training, night flying does make extra demands on the tyro pilot. This would have applied especially to one not native to Britain, and to one who, additionally, had learnt to fly under the Empire Air Training Scheme in the clear skies of uncluttered Canada. Accordingly, as they flew the dual exercise, the instructor would refresh the pupil on the methods of gaining navigational assistance at night in the event of his becoming uncertain of his position when flying alone.

The instructor would demonstrate, for example, how a pilot could locate his position in relation to the coded 'pundit' beacons the active airfields would be showing; or how he could call into play occulting searchlights which, on request, would swing their beams to indicate the direction of an active airfield. Alternatively, if such lights were obscured for some reason, and the pilot was still unsure of his whereabouts, there was the 'Darky' network of listening stations which, by night, just as well as by day, could pass an aircraft from one to the other and so bring it to the nearest active airfield. Clear visibility, of course, was the most important aid of all, but to have proved the route just a short while before sending pupils solo eased the minds of authorising officers, instructors, and pupils alike.

On the night of 18 October 1943, when Pilot Officer Dennis Kyne, of the Royal New Zealand Air Force, was sent off by himself, he had already flown the dual sortie. The route called for an eighteen-mile, south-westerly leg to the pundit light-beacon indicating Condover airfield; then a northerly

ten-mile leg to the Shawbury pundit, probably then, as in later years, slowly coding 'SY' in morse –
but only in peacetime, with no intruders on the prowl, actually located on the airfield itself. The
final leg would take Pilot Officer Kyne the seventeen miles back to Wheaton Aston. It was an
undemanding exercise which, taking everything into account, would see him back in the circuit in
some twenty-five to thirty minutes. Only for the New Zealander things went sadly wrong. For Pilot
Officer Kyne's aircraft did not return to base, and when it was eventually located it was found to
have crashed on desolate moorland fifty-two miles to the north-east of Wheaton Aston.

The investigation would quickly discover that the Shawbury pundit, a beacon critical to Pilot
Officer Kyne's navigation in marking the northern limit of his pattern, had become unserviceable
only a short while after he had taken off. Which meant that, on his northerly leg, searching ahead
over otherwise blacked-out Britain, he would have seen only darkness, instead of the reassuring
pulse of light which had marked the turning point on the dual sortie. At his stage of training it must
have seemed only sensible to fly on just a little more; headwinds do spring up and alter estimated
arrival times, after all.

And things had certainly altered at Wheaton Aston, confounding the best efforts of the authorising
staff to ensure that their pupils were not sent off in unduly adverse conditions; for just as the second
wave of mainly solo pupils had got airborne, so the weather had deteriorated markedly, in concert,
it might seem, with the failing Shawbury pundit. Most aircraft had returned to base as the weather
closed in, but one other, although initially causing some alarm, was found to have diverted, leaving
just LX518 unaccounted for. After the prescribed lapse of time with nothing heard overdue action
was taken as a matter of course, all agencies being contacted for information; but without result.
Indeed not until four days later was Pilot Officer Kyne's body discovered amid the wreckage of his
Oxford, high on the Howden Moors.

In 2005 Farmer Kenneth Wilson, of Greenwood Farm, near Hathersage, was able to throw light
on the manner of its finding. 'We were beating for a grouse shoot on Howden Moor', he said, 'when
we came upon the wreckage, strung out over a half a mile or so. Then we saw the pilot, still strapped
in his seat. I remember one of the farmers asking, as if in hope, "Is it a dummy?" But it clearly
wasn't. After that, we stayed there, mounting a sort of guard while people went to raise the alarm,
and brought back some servicemen.' He smiled suddenly. 'I remember they also brought us Spam
sandwiches. And that I quite liked them!'

2006, the terminal
impact site, beside the
highly frequented path

Farmer Mr Kenneth
Wilson, of
Hathersage; on a
grouse shoot when
the crash was
discovered

Debris tumbled into a
gully by the salvage
team

What caused Pilot Officer Kyne to stray so far north had to be a matter of speculation, but fifty-two miles was, after all, less than twenty minutes' flying time for an Oxford. Examination of the wreckage showed that Pilot Officer Kyne had not run out of fuel; accordingly the investigation turned to the procedures he might have adopted to get assistance.

It seemed clear that he had not made use of any radio facilities; indeed the 'Darky' posts in that area had been busy throughout the period, yet nothing had been heard of him. Further, his automatic alerting device, the 'Identification-Friend-or-Foe' equipment (IFF), had not been switched to the correct channel; although that alone would hardly have saved him, even had a shepherd aircraft been able to locate him in time. As it was, it seemed that he had become totally lost, steering blindly north and north-east in a vain endeavour to fix himself. Except that, while unknowingly moving over higher and higher ground, he had maintained the height on his altimeter laid down for the low-lying Wheaton-Aston-area navigational route, until eventually his cruising aircraft had impacted on Howden Moor at an altitude of 1,700 feet above sea level, without catching fire, but instantly killing Pilot Officer Kyne.

In 2006 a burn scar beside the footpath, caused by the fire set during the clearance operation, and still liberally strewn with molten metal, marked the terminal impact point. Additionally a fair amount of wreckage remained where the salvage team had tumbled it into a gully just a few yards to the north; like the burning, a precaution against its distracting future air searches.

## Airspeed Oxford Mk.1 NM683,　Rushup Edge, lower northern slopes

SK 10944 83827 270m

Navigation Training Unit, Pathfinder Force, RAF Warboys (north-east of Huntingdon), No.8 Group, Bomber Command
4 March 1945

Occupants: all injured:
Flight Lieutenant Brian Gipson, DFC and bar, pilot
Flight Lieutenant Barclay, DFC, navigator, staff instructor
Flying Officer Skone-Reese, DFC, navigator trainee
Flight Lieutenant D.I. Jones, passengering pilot

In March 1945, even though the war in Europe was drawing to its close, opportunities for relaxed flying would still have been rare. They would, therefore, have been warmly welcomed, and certainly not least by aircrew personnel, veterans of at least one operational tour on bombers, who were currently staffing and undergoing courses with the Navigational Training Unit of Bomber Command's Pathfinder Force, then located at RAF Warboys, near Huntingdon. One such veteran was staff member Flight Lieutenant Brian Gipson, a pilot who had, in fact, completed two Pathfinder tours besides. But then none of the fliers on board Oxford NM683 was a novice to operational flying, as their decorations bear witness, and even passengering Flying Officer Jones had logged very nearly 1,500 hours.

The terrain, towering awesomely ...

The duty in hand was basically a simple communications detail; Flying Officer Jones had to be delivered to Royal Naval Air Station Stretton, near Warrington, and following common practice, the requirement was met by laying on a mapreading cross-country exercise.

The direct track would have taken the aircraft over Derby, and then Ashbourne, but the weather was good, and the cloud, although clinging low over the high ground, was as forecast, and indeed did not change throughout the period. It is highly likely, therefore, that the crew decided to head northwards over the Peak District to take advantage of the scenery; certainly when cloud blotted out the ground the decision was made to descend below it. Only the descent was inadvertently made into the Vale of Edale, and when the cloud broke before him, Flight Lieutenant Gipson found himself heading at slightly-above cruising speed into the virtually precipitous flank of Rushup Edge, towering awesomely to lose itself in the mists high above him.

Hastily – as one might well imagine – he heaved back on the stick and powered up. And although he could have had scant hope of clearing the ridge, he managed to rear the aircrafts' nose so high that, against all the odds, it flattened itself against the ground rather than driving full tilt into it. By equal good fortune there was no fire, and although NM683 was totally destroyed, and all on board suffered some degree of injury, everyone survived.

When interviewed in late 2004 there were villagers who still remembered that day, retired postman Mr Alan Chapman, of Barber Booth, among them. 'The Oxford was like a great butterfly pinned to the hillside,' he recalled, 'and how the pilot managed to land it on that steep slope mystified us all. I remember the local people and the RAF clearing the wreck, and simply rolling the engines down the hillside.'

There was an inquiry, as a matter of course, which found that the pilot had destroyed his aircraft and injured his crew by descending through cloud without having ascertained his position beforehand; thereby contravening flying regulations. Only it seems clear that operationally-gained reputations had a lot to commend them, for although directing that the staff pilot and the navigator be reproved, the hierarchy of Air Officers left it to the officer commanding the navigational unit – with his comparatively limited powers of punishment – to administer what was, in effect, an avuncular slap on the wrist.

In 2006 there was still a moderate pool of wreckage to be seen, tucked into the side of a re-entrant gully; a location which made this another of those sites where it was possible to stand directly above the cache and fail to see it.

Crash site, facing the Vale of Edale, Manor House Farm, and Barber Booth

Surface debris remaining in August 2006

## Airspeed Oxford Mk.2 AB662, Gatefoot Farm, New Mill, Shepley

SE 18221 08521 285m impact with barn
SE 18175 08395 300m debris spread
No.14 (Pilots) Advanced Flying Unit, RAF Ossington (near Newark), No.2 Group, Flying Training Command
14 April 1942

Pilot: solo pupil pilot, killed:
Sergeant Melvin Harry Smith, Royal Canadian Air Force

In the early hours of 14 April 1942, Sergeant Melvin Smith, an American from Illinois, serving with the Royal Canadian Air Force, was dispatched from RAF Ossington, near Newark, to carry out solo night circuits and landings. It would have been normal enough to temporarily clear from the circuit in order to practise homing to the airfield and rejoining the landing pattern, but the time came when Sergeant Smith lost sight of the flare path altogether and realised that he no longer knew where the airfield was. This was not that surprising, for the flare path, the sole lighting showing in the blackout, was formed by nothing more than two faltering lines of paraffin-fuelled gooseneck flares; the burners employed, moreover, being hooded, and fully visible only from the approach direction.

Sergeant Smith might have been expected to relocate himself using contingency procedures which would have been demonstrated to him on previous sorties. As it was, he strayed some forty-six miles from low-lying Ossington, and at 0500 hours crashed into a barn on a 1,000-feet-above-sea-level hillside at New Mill, near Holmfirth. The aircraft disintegrated on impact, killing Sergeant Smith outright.

Mrs Catherine Wilson, Shepley, witness

In late-2005, Mrs Catherine Wilson, of Gatefoot Lane, readily recalled the day of the crash, although she had always thought the aircraft was a much lighter trainer. 'It had crashed along the barn just across from us,' she recalled, 'but we weren't allowed to go over there until it had been cleared away. Fortunately it hit the barn, rather than the house, so nobody in the farm was hurt.'

Mr Frank Brook, in 2005 of New Mill, but formerly resident in Gatefoot Farm, had even less difficulty in recalling the shock of the aircraft's arrival; and he had no doubts about its type. 'It was an Oxford,' he said, 'and it came from the Shepley direction and crashed into the gable end of the barn. It took off the roof, then scraped along one wall, but just missed where our family was, in the house at the end. One of the big radial engines finished up beside the house, but the other rolled downhill to the Junction Pub – it's now The Crossroads. The rest of the wreckage had broken down the drystone walls bordering the road and finished up in the field beyond. In fact, that's where we found the pilot's body: he was Canadian Air Force.'

Mr Frank Brook, New Mill, witness

He paused, considering. 'Before that, I remember Dad calling for a match because all the electrics had gone. Until my sister pointed out that the whole place reeked of petrol.' He grinned. 'And I remember one of the local men, a Home Guard, arriving, and although we'd been wandering about all over, ordering, "All *civilians* out of the field." Then the army came from Shepley, and in the end

The terminal crash site, beyond the drystone wall

the RAF took away the wreckage in their Queen Marys. Fortunately there was no fire, and the house was untouched. Then, too, a great stone from the barn had fallen down and landed between two cows, but without touching either. And we got compensation for rebuilding. In fact, original stones from the barn were used to make the coping stones on the boundary wall.'

By late 2005 Gatefoot Farm and its barn had been transformed into private residences and showed no signs of the fatal crash of 1943; indeed the owner of what had formerly been the barn had no inkling of the tragedy that had once occurred there. On the roadside drystone wall in line with the barn, however, the coping stones originating from the damaged barn, mute though they were, still told the tale.

The corner of the erstwhile barn struck by Oxford AB662

## Lockheed P-38J Lightning 42-67207, Tintwistle Knarr, Longdendale Valley

SK 03932 99080 444m

United States Eighth Army Air Force, 8th Air Force Composite
Command, 496th Fighter Training Group, 554th Fighter Training
Squadron, AAF345 (RAF Goxhill), 12 miles north-west of Grimsby
10 May 1944

Pilot: killed:
Flight Officer Hugh Allen Jones, United States Army Air Force

By 1944 the twin-boomed P-38 Lightnings were making their mark as escorts for the American long-range daylight bombers penetrating deep into enemy territory. This was not without cost, of course, so a constant stream of replacements for both machines and pilots was required to keep the operational squadrons up to strength, the job of initiating such new pilots into European-theatre conditions falling to fighter-training groups like the Goxhill-based 496th.

On 10 May 1944, Flight Officer Hugh Jones was detailed as one of a section of P-38 pilots who were to carry out a sequence of exercises. These were to include cine-gun practice in engagements with other P-38s; then formation flying, single-engined operation, and navigation on instruments at a specified 'over 5,000 feet' altitude; an intriguing mixture for any leader to tie into a coherent sequence. However, on getting airborne, Flight Officer Jones failed to join up with his own section, and instead, joined a pair who had been briefed to carry out a similar mixed-bag sortie.

The leader of this pair, accepting the stray lamb which had appeared on his right wing, headed west, and was to hold that general heading for twenty minutes while exercising his extempore trio in various instrument manoeuvres, his eventual intention being, as he later testified, to 'pin-point on Manchester'. As he neared the zone of high ground, however, he encountered thick cloud, and having descended to 2,500 feet in an attempt to find space beneath it, discovered that it extended to ground level. He then initiated a left-hand half-circle in order to bring his three aircraft into clear air once more; except that, on emerging from cloud just thirty seconds later, it was to discover that Flight Officer Jones had failed to keep station, and was missing.

Later, the American authorities were advised that Flight Officer Jones's machine had crashed and burnt out on the shoulder of Tintwistle Knarr, above Longdendale's Valehouse Reservoir. Examination of the wreckage then revealed that the P-38 had crashed inverted and at a shallow angle, from which the accident investigators concluded that Flight Officer Jones, no longer able to keep station, and so being forced to an instant reliance on his flight instruments in cloud, had lost control. Loss of control could also have occurred if, on transferring his attention from his leader's machine into his own cockpit, he had found his gyroscopically-stabilised flight-attitude instruments toppled – the result of a few minutes of tension-breaking follow-my-leader aerobatic chasing, perhaps? But this would have been no cause for concern had Flight Officer Jones only managed to maintain station in that final turn, for then he would have had no call upon his own instruments. The state of his flight-instrument gyros aside, however, being relatively inexperienced, and beyond that, trained for the most part as a 'clear-sky' day-fighter pilot, it is probable that he simply found himself unable to cope with the demands of a shock transition onto instrument flight.

But there was another factor, for, having once lost control when the formation turned at the leader's declared 2,500 feet on the altimeter, and over ground elevated to 1,640 feet above sea level, the 900 feet of sky Flight Officer Jones had been left with was precious little for him to either regain control or bale out; even had he broken cloud before impact.

Unsurprisingly the accident was attributed to '100% pilot error, with Error of Technique underlain by Inexperience'. Inexplicably, however, the compilers of the statistical section of the accident report, while recording Flight Officer's Jones's 300 hours' total flying, not only omitted his recent instrument-flying history, but positively dismissed instrument flying as 'Not a factor'. Notwithstanding which the final recommendation was 'That more instrument flying, and more cloud flying technique, be taught in the Operational Training Unit Course'.

In July 2006, Farmer Wright Cooper, of Tintwistle, spoke sombrely of that day. 'I was shepherding on Robinson's Moss,' he recalled, 'when this plane dived almost vertically into the ground. I was only a few hundred yards away, so I rushed across, but found that there was nothing to be done. The pilot's torso had been flung clear. And everything else was in pieces too. Some Water Board men had been working on the lower slopes and they soon joined me. Then one of them went down to Bottoms Reservoir office, and had the alarm raised.'

2006, Farmer Mr Wright Cooper, of Townend Farm, witness

As Mr Cooper had found, and as the American investigating officer recorded, when the aircraft impacted and exploded, its wreckage was spread across an area 100 yards long and fifty wide. 'The Americans,' Mr Cooper explained, 'winched most of the big stuff down. They'd wind in the cable as far as they could, then re-position their winch lower down, until eventually they reached their vehicles. Just the same, a lot of bits were left.' By 2006, however, the leavings had dwindled to a moderate pool of debris, together with a memorial cross; additionally two stakes had been raised to form a marker. And the latter proved a felicitous touch, for with the surrounding terrain so broken, with heather and scattered boulders abounding, the debris ring still proved tricky enough to re-locate.

The crash site in 2006, looking south-east

### North American P-51D Mustang 44-64084, Plainsteads Farm, Monk's Road, near Glossop

SK 02620 91369 337m
United States Eighth Army Air Force, 2nd Air Division, 4th Fighter Group, 336th Fighter Squadron, AAF356 (RAF Debden), near Saffron Walden
29 May 1945

Pilot, killed:
Flight Officer Darnaby H. Wilhoit, United States Army Air Force

On 8 May 1945, the Second World War in Europe ended, but with the Japanese War still raging it was decided to redeploy Mustangs to the Far East, the first stage in this transfer being to position the aircraft to Speke, the airfield most convenient for the Liverpool Docks. Accordingly, on 29 May 1945, a fleet of twenty-three Mustangs took off from RAF Debden on the one-hundred-and-sixty mile ferry. They were under the command of a first lieutenant pilot, Harold H. Frederick, a leader personally appointed by the 4th Fighter Group's senior operations officer.

As they commenced their let-down towards Speke, however, the whole operation became a debacle, with two pilots fatally crashing: the leader himself, but also Flight Officer Darnaby Wilhoit, in Mustang 44-64084; additionally, the leader's closely formating wing man only narrowly missed disaster, while several other pilots used up one too many of those proverbial nine lives. But complicated as the situation became, the seeds of the debacle had been sown before departure, permitting hindsight to be legitimately used to indicate some of the errors made, and to follow the vagaries of fortune that attended the ill-starred operation.

A leavening of seasoned pilots having been assigned to the task by Group Operations, First Lieutenant Frederick was then left to organise it. There were to be three fighter squadrons involved, but he elected to combine all the aircraft into a single formation flying in five elements of four, with one threesome.

Early on the morning of departure the weather forecast showed heaped frontal clouds sitting on all the hills of the intervening Peak District. At the same time actual reports from Speke showed low scud, and visibility markedly reduced by both rain and industrial smoke. Just the same, Group Operations approved a direct-routing which would overfly Leicester East airfield then transit the western Peak District before descending into Speke. Additionally, the controlling authority detailed 3,000 feet as the safety height to be flown. Only while First Lieutenant Frederick gave a comprehensive pre-take-off brief, even detailing the parking of the aircraft at Speke, several pilots recorded that he described the terrain on the direct route (across the Peak District!) as 'flat and level'.

As take-off time approached the Group Operations Officer ultimately responsible for the whole operation was advised that conditions had barely altered in the Speke area. But although he would later criticise his appointed leader for not checking the latest met before departing – and for not administratively clearing the flight in the approved manner! – he seems to have made no move to get this daunting information passed on, still less to delay the formation, which duly got airborne at 1005 hours.

As would have been expected of a flight into frontal conditions, it proved necessary to climb steadily in order to remain in clear skies, so that on passing Leicester the formation was at 6,000 feet over unbroken cloud. What could not have been anticipated was that a microphone should jam on, effectively blocking the communications channel for the whole formation. And this persisted throughout the flight, for when a frequency change was effected the inadvertently offending aircraft merely changed too. Just the same it seems strange that, although the flight was to cruise north-westwards for some forty-five minutes more, no action was taken to identify, and so eliminate, the inhibiting interference.

But all went well until, using time-and-distance reckoning alone, First Lieutenant Frederick closed the formation up, and began to lead them down by sections through the now unbroken overcast. What followed  has to chill the blood of any modern flier, but the reported experience of just two elements, Red and Blue Sections, will paint the picture.

The leader of Red Section descended in his turn to 2,400 feet on his altimeter, then, still in thick cloud, levelled off, looking for a hole. Not seeing one, he eased down further, and eventually broke cloud in rain and industrial smoke at an estimated 1,000 ft above Burtonwood airfield. Despite the jammed microphone (most likely aided by sheer proximity) he managed to contact Burtonwood and get a heading for Speke, where he landed. His number four, in the interim, having advised that he was flying wide to the left of the element in the descent because of a trim problem, heard the heading passed for Speke, adopted it, followed it through the gloom, and actually managed to rejoin Red Section before the landing; making Red Section's a very creditable, if decidedly nail-biting, effort all round!

Blue Section, the next in line to descend, was not so fortunate. Blue Leader led his section down to 1,500 feet on his altimeter, but finding himself still in cloud powered up and began to climb out again. In so doing, however, he lost his three followers, and did not break clear himself until 9,000 feet. Once on top, and now alone, he found a gap, and recognising Manchester, made a visual descent. But even having crept beneath the cloud he failed in three attempts to reach Speke and once again climbed, this time being forced up to 11,000 feet before rediscovering clear air. Finally, getting a heading for Speke from Burtonwood, and once more descending as best he could, he managed to locate the field, and landed; to receive the news that his number four, Flight Officer Darnaby Wilhoit, had fatally crashed.

Of the remainder of the twenty-three Mustangs, leader First Lieutenant Frederick would crash thirty-five miles to the north-east of Speke, his formating number two clipping the ground but surviving to climb away and return to Debden. The rest, in pairs or as singletons, would either probe their various hazardous ways into Speke, or abort the mission and return to Debden.

Flying P-51 44-64084, in Blue Section, Flight Officer Darnaby Wilhoit, the subject of this narrative, was one of those who, having lost station, had elected to continue to find Speke independently, and no doubt assuming that the ground thereabouts was relatively flat, as it had been described in the communal briefing, had continued to nose down through the overcast. Unhappily he had still been only slightly west of Kinder, and flew disastrously into the ground at Plainsteads Farm, immediately across the valley from The Grouse Inn, above Glossop, striking at 1,200 feet above mean sea level.

Witnesses, their attention drawn skywards by the noise of several aircraft manoeuvring above the overcast, saw Flight Officer Wilhoit's machine break cloud at a low altitude, turn hastily, as if to avoid a hill, then disintegrate as it struck the ground. The impact created a deep crater and a fan-shaped spread of debris, both of which minimised the resultant fire; accordingly, Flight Officer Wilhoit's watch, found to have stopped at 1054 hours, furnished poignant proof that his final flight had lasted just forty-nine minutes.

In terms of collateral damage, the exploding aircraft partially demolished two drystone walls and sent a four-year-old horse, hitherto grazing in the field, panicking through another two, the animal suffering superficial cuts about the legs and chest but no more serious injuries. The aircraft wreckage being easily accessible from Monk's Road and the American salvage team moving swiftly, the site was cleared by 1730 hours the same day.

No surface evidence remained at the site by 2006, but a metal-detector sweep revealed the extent of the debris spray outwards from the impact site, itself located just beyond the gateway to the field.

The crash site of Flight Officer Darnaby Wilhoit's Mustang

## North American P-51D Mustang 44-72181, Castleshaw Moor, north-east of Oldham

SD 99902 11184 403m

United States Eighth Army Air Force, 2nd Air Division, 4th Fighter Group, 336th Fighter Squadron, AAF356 (RAF Debden), near Saffron Walden
29 May 1945

Pilot: killed:
First Lieutenant Harold H. Frederick, United States Army Air Force

In the preceding section, describing the fatal crash of Mustang 44-64084, near Glossop, it was explained that on 29 May 1945, a formation of twenty-three Mustangs, each machine chosen for its low flying hours, was dispatched from Debden, near Saffron Walden, on a ferry flight to Speke. The present narrative, while necessarily restating certain points in recounting the fate of the formation leader, First Lieutenant Harold Frederick, focuses additionally upon the ensuing politicking.

The Senior Operations Officer of 4th Fighter Group had, it will be recalled, personally assigned command of the formation to First Lieutenant Frederick, who, though of undeniably junior rank, was a relatively experienced pilot who had logged just under a thousand hours of flying, of which some four hundred were combat time. First Lieutenant Frederick had already led the 4th Fighter Group on a wartime mission and was presently holding the post of Assistant Operations [Intelligence] Officer for the 336th Fighter Squadron. Accordingly, having ensured that First Lieutenant Frederick was provided with a fair proportion of experienced pilots for the lift, Group Operations then left him to make his own arrangements.

First Lieutenant Frederick decided to operate the aircraft from all the three squadrons involved as a single formation; no great matter in itself, for by splitting the twenty-three aircraft into elements of five double-pairs and a single threesome, each element leader would be ultimately responsible for his own section. In truth, organising the lift was not a particularly onerous task; given good weather and a reasonable degree of luck.

There was to be no good weather, however, for on the morning of the

First Lieutenant Harold H. Frederick, USAAF (courtesy Mr Alan Jones, vice Mr Ron Collier)

flight cloud was heaped upon the high ground while showers, scud and industrial haze reduced the visibility at Liverpool. Just the same Group Operations approved the choice of a direct routing over the Peak District, merely stipulating 3,000 feet as a safe height.

Nor was the aforementioned 'reasonable degree of luck' to be granted to First Lieutenant Frederick, for the lift was to end in an imbroglio with some aircraft landing in Speke, some aborting and returning to Debden, with two pilots dying, including First Lieutenant Frederick himself, and with First Lieutenant Frederick's wingman having a near-miraculous escape from following him into the ground.

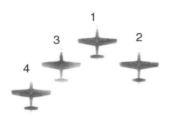

An element of two pairs flying in Left-Hand Finger-Four formation

First Lieutenant Frederick's element. In the descent numbers three and four separated as a pair, but on encountering cloud-covered high ground split up themselves. Number three subsequently rejoined the by-then damaged number two and returned in company with him to Debden, where number four also landed

On arriving in the Liverpool region, and having ordered the main formation into sections, First Lieutenant Frederick headed his own section down through cloud. Failing to locate Speke, however, he climbed again, but on breaking clear at about 10,000 feet, discovered that he had lost his numbers three and four. Just the same, he set himself up to make a further attempt, unaware as he did so that in the course of repositioning he had moved north-eastwards, and that as he led his number two down once more he was, in fact, a full forty miles away from sea-level Speke, and over the 1,300-feet-above-sea-level moorlands beyond Oldham.

So it transpired that his number two, still grittily sticking to his leader's starboard wing, with mist streaking past in his peripheral vision, suddenly saw the other's aircraft disintegrate in a 'ball of fire', felt a jar on his own port wing, and pulled aside, not climbing for height, but holding low, preferring to keep even doubtful visual contact with the ground rather than risk an instrument climb in his damaged state.

Settling, the erstwhile number two could see that his left wingtip was badly crumpled. A slow-speed handling check proved satisfactory, however, and when he then fell into company with his number three, by now himself a singleton, both of them turned for Debden, where their number four had already made a safe landing.

First Lieutenant Harold Frederick's aircraft, tragically, had indeed exploded in flames as it struck Castleshaw Moor, further disintegrating as it bellied over the hummocks, giving him no chance of surviving whatsoever.

But neither was he to be given any better chances back at base. For the Senior Group Operations Officer, in an ostensibly chest-baring statement, appeared to take full blame upon himself, reporting that 'The entire mission was poorly managed by the Group Operations Officer who accepted too many factors without closer scrutiny'. He then contritely observed that the mission should 'not have been left to independent units', and that a less than thorough supervision had been exercised. He further wrote of the rigorous control of flying activities he intended to exercise in the future, stoutly confessing, 'This does not excuse the previous laxity that is considered to be a major factor contributing to the disastrous accidents.'

And then, in the interests of showing just how remiss he had been in ever appointing First Lieutenant Frederick to the lead, he charged that the first lieutenant, in addition to not having correctly booked out, and not having updated his met information, had, through his lack of judgement in not aborting the mission in view of the weather and the lack of radio contact, been one hundred percent responsible for the accident; indeed for all the accidents and incidents alike.

This apparently career-sacrificing *mea culpa*, however, fell just a little short of convincing when his immediate superior reported upwards, pointing out that the worthy Senior Group Operations Officer 'had just taken over the operational duty and was not responsible on the day of this incident and ... that the previous operations officer had failed to take proper supervisory action': that he, as commanding general, had neither taken, nor even contemplated taking, any disciplinary action against his new Senior Group Operations Officer.

On the other hand First Lieutenant Frederick's squadron commander, whose involvement in the matter seems minimal, to say the least, was immediately relieved of his post and sent packing to the United States. The commanding general did, however, amend the new Senior Group Operations Officer's percentage of cause, apportioning it as 30% to supervisory personnel, 20% to the weather, and only 50% attributable to the flight leader.

At the crash site there may be some additional interest to the aircraft-enthusiast walker in that the particular P-51D in which First Lieutenant Frederick flew to his death had, until that ferry, been the personal aircraft of Colonel Everitt W. Stewart, the 4th Fighter Group's revered commander from February until September 1945. Dubbed '*Sunny VIII*', it had been resplendently maintained, but although some elements of it still remained at the crash site in 2006, no paintwork, not even its eleven swastika victory-symbols, had survived, only crumpled aluminium sheets and riveted spars, often enough hidden from sight by the rough and seasonally haylike hummock-grasses of wind-razed Castleshaw Moor.

2006, P-51D Mustang, 44-72181 (styled 'Sunny VIII')

## De Havilland DH89 Rapide G-ALBC, Edale Moor, Kinder

**SK 10160 88241** 607m

Solair Flying Services, Birmingham

30 December 1963

Crew: both injured to varying degrees:

Captain Dennis Holmes

Co-pilot John McWhirter

Although only 700 de Havilland DH89 Dragon Rapides were to be built, and although production ceased in 1946, the 1934 transport was to become one of the United Kingdom's most cherished designs. Many were commandeered by the RAF on the outbreak of the Second World War, when, renamed the Dominie, they were used for training and communications purposes. However, for years after that the Rapide's tapered wings, streamlined but fixed undercarriage, and its by-then singular biplane configuration, made it a familiar novelty in the sky.

Indeed, several were still airworthy beyond the turn of the century, the type being used for pleasure flying at Duxford, just as it had been in the late nineteen-forties at the embryo, canvas-tented Heathrow when the author's father paid seven shillings and sixpence (35.5 pence!) to send him – in the care of a lady captain – on a fifteen-minute flight. Remembering what wages were then, this was an enormous outlay; but, in truth, as an equivalent fee, not all that very far removed from the twenty-five pounds charged at Duxford in 2006. [Flying instruction in 1956, just by-the-by, cost £3 an hour.]

With its light construction and easy adaptability, whether for freighting, passenger-flying, or parachute dropping, the Rapide was understandably popular with hopefully-emergent airline companies, among them the Birmingham-based Solair Flying Services, which used Rapide G-ALBC for photographic surveys.

On 30 December 1963, having completed their assigned task, a Solair crew, Captain Dennis Holmes and his co-pilot, Mr John McWhirter, were returning to Birmingham from Middleton-St-George, a wartime RAF airfield and, for many years since, Teesside Airport. Approaching halfway along his 140-mile course, Captain Holmes, encountering stronger than anticipated headwinds, it might be – or, conceivably, becoming uncomfortable with his fuel consumption – decided that it would be politic to divert to Manchester and refuel. However, while his direct routing to Birmingham would have taken him well to the east of Ladybower, and over relatively low-lying terrain, his change of course to Manchester took him skimming over the crag-rimmed plateau of Kinder Scout, an expanse of moorland raised to an average height of some two thousand feet above sea level.

As might have been expected from a weather pattern giving high winds and billowing cloud, strong vertical gusts obtained over the plateau, and when a downdraught embraced the presently ground-hugging machine, it effectively sucked it from the sky at such a rate that its twin 200 horsepower Gipsy Six engines were quite unable to counteract the descent.

The machine struck heavily and disintegrated, but providentially there was no fire, for both crew members were incapacitated. Co-pilot McWhirter suffered head injuries which, while painful, eventually turned out to be slight. But Captain Holmes sustained a broken leg which immobilised him amidst the wreckage.

The downdraught had struck too swiftly to permit a distress call, so both knew from the outset that they were in for a cold and uncertain wait. In fact, it was to be colder and more uncertain than they might have anticipated, even at that, for although they were spotted by a helicopter before darkness fell, conditions had so worsened by then that the helicopter crew were unable to even contemplate landing. Indeed it was to be the fortunate chance of a glint of moonlight on a metal panel that eventually led a blizzard-bucking mountain rescue team to the site. Even then it was a matter of leaden-footed hours before Mr McWhirter was helped, and Captain Holmes carried, off Edale Moor and down to where proper care could be given.

One of the first on the scene had been Mr Gordon Miller, by title 'Area Ranger for Kinder – including Edale, Castleton, and Hayfield', who, in 2006, recalled that the first thing both pilots asked about, and continued to be concerned over above all else, was the safety of the camera and the films; that only when assured that these had been secured would they turn to their own requirements.

What the long-defunct Solair thought of its captain being caught out by a downdraught is not recorded, but there was nothing to be done with the remains of the stately old Rapide beyond incinerating what would burn in order to obviate its distracting from any future airborne searches. Indeed, Area Ranger Miller spoke graphically of the bonfire, photographed by his associate, Peak Park Ranger Jim Buie, and particularly of 'the writhing iridescence' as petrol-soaked, painted wood and doped fabric flared up in the breeze.

Because of the relative remoteness of the crash site there was still a substantial amount of wreckage at the scene in July 2006, notably the cylinder block of one of the engines; but little else identifiable; just a general scattering of intermingled wood and metal fragments. And little enough beyond the site. Nothing but the nearby lift of boulders above a moorland otherwise largely featureless; and deeply rutted to any horizon the uncertain Kinder weather may allow by a myriad twisting groughs and hags.

As will be appreciated with a site lying in such tortuous terrain, a careful search-about might well be called for in order to locate the correct gully.

Rapide G-ALBC, photograph by courtesy of Peak Park Ranger Jim Buie

Debris at the crash site of Rapide G-ALBC in 2006

## North American Sabre Mk.2 19234, Holme Moss

SE 09106 05071 536m
Royal Canadian Air Force, No.137(T) Flight, Ringway (Manchester)
14 December 1954

Pilot: killed:
Flying Officer Patrick V. Robinson, Royal Canadian Air Force

In 1954 the Royal Canadian Air Force was occupying RAF stations in Britain as part of its 'Cold War' commitment. On 14 December 1954, one of its Sabres, No.19234, part of a batch to be made over to the Greek Air Force, had been undergoing servicing at the maintenance depot at Ringway, Manchester. Emerging from the hangar towards evening, now sporting its Greek colours, it was to be test-flown by Flying Officer Patrick Robinson. Some time after take-off, however, and in conditions of poor visibility, the machine was seen to pass relatively low over Holme in the direction of the 1,700-feet-above-sea-level Holme Moss. Then, shortly after it had passed into the gloom, the concerned watchers, seeing a brief glow high in the mist followed by the sound of an impact, knew only too well what had happened.

Rescue efforts were soon under way but the weather made the crash difficult to find; and even when the site was eventually located it became clear that the task was one of salvage rather than of rescue. For the Sabre had flown directly into the moor and skidded on, shedding wings and other components as it went. It had also torn Flying Officer Robinson from his ejection-seat harness, thrown him through the canopy, and tumbled him a full eighty yards further on along the line of flight.

The inquiry had little to do in finding that the aircraft had simply been flown too low, Flying Officer Robinson having taken no account of the terrain.

In 2006 there was a substantial amount of wreckage still to be seen, gathered in three sites around the reference given, the three sites reflecting reasonably well both the line of approach and the track of the Sabre after impact.

The main debris site, Holme Moss, 2006

## North American FMk.4 Sabres XD707 and XD730, Kinder Scout and Black Ashop Moor

SK 06926 89664 595m Kinder: initial impact point, start of debris trail
SK 07268 90236 470m Black Ashop Moor: wings, gear, with an engine in an adjacent grough
SK 07300 90100 480m Black Ashop Moor, two debris pools
SK 07548 90390 437m Black Ashop Moor, the second engine
No.66 Squadron, RAF Linton-on-Ouse, No. 12 Group, Fighter Command
22 July 1954

Formating pilots: both killed:
Flying Officer James D. Horne, section leader (XD707)
Flight Lieutenant Alan Green, formating pilot (XD730)

When Russian-built swept-wing MiG-15 jet fighters were encountered in Korea in 1950, British manufacturers had nothing to match them. British transonic swept-wing fighters were under development to replace the straight-winged subsonic Meteors and Vampires, but until the Hunter arrived in 1955, Canadian-built Sabres filled the void. Held to be pleasant to fly, most of the Sabres were based in Germany, but No.66 Squadron was among those units equipped with them in Britain.

So it was that on 22 July 1954, four of the No.66 Squadron Sabres were recovering to Linton-on-Ouse, near York, after a high-level interception sortie flown in the course of a major annual-evaluation war-game. For the descent, the formation leader had split his section into pairs, each pair entering cloud independently at 12,000 feet. Some time later, as his pair passed 5,000 feet, still in cloud, the overall leader transmitted an advisory warning to Flying Officer James Horne, now leading the second pair, against descending below 3,000 feet on their present heading: the more realistic safety height of the future was to be 3,800 feet.

The foursome had noted already that Flying Officer Horne's radio was weak at times, so he may not have heard the warning; certainly, he did not acknowledge. Indeed nothing more was heard of him, or of his number two, until three days later when a walker came upon a body on The Edge, high above Black Ashop Moor.

Until this discovery bad weather had hampered the search, although the keeper of the Kinder Reservoir had reported being alarmed by two jet fighters roaring at very low level towards cloud-covered Kinder. Despite his concern, however, he had heard no subsequent impact.

These aircraft had undoubtedly been the two Sabres, although what made Flying Officer Horne take his number two that low will never be known. A likely scenario, however, is that he saw a clearance below him, and dropped into what turned out to be a 'sucker's gap' – a beckoning clearance which then closed in around him. Certainly, in his evidently hasty pull for a safe height, he managed to clear the edge of Kinder, but equally evidently something untoward happened after he had done so, for both aircraft struck the ground in a single impact point not many yards into the plateau.

To conjecture further, although Flight Lieutenant Alan Green, the number two, was more experienced than his leader, he was still settling in having been posted from another squadron. It could be then, that, caught out by the hastily initiated transition from level flight to very steep climb, he had – understandably – twitched just that little bit, causing his wingtip to lock with his leader's tail. Or what is equally likely, bearing in mind that both aircraft were in very steep climbing attitudes, is that, in reaction to his leader's over-hasty pull, Flight Lieutenant Green had pulled even harder, got high, and being momentarily unsighted from his leader, had collided in blindly pushing back into position.

The court of inquiry, however, did not treat with such speculation, finding only that Flying Officer Horne, as section leader, had failed to observe the area safety height – which he should have been familiar with regardless of any missed transmission – although it found some little mitigation in his faulty radio. It specifically noted that no blame was to be attached to Flight Lieutenant Green, whose sole responsibility had been to formate upon his leader.

200A Mr Graham Atkin, who discovered the tragedy

The walker who had stumbled upon the tragedy was Mr Graham Atkin, who described the experience in 2006. 'It was the Sunday of that week, at about midday,' he explained, 'and I was heading for Fairbrook Naze. I'd left Ashop Head some way back when I saw something white ahead of me. At first I thought it was snow – but in July? It was, of course, an only partly-deployed parachute. And then I saw the body of the pilot. He'd clearly been there for some time, and equally clearly, although this was the first dead person I'd ever seen, there was nothing to be done for him. So I angled my way down into Black Ashop Moor, heading now for the Snake Inn, and initially stepping over scores of cannon shells and bits of metal. I didn't see any of the major wreckage down in the valley, so by angling off I'd obviously passed to the right of that. Once at the Inn I dialled 999 and reported the crash. Then I caught the bus into Glossop [the good old fifties!], to the police station. They'd made phone calls, among them to the RAF Mountain Rescue Unit at Harpur Hill, and now they took me to Hayfield where I led them back up via William Clough to where the pilot was. A policeman took down my statement in his notebook. Then, I suppose, I left them all to it, and went on down again: how fit I must have been back then!' He paused. 'Some days later I had to attend the coroner's inquest at Marple. And really, that was that. I've always supposed the two planes simply crashed into the hill in the cloud, but, as it happens, only a couple of years ago I was leafing through a book on Derbyshire where the author had it that they had been led into the cliff by a ghost aeroplane! What a lot of rubbish! But then people tend to make up these stories of ghost aeroplanes in the Peak.'

'I remember,' he added, 'in about 2000, Alan Jones visiting to talk me through what I saw that day. Apparently he'd actually found the pilot's ejection seat.'

In fact, researcher Mr Jones had spent a considerable time examining the variously scattered sites of the two Sabres, on one occasion actually breaking an ankle in the process and having to be stretchered off Black Ashop Moor! 'We found that particular pilot's ejection seat', he said, speaking in 2006, 'just off the plateau, jammed into the first tiny gully on the Black Ashop Moor side of the path. Although by that time it had been flooded full of rocks.'

Given the juxtaposition of body and ejection seat it is possible that the pilot had tried to eject, but that, early ejector seats not having the ground-level, zero-speed capability they later acquired, the attempt had been made in descending flight, and fractionally too late. It seems more probable, however, that he had been unconscious throughout, and that he and his ejection seat had been separated as the two aircraft continued to disintegrate; a more kindly sequence of events, and hopefully, the correct one.

Much evidence of this accident still remained in 2006, the debris trail stretching from the impact point, just inside the edge of the Kinder plateau, for a thousand yards north-eastwards into the depths of Black Ashop Moor, where major components lay.

2006, the Sabres' initial impact site, Kinder Edge, looking towards Kinder Reservoir

2006. Black Ashop Moor, looking south-west, back along the trajectory

2006, F-86 Sabre engines at main site, Black Ashop Moor, and to the north-east of the main site

## Supermarine Spitfire K9941, Back Lane, Hooton Roberts, Rotherham

SK 48601 96945 46m
No.72 (Basutoland) Squadron, RAF Church Fenton, No.12 Group, Fighter Command
21 August 1939

Pilot: solo:
Sergeant Donald Victor Peacock, killed

On 21 August 1939, Sergeant Donald Peacock, of No.72 Squadron, was engaged in local flying from RAF Church Fenton when his engine began to malfunction; ultimately this led him to stall, and then to nosedive into a field off Back Lane at Hooton Roberts, near Rotherham. There was a fire after impact, but the coroner determined that Sergeant Peacock had been killed instantly when his head struck the instrument panel.

In late-2005 Mr Rex Plowright, of Hooton Robert, a lad of ten in 1939, described what he saw. 'We'd been playing in the yard at Holly Farm,' he said, 'when we heard this plane coming down, and then this great bang. It was a Spitfire, and it dived straight into what was then Cartwright's Top

Field, above Back Lane, causing a crater. All of us got bits, of course – later, we'd collect shrapnel off the streets when they raided Sheffield – but very soon the police arrived, and then the RAF, and we were sent packing. The RAF were there for quite a while, collecting the bits, but the buried engine was taken later, and the crater backfilled.'

Mr Plowright's older brother, Roy, was yet more closely involved, as he related in July 2006, speaking from his home in Weston Super Mare. 'I was working in the Holly Farm stack yard with the Cartwright's labourer, Ken Howe, when we saw this aircraft, its engine sounding odd, appear out of the low cloud, then disappear up into it again. Only instants later it emerged again, in a spin, and crashed. We dropped

The screened-off cockpit section, showing No.72 Squadron's code SD, valid April to September 1939; photograph by courtesy of Mr Roy Plowright, witness

what we were doing but both the Cartwrights – the farmer, and his wife, Lily – and 'Tel' White had been nearer, so that as we got close Mrs Cartwright came running back towards the house, desperately calling out, "Get a knife! Get a knife!"'

Mr Roy Plowright

Despite the war fever filling the press of the day, reporting restrictions had not yet been imposed, and accordingly the crash was well covered by the *Rotherham Telegraph* which interviewed Mr David Cartwright, the incumbent of Low Farm, and Mr Telson White. 'We saw the plane from the farmyard,' Mr Cartwright said. 'Its engine was missing, and we watched it come lower and lower over the village. Suddenly the engine picked up for a minute and the pilot appeared to be trying to climb again. The next minute it was hurtling earthwards.' The paper noted how the two men had 'braved the blazing fuel tanks as, working with desperate speed, they cut the straps and the helmet tube [probably the oxygen tube] to extricate the pilot.' It also commented on the fact that, 'Despite the terrific impact none of the eight machine guns which are installed in the wings was broken.'

A motorist driving down the hill at Hooton Roberts had also seen the machine in difficulties, and reported, 'It got into a spin and then vanished behind the hill. A moment later I heard the crash. I went straight to a telephone and reported it, then drove to the scene.'

Sergeant Peacock's father told the coroner's court that, since joining the RAF four years before, his son had always stressed how 'careful the RAF was to ensure that its aircraft were airworthy before letting pilots take them up'. The coroner, for his part, stated that he intended to elicit no more details than would enable him to issue a burial certificate; that he did not intend to ask technical questions which 'might give rise to objection "on the grounds of the times we are now living in".' He added, 'It is, perhaps, not expedient to give much publicity – if any – to points of that kind.' The coroner's diligence in avoiding delving too deeply into matters that might affect national security was timely, for the anticipated war broke out just under two weeks later.

Regarding the sequence of events leading to the crash, it seems that Sergeant Peacock, faced with a malfunctioning engine, had commenced a forced landing, but that when the engine picked up, had hoped for the best, lifting the nose to climb away; only to lose power completely, after which, caught nose high with falling airspeed, the stalling aircraft had spun into the ground.

In 2006, Mr Geoffrey Ogley, of Hilltop Farm, remembered his friend, Mr Bernard Wheelhouse, of Holly Farm, describing the crash, and the subsequent visit, just days later, by the pilot's saddened family. For his part, Mr Wheelhouse's son, John, the 2006 incumbent, was able to verify the actual impact site. 'Some twenty-five years ago,' he explained, 'a metal-detectorist got permission from the then-owner, Mr Beaver, to dig in the field. I had a JCB handy, and we found several bits of aircraft metal, most of which the chap took. The rest, which I kept, have long since disappeared.'

Certainly, in early 2006 there was no sign of the crash on the hilltop of what, by then, had become known as Beaver's Top Field.

The impact site of Spitfire K9941, Hooton Roberts

Mr Geoffrey Ogley

Mr John Wheelhouse

### Supermarine Spitfire, Wessenden Head Moor, north-west of Black Hill

SE 07493 05492 536m

In the 1980s researcher Mr John Ownsworth and some colleagues took this reputed crash site seriously enough to spend a day metal-detecting, but found no evidence. Certainly nothing aircraft-related was to be seen in 2006. Nor was any archive evidence discovered. As with similar sites having such provenance, this one is recorded for posterity.

### Supermarine Spitfire, Irontongue Hill, Higher Swineshaw Reservoir

SE 01498 00599 408m

Some sources hold that the wreckage of this aircraft was totally buried, but as far back as 1949 Mr Jim Chatterton, of Tintwistle, found 20mm cannon shells, as he noted, 'on Irontongue Hill, just below the summit, on the south-western side of the hill; a large, sparsely grassed area.' In the seventies, researcher Mr John Ownsworth spent a day metal-detecting the site with him but found nothing. A search in 2006 also proved negative, nor have any other details emerged from records. This is another site with provenance enough to be worth recording for a posterity in which more sophisticated detectors might advance research.

### Supermarine Spitfire Mk.2A P7883, Rushup Edge, Edale

SK 10854 83536 505m impact point of aircraft
SK 10890 83455 520m terminal point of aircraft
SK 10380 83745 424m map, in hollow
SK 10356 83845 394m Mae West
SK 10561 84264 294m pilot
SK 09284 82558 451m debris left near road for disposal
No.53 Operational Training Unit, RAF Hibaldstow (near Brigg), No.9 Group, Air Defence of Great Britain Command
10 December 1943

Pilot: injured:
Sergeant Ronald A. Mitchell

While Fighter Command, with its Spitfires and Hurricanes, has passed into history as the saviour of the country during the Battle of Britain, it should be remembered that the fighters would most often have been flying blind had it not been for the air-defence control system built up prior to the Second

World War. Until 1936, when the various RAF Commands emerged, the defences had been co-ordinated in what had been known since the First World War as the Air Defence of Great Britain (ADGB), and so important was the national-defence role that the old title re-emerged on 15 November 1943. However, the change was soon reversed, and on 15 October 1944, Fighter Command flourished once again. But on 10 December 1943, during the interregnum, when an accident report was raised on Spitfire P7883, an aircraft of No.53 Operational Training Unit (OTU), whose controlling station was RAF Kirton in Lindsey, it was duly recorded as coming under of the aegis of ADGB Command.

Not that on the day in question Sergeant Ronald Mitchell was engaged in air-defence duties as such, for as an OTU pupil he was practising formation flying in company with three other Spitfires airborne from Kirton's satellite airfield, RAF Hibaldstow, near Brigg, in Lincolnshire.

The formation leader had been briefed to operate within a specified local area, but as the sortie progressed so deteriorating weather forced him to shift ever-further westwards in order to remain in air clear enough to allow him to carry out the evolutions to be practised. These would have included flying in close formation, but also in the looser, more tactically-flexible finger fours; possibly carrying out dummy attacks and interceptions, pair against pair, and certainly relaxing in exhilarating line-astern, follow-my-leader tailchases, the leader doing his utmost to shake off his faithful followers.

But periodically the leader would have – *should* have might be more apt here – advised his section of their whereabouts in case any of them should get separated. Certainly he would have opened them out, affording them the chance to check around their cockpits for temperatures, and pressures, and above all, fuel states, for at the high power settings often demanded in formation the Spitfire would guzzle its 85 gallons of fuel at a rate of 130 gallons an hour! And it was on one such break that Sergeant Mitchell found, undoubtedly to his consternation, that his fuel-gauge needle was hard to the left, indicating zero.

 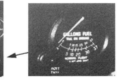

Spitfire fuel gauge (bottom-right dial), the top-pivoted needle hard over left, to zero

Understandably enough, Sergeant Mitchell was rattled. For a start, he lost the formation, but then, having called for, and obtained, an easterly homing for base, he cruised off to the west! Not a thing to be recommended in an aircraft seemingly out of fuel, but one for which there is a certain rationale; for Sergeant Mitchell expected to be over coastal Lincolnshire, not over inland Derbyshire, so to get a homing ostensibly sending him out to sea would have fought against every directional sense. Consequently, initially unable to carry out the mental gymnastics required, he turned instead towards the west, and even deeper into Derbyshire's high ground, rather than towards the east, and his low-lying Lincolnshire base.

At what stage he realised his error, and whether he had corrected it, is not known, for while his formation leader was still endeavouring to set up a rendezvous, Sergeant Mitchell saw a sudden darkening of the cloud, and only just had time to bring the nose up before flying into the ground.

There was no fire, but he was left with a broken leg, arm and nose, on a high, remote moorland that was most certainly not Lincolnshire, and upon which a December blizzard had now closed with a vengeance.

So it was that searching aircraft, having only the haziest idea whereabouts Sergeant Mitchell had dropped out of formation, had little chance of locating him. Indeed it was not until after another twenty-four hours that a ground search was even mounted; and then it was to be a purely extempore effort, some might say a truly 'British' affair, as two of the original members of that initial search party well remembered in late 2005.

Mr Ron Townsend, a retired Sheffield steelman, was able to refer to his 1943 diary, kept when he was a member of the Peak Climbing Club. 'It was a Saturday,' he recalled, 'and there was a blizzard blowing. But a group of us had planned a midnight walk on Kinder. So at about half-past ten we'd had a few preparatory drinks with Bill Heardman in the Church Hotel, Edale – it's The Ramblers' Inn now – when a police inspector came in and told us that a plane was missing. Apparently a farmer had heard a loud bang after one had passed low over Brown Knoll the day before, and a search plane had since reported seeing a wing on Rushup Edge.'

He pursed his lips. 'Well, we shelved our planned walk, and split up into parties, with mine searching its way upslope from, and parallel to the old drovers' path of Chapel Gate. The weather was still atrocious, but eventually we stumbled upon an aircraft map in a hollow just above the path. Which gave us an indication that the pilot might still be alive. At which point we were joined by our colleagues descending from Rushup Edge who had found the plane – a Spitfire – but not the pilot.'

Mr Jack Bricklebank, in 2005 a resident of Eyam, had been with the party searching high along the shoulders and upper surfaces of Rushup Edge. Like Mr Townsend he was then a reserved-occupation steelworker in Sheffield, but he would later fly solo during assessment selection as a Fleet Air Arm pilot, although eventually settling for wartime service in the Royal Navy, finishing up in Japan.

The initial impact point, above Barber Booth

'When we came upon the aircraft,' he remembered, 'my impression was that he'd belly-flopped. That is, he'd realised how close he was to the rim, and pulled back, but struck quite hard, then skipped, before finally pancaking in. So while the wings had broken off the fuselage was pretty well intact. We looked into the cockpit, but it was empty. So we realised the pilot must have survived the impact, at least.'

At that stage they had no reason to believe that the pilot had been seriously injured, but they reasoned that, realising how vulnerable he was in the Arctic conditions obtaining on the exposed heights, he had decided to leave the area of the wreck and make his way down to shelter. They knew that the nearest road lay eastwards, towards Mam Tor, but they knew too that during the late-afternoon blizzards of the day before the swell of Lord's Seat would have made that way seem untenable. The same applied to the prospect back along the trail of the aircraft, where the precipitous, snow-covered slopes, when glimpsed through the flurries, must have appeared as bottomless chasms, with hazarding crags. To the west, on the other hand, the broad ridge sloped gently downwards.

Looking west from the crash site: Sergeant Mitchell's route down

After nearly thirty-six hours any footprints in the snow had been obliterated by high winds and the continuing snowfalls, but they decided to follow the downsloping westerly ridge as the most likely bet. And so it was that as they slithered down to the largely snow-obscured Chapel Gate they came up with the lower party who had just found the map.

'We all dropped below the track,' resumed Mr Townsend, 'and almost at once came across a yellow "Mae-West" lifejacket, partially buried in snow, but liberally bloodstained. So although we knew then that we'd successfully second-guessed the pilot, we knew too that he had, in fact, been injured.'

'But', he traced his finger on the map, 'although we searched the valley bottom down to Dalehead, we could find no sign of him. And so at about four in the morning we made our way back to Edale. We had a meal, and then decided to set off again. Only by that time a full-scale official search by fifty or so police and Home Guard had got under way, and as we reached Barber Booth we were told that the pilot had been found in a gully not that far above the mouth of the Cowburn Tunnel.' He smiled, but rather grimly. 'He was alive! Which was certainly gratifying. But the feeling among all of us was that the farmer's report should have been acted upon much sooner.'

The court of inquiry was unable to settle upon an actual cause for the crash, although bad weather was advanced as a major factor, with Sergeant Mitchell's having lost the formation and then flown a reciprocal course exacerbating matters. The fuel gauge, it was suspected, had been faulty, and it was recommended that more attention should be paid to the Form 700, the RAF's equivalent of civil aviation's 'aircraft technical log'. But when they criticised the formation leader for having strayed

Former Sergeant
Ronald Mitchell in the
1980s

from the prescribed area then higher authority demurred, ruling that this had been perfectly understandable in view of the weather, and putting far more emphasis on the contribution of the faulty fuel gauge.

If Sergeant Mitchell's ordeal had been protracted, his recovery to health was to be equally so; but after six months off flying he was back in the air once more. Mr Peter Jackson – in 2006 a part-time Ranger and Information Officer at the Fairholmes Information Centre – met him in the 1980s. 'He particularly impressed me by the way he made a joke of his chequered flying history,' Mr Jackson remembered. 'He told us how, shortly after getting his wings he'd had a mid-air collision near Edinburgh, and crashed. After which he'd flown into Rushup Edge, and crashed again. Which convinced him the shooting war itself had to be safer; except that just a few days before VE Day [Victory in Europe Day, 8 May 1945] he was in a Mustang over Germany when he was shot up by a – supposedly friendly – Russian fighter!'

Not that even this put him off flying, for as Mr Jackson quoted him, 'I remained in the RAF until 1947, went on to first-generation jets, and had to be pulled kicking and screaming from the cockpit when it came time to leave the Service.'

Where the crash site is concerned, Mr Maurice Oaks, of Barber Booth, who got the job of clearing it, maintained that little was left behind. In 1980 Mr Oaks escorted researcher Mr John Ownsworth to the site and described how he had sledged the wreckage behind his tractor, parallel to the ridge path, to a point on the road where a Queen Mary had been waiting [at SK 09300 82520].

When Mr Bricklebank was told of this clearance, however, he smiled. 'There'd been souvenirs enough earlier on. For a start,' he confided darkly, 'Ben Twig, my walking companion, who found the Spitfire with me, went back and took out the altimeter.' He paused, his smile becoming pensive. 'He's long gone now, good old Ben. But he became one of the earliest members of the RAF Mountain Rescue Service.'

The terminal site of Spitfire P7883

## Douglas C-47 Skytrain (Dakota) 42-108982, east of James's Thorn, Ashton Clough, Bleaklow

SK 08069 94736 528m impact site, east
SK 08045 94736 530m impact site, west (see below for other, related sites)
United States Ninth Army Air Force, 9th Air Force Support Command, 314th Troop Carrier Group, 32nd Troop Carrier Squadron, AAF527 (RAF Leicester East)
24 July 1945

Occupants: seven; two passengers, five crew, all killed:
First Lieutenant George L. Johnson, United States Army Air Force, pilot
First Lieutenant Earl W. Burns, USAAF, co-pilot (monument raised)
First Lieutenant Beverly W. Izlar, USAAF, navigator
Sergeant Francis M. Maloney, USAAF, radio operator
Sergeant Theodore R. McCrocklin, USAAF, crew chief
Corporal Grover R. Alexander, USAAF, passenger
Leading Aircraftman John D. Main, RAF, lift-hitching passenger

From 1936 the American Army Air Corps played an active part in the development of the Douglas airliner that metamorphosed into the DC-3 – the Dakota to the British – spawning in turn the C-53 Skytrooper and the C-47 Skytrain variants. By 1941 the Air Corps had become the Army Air Force and the C-47 Skytrain its standard transport aircraft, which, with a strengthened floor and a wide cargo hatch, proved capable of carrying out a seemingly infinite number of tasks. So it was that, when C-47 42-108982 was dispatched from the American base at RAF Leicester East to that at RAF Renfrew (subsequently Glasgow airport) it was carrying not only passengers but a jeep, lashed aft.

Dependable as the C-47 was, however, this one was not to complete its flight, for just sixty-nine miles into its two-hundred-and-thirty-mile route it was flown into the cloud-covered hillside high on Bleaklow's Shelf Moor where it disintegrated, much of it burning, leaving no survivors. The jeep, for its part, burst its lashings and was propelled forwards with such violence that it smashed its way through the passenger seating zone and out of the aircraft; closely mirroring the jeep at the crash of Skytrain 41-38608, at Bosley (*The Central Area*, pp.113-4), in illustrating the danger of stowing main-cabin freight to the rear of passengers; the practice later adopted on types with no under-floor freight hold being to load cargo forward of passengers when operating in the passenger-cum-freight role.

Before his departure, the pilot, First Lieutenant George Johnson, had been advised to follow an east-coast routing in view of reported strong winds and low cloud ceilings over the High Peak. Notwithstanding which he made the perfectly proper command decision to fly the direct, time-saving track. Only less properly – indeed fatally for his crew – he then chose a demonstrably unsafe cruising altitude, taking too little account of the height of the en-route terrain, and just as little of either the low cloud or the vertical currents the strong winds would breed.

It says much for the rugged construction of the Dakota that, despite the force of the impact and the subsequent fire, the rear fuselage and tailplane were relatively intact when the wreck was discovered by an off-duty airman, identified by the *Glossop Chronicle* as a Sergeant Pidgeon, two days later. The salvage teams disposing of the wreckage, however, spilled much of it down the adjacent Ashton Clough.

In July 2006 there were two distinct sites in the area of impact, each with debris and each still largely devoid of vegetation. In addition, below the fence erected in 2003, an undercarriage member lay on the shoulder of Ashton Clough. Finally there was the rest of the wreckage trail extending down the Clough to Shelf Brook and Doctor's Gate. Indeed, until 2000 or so both engines were to be seen, since when the best-preserved one had either been removed by enthusiasts or buried by floods. In which context, speaking of a major airframe section, long since become seemingly integral with an accumulation of soil and rocks, Mr Mike Brown, of Glossop, an inveterate crash-site visitor throughout his boyhood, asserted, 'When we'd first go there, in 1957 or so, that aft-fuselage section, just before the tail, provided a good shelter from the rain, and would just hold three lads.'

## Lower sites as recorded in July 2006:

SK 08139 94627 478m undercarriage components, grass shoulder of the clough

In Ashton Clough, descending:
SK 08155 94594 446m fuselage section
SK 08144 94576 440m fuselage member
SK 08130 94577 437m panel
SK 08107 94496 424m undercarriage component
SK 08075 94434 390m reduction gear
SK 08067 94317 377m engine
SK 08057 94287 355m panel
SK 08051 94254 345m fragment

This particular crash made no banner headlines when reported in the *Glossop Chronicle* a week later, being covered in a modestly-heralded single paragraph on page five. It did, however, make near-epochal news as far as the Peaklands' air crash scene was concerned, the newspaper observing, 'The end of hostilities in Europe has lifted

Skytrain impact sites in 2006, looking west towards James's Thorn; the 2003 fence is downhill

February 2003. The westerly impact site, with the 2002 family tribute to co-pilot First Lieutenant Burns

A landing-gear member on the grassy slopes, 2006. Left and up to the impact point; down and right to the Ashton Clough sites

Left: A major fuselage section in Ashton Clough; in the 1950s it 'would hold just three lads ...'

the security blackout which has curtained the numerous crashes on the moorlands during the last five years. Last week's crash is just one more to be added to the already long tragic list which has grown since 1939 and in which there have been very few survivors.'

In late 2002, a tasteful, Perspex-sealed, A4-sized testimony to the co-pilot, First Lieutenant Earl Burns, appeared at the site. Placed there by members of his family, following research by aviation enthusiasts, it clearly annoyed some walker's sensibilities, for by the following July it had been smashed. Yet if it was the depiction of the American flag which riled, on the eve of the controversial second conflict in Iraq, clearly the Remembrance Day crosses also found disfavour, for their limbs had been pointedly snapped across.

At that time this was a pattern of vandalism repeated on the ex-Staffordshire Home Guard memorial at the Merryton Low trig column, and also at the Bleaklow Defiant site, where a tiled plaque was smashed in a way that owed nothing to the elements.

Merryton Low trig point. Memorial to those ex-members of the Staffordshire Home Guard later killed in regular units. Memorial crosses deliberately snapped

Above: 2005. The vandalised memorial to First Lieutenant Earl Burns

Memorial tile to the Defiant on Bleaklow, deliberately smashed

## Short Stirling Mk.3 LJ628, Upper Commons, east of Margery Hill summit, Howden Moors

SK 20291 95633  469m impact area
SK 20142 95520  480m terminal area, debris in gully
SK 21326 95900  361m wing fragments in Ewden Beck
No.1654 Heavy Conversion Unit, RAF Wigsley (west of Lincoln), No.5 Group, Bomber Command
21 July 1944

Crew: ten aboard, two injured:
Squadron Leader Hadland, pilot, flight commander, observing
Flying Officer O'Leary, screening pilot
Flying Officer L. Gardiner, pilot under training
Sergeant McDonald, navigator
Sergeant James Coulson, bomb aimer, injured
Sergeant John Gittings, screen flight engineer
Sergeant Ludlow, flight engineer under training
Sergeant Tex Burroughs, wireless operator
Sergeant Lennox van Nierkirk, Royal Rhodesian Air Force, air gunner (rear turret), injured
Sergeant Austin, mid-upper gunner, Royal Rhodesian Air Force

Stirling losses became so heavy compared with those of the higher-flying Halifaxes and Lancasters that in September 1944 it was removed from bombing operations; just the same it continued to serve on such duties as minelaying, glider-towing, electronic countermeasures, clandestine operations, and transportation. In addition it was used for four-engined training prior to conversion to Lancasters or Halifaxes, with crews posted onto it being trained by No.1654 Heavy Conversion Unit (HCU) located at RAF Wigsley. One such crew, earmarked for Lancasters, which got airborne for its initial Stirling training sortie on 21 July 1944, was that gathered about him by HCU-trainee Flying Officer L. Gardiner.

The normal crew complement of the Stirling was seven men, but even for a training flight this one was top heavy, with ten occupants, for in addition to the normal Conversion Unit's instructing – or 'screening'– staff, the unit's flight commander was aboard to carry out an overall monitoring.

The sortie, being the initial introduction to the Stirling, was planned to be wide ranging, but started with a climb to height, followed by a fly-around during which various engines were stopped in order to familiarise the pilot and flight-engineer trainees with the technical problems and altered handling qualities when either an outer or inner engine was lost. With all engines re-instated the aircraft was then descended preparatory to practising landings and take-offs back at Wigsley. However, in the descent, after forty minutes in the air, having flown for the most part over complete cloud cover, and with everyone patently concentrating rather too much on what was going on inside the aircraft, a cry of alarm from the front turret changed the whole picture.

Looking up at the warning, the operating pilot saw, rushing towards him through the enveloping mist, what the bomb aimer in the front turret had seen just instants before, rough moorland where only sky had been expected; moorland which, despite an instant application of full power and even brutish back pressure on the stick, so rapidly outclimbed the bomber that the aircraft struck heavily, and proceeded to disintegrate over a two hundred yards' slide. Providentially, there was no fire.

In the immediate aftermath of the crash two separate pairs of crew-members variously set off across the moors – one pair reaching Ewden Lodge Farm – and eventually brought assistance. Subsequently, although both the bomb-aimer and the rear-gunner received injuries which required surgery, all eventually returned to flying duties. Indeed, with the exception of the bomb-aimer, who, when fit, was moved to another crew at the Lancaster Finishing School and later completed an operational tour, the other six remained together. These moved on to a different Lancaster squadron from their erstwhile bomb-aimer where they too safely completed a tour of operations.

It became apparent to the court of inquiry that in the course of the sortie the aircraft had been allowed to drift far further west than anyone on board had suspected; moreover, that only the sketchiest attempt had been made to fix the aircraft's position before commencing the descent.

Similarly it was evident that during the engine-out-handling phase of the flight, and during the initial descent, the undue pre-occupation of the pilots and flight engineers had led to a gradual and undetected frittering away of height. This was not a situation that would have been apparent to very many of the crew members, for each would have been busy with his own specialisation. Not only that, but had anyone noticed the altimeter, it would have shown an apparently healthy 1,500 feet or so, having been set to zero on the 70 feet-above-sea-level runway of RAF Wigsley; certainly nobody aboard conceived that they had drifted over, and were now letting down over, the 1,560 feet-above-sea-level Upper Commons area of Broomhead Moor!

There followed condemnation, from the officer commanding the unit upwards through every higher echelon, of all those members of the crew responsible for having omitted to acquire an adequate fix before beginning the descent. But although the Air Officer Commanding would rule, and his superior, the Air Officer Commanding-in-Chief, would concur, that the accident was 'caused by the disobedience [by the pilot] orders for breaking cloud', the incident was clearly regarded as one of the hazards attendant upon intensive training; for it became a case of flying-logbook endorsements in red, formal reproofs for both pupils and instructors – slapped wrists all around – then back to the task in hand.

In the 1980s the former Sergeant John Gittings, the one-time screen flight engineer, met Peak Park Ranger Peter Jackson and spoke of the impact. 'I was in the astrodome,' he recalled, 'expecting the clouds to part and show us Wigsley's runways, when suddenly I felt this massive bump, and saw lumps of earth flying past.'

The former Sergeant John Gittings in the 1980s, courtesy of Mr Peter Jackson

Mr Alwyn Haigh, of West Nab Farm, Bradfield, was a schoolboy in 1944, but in 2006 he retained vivid memories of the crash. 'It was a really foggy day,' he recalled, 'and for some time we'd heard this aircraft overhead. Eventually it came very low indeed, although it never broke cloud. Then we heard it had crashed.' Mr Haigh's first visit to the site had come just days later. 'Not long after we passed the Broomhead Moor Shooting Lodge we could see what turned out to be one of the wheels.' He paused. 'One of our souvenirs was a gyroscope, but although there were no sentries on the plane, the roads were guarded, and so eventually we ditched it.' Having reflected, he went on, 'What stuff the RAF wanted they took on crawler tractors over White Carr Ridge and the track to Cottage Farm, on the Mortimer Road, but they left loads at the site.'

Mr Lewis Couldwell, who was brought up in Garlic House Farm, remembered that several bits of wreckage were spilled off during the wartime salvage operation, with some unaccountably wandering off even that route. 'When we were out beating from the shooting lodge and had to drop down into Ewden Beck on our way to the northern side of the moor, we'd shelter from the rain under a wing that was propped over some rocks; though how it had got down there, we never did discover, for most wreckage they salvaged, but didn't trans-ship from Mortimer Road, was dumped onto Ewden Height – among the targets, some of which they'd shoot at from over near North America Farm, beyond Range Moor Top, to the north-west.'

Certainly, in 2004, a great deal of debris was still strewn along the line of approach at the main site, whole panels flapping forlornly, and most notable of all, the great struts and vast, smooth-tyred wheels that would have cushioned the machine back to the tarmac, had it indeed been, as the screen pilot supposed it to be, over Lincolnshire, and not over the blandly-featureless Long Pole Ridge of moorland Upper Commons.

Debris beside Ewden Beck, 2006

Gully debris in 2004; and gully in 2006, cleared of large items

With the crash site being so remote, and the Stirling being such a large aircraft, this very substantial amount of wreckage seemed destined to remain for all time. Early in 2005, however, 'The Stirling Project' preservation group obtained Service assistance to airlift the major items from the site for use as templates in the creation of a static-display Stirling. Just the same, enough debris remained in 2006 to tempt the interested walker onto this otherwise largely unfrequented, and for the most part, trackless, moor.

Walkers joyously heather-bashing across to this site, however, might usefully note the caveat included in the Hawker Hunter narrative, and further evidenced in this, that the moor was used as a World-War-Two firing range, and that any ordnance discovered will be potentially lethal.

2004, vast, smooth-tyred wheels

### Fairey Swordfish Mk.1 P4223, Heydon Head, Black Hill

SE 08338 04762 572m
No.751 Squadron, Royal Naval Air Service Ford (Littlehampton), West Sussex
25 January 1940

Pilot: killed:
Sub-Lieutenant Gerald Vyvian Williamson, Royal Naval Volunteer Reserve

For a single-engined, carrier-borne aircraft the Swordfish was surprisingly large, enhancing its short-landing and take-off capabilities with leading-edge slats and lift-augmenting ailerons. Its normal crew complement was three, but on 25 January 1940, when four new aircraft were to be ferried to Royal Naval Air Station Ford, near Littlehampton, from No.22 Maintenance Unit at RAF Silloth, on the Solway Firth, only pilots were detailed for the task. Considering the time of year, however, it could well be that when Sub-Lieutenant Gerald Vyvian Williamson and three other Swordfish pilots set out from Ford to collect the machines, their non-involved crew members were only too glad to wave their pilots god-speed on the odyssey that would culminate in a chilly three-hundred-mile delivery flight.

Just over a third of the way into that southbound delivery flight, however, it was realised that Sub-Lieutenant Williamson was no longer holding station. Not that this was a matter for undue concern, for although new to the Senior Service, Sub-Lieutenant Williamson had ten years of flying experience behind him; indeed he had been one of the 4,000 Britons holding flying licences (and 35,000 without!) who had applied to join the Civil Air Guard in July 1938. Moreover, as a founder member of the Yorkshire Light Aeroplane Club he knew both local winter flying conditions and the region where he had been missed as well as anyone. Except that he never did arrive back at RNAS Ford.

Indeed nothing more was to be heard of him for a full month, until, on 13 March 1940, Roadman

Mr John Davies, later of Railway Cottages, Crowden, while clearing snow on the Woodhead-Holme Moss road, was struck by an unfamiliar object silhouetted on the skyline, and decided to investigate. As he told researcher Mr John Ownsworth in 1970, his curiosity took him up a two-mile lift of icy moor towards Heydon Head, there to discover the wreckage of the missing Swordfish; and the corpse of Sub-Lieutenant Williamson, still firmly locked into the safety straps.

During Mr Davies' climb the weather had begun to deteriorate, but undaunted by this, if somewhat unsettled by his macabre discovery, the road-mender then made a Homeric trek through what became blizzard conditions down to the George and Dragon public house on the Woodhead Road, and the nearest telephone.

As the hours passed, the storm intensified, so that when Mr Harry Shaw, then the incumbent of the Fleece Inn, Holme, led an RAF recovery-cum-salvage detachment to the scene, conditions had become hazardous. Nor did they improve. For although Mr Shaw organised a search party when, as evening approached, the eight men still engaged on the salvage element of the task had not returned, it was to be well into the next day before they were located on Sliddens Moss, having become disorientated and headed ever deeper into the moors rather than towards the nearby Holme Moss road and their transport. It was with great relief, therefore, that they were led down to Woodhead, and thence to Holmfirth, where two of the eight had to be hospitalised with frostbite.

In fact, even those who had not been frostbitten were to spend a full five days recuperating in Holmfirth's Victoria Hotel before being permitted to return to the moor and complete their task of reducing the wreckage.

The aim of burning and burying what wreckage it was not feasible to remove was to obviate its taking the attention of future search aircraft; only debris tends to surface through peat – so that barely eighteen months later a Lysander pilot, injured and trapped in wreckage some three miles to the west, would watch in frustration as a searching machine persistently circled over the Swordfish site [Lysander V9403, p. 96, in this volume].

The Swordfish investigation determined that Sub-Lieutenant Williamson had crashed some seventeen miles east of his planned track, and there being no evidence of mechanical malfunction, found that he had simply flown into cloud-covered ground.

There was still a fair amount of debris at the crash site in 2006, a site overlooked these many years by a television mast frequently lost within clouds of the sort which seemingly ensnared the sub-lieutenant. But then the numerous groughs lacing this moorland summit tend to hide the spot from all but the most serious searcher. And so, despite its proximity to both a major Black Hill footpath and the Holme Moss road, the site retains a certain stark forlornness.

Yet how much more forlorn it must have been during that lonely, sightless, and unseeing vigil back in January 1940, when long chill nights succeeded foreshortened icy days throughout the rigour of a winter month, and not a living soul strayed by!

2005. Wies White, in sombre settings, yet gratified that her GPS gift had relocated the site after the author's three failed attempts

## Fairey Swordfish, unidentified, Cross Cliffe, Glossop

SK 04021 94033 83m
Royal Naval Air Service
June-July 1945

Recalling this set down in July 2006, Mr Derek Slack, of Glossop, remembered, 'It happened in 1945, between VE Day [8 May] and VJ Day [15 August]; I was about 10. Either I heard, or actually saw, this aircraft passing very low nearby, very close to the mill chimney: there were many more chimneys then. Anyway, we ran and got to it within five minutes of its putting down. It was a Fairey Swordfish, in grey Naval camouflage, and we gathered that it had got lost and run out of fuel. It didn't seem damaged, and the pilot made off under his own steam. He'd touched down parallel to Hurst Brook, just about where, nowadays, Slant Close leads off Shirebrook Drive. The plane then sat there for some days – they didn't seem in any hurry to recover it –, then the wings were taken off, and it was loaded onto an RAF low-loader trailer; indeed I still recall marvelling at the tailgate notice saying, "Caution, 80 feet long".'

Mr Jack Holden, founder of the estimable Glossop Moorland Rescue Team (subsequently to become the *Mountain* Rescue Team), had equally vivid memories of the set down. 'Rumour flew around that this aircraft had landed, so we ran towards Slant Row from Silk Street, and found this Swordfish, facing up slope, on its booted wheels.' He paused, and then said diffidently, 'Derek [Slack] tends to know what he is talking about, but I wonder about the date here: I'd have put it some years earlier, because in 1944 I was already flying training in the RAF.'

Mr George Sherratt, of nearby Carr House, was aware that a 'spotter' plane had put down in the vicinity, 'I didn't see it myself,' he explained, 'I was still at Whitfield Barn Farm then; but it seems the men guarding it bivouacked in the barn. Only a tiny section of the track they used to get it out to High Street East remains now, beside where the Shirebrook Drive mini-roundabout is. What always intrigued the friend who'd tell me about it, though, is that the recovery people didn't bog down with their articulated Queen Mary in the field itself. For when the developer wanted to put up the bungalows he had to dig deep to get down to gravel to support his footings.' From her bungalow, sited on land which would have been skimmed by the landing aircraft, Mrs Joyce Heginbottom, of Slant Close, indicated the pleasantly landscaped estate around her. 'Lovely now; but yes,' she agreed, 'when we were growing up all this was just flat, rough, and seasonally marshy.'

Built-over landing path of Swordfish; Hurst Brook is to the right of shot

The fact that the author became aware of this aircraft set down only days before publication, precluded any comprehensive archive research. It was established, however, that no crash-report on the incident was raised by the RAF, although they recovered the machine; nor could any further information be found in the time available by RNAS Yeovilton, for all the good offices of the Fleet Air Arm Museum Archives Department. Significantly, however, Mr Jim Buie, Secretary of the Greater Manchester Fleet Air Arm Association, proffered that between June and July 1945 scores of Swordfish were being flown into Barton (Manchester) where David Rosenfield Ltd had obtained the contract for scrapping them; it rather looks, therefore, as if this particular veteran had decided to depart with rather more dignity than those who condemned it to the scrapyard had intended.

## Republic P-47C Thunderbolt 41-6227, Horsehill Tor, Hope Valley

SK 09344 84337 492m
United States Eighth Army Air Force, 56th Fighter Group, 63rd Fighter
Squadron, AAF123 (RAF Horsham St Faith), Norwich
25 April 1943

Pilot: baled out, fractured spine:
Second Lieutenant John E. Coenen, USAAF

Although the P-47 Thunderbolt was the heaviest of all the single-engined fighters, it still had the called-for nippiness in roll. Only this was not an attribute to make it the most stable of platforms for rough-air flying on instruments. As Second Lieutenant John Coenen was to be reminded when he got airborne on 25 April 1943, Easter Sunday.

As a temporary relief from his secondary-duty role as assistant squadron intelligence officer, Second Lieutenant Coenen must have welcomed the chance to get airborne from his Norfolk base on a stores run to Liverpool's Speke airfield; notwithstanding that this particular Easter Day bore scant resemblance to those depicted by Hollywood, having high and gusting winds with rainclouds hanging damply over every hill.

The outbound flight was uneventful, and having collected his consignment of spares, Second Lieutenant Coenen got airborne once again. However, after only a few minutes he ran into the bad-weather conditions he had managed to skirt on the outbound leg. Indeed conditions over the Peakland hills proved so unfavourable that almost immediately he decided to turn back and land at Burtonwood, the large American utility – their Base Air Depot – to the east of Liverpool.

Second Lieutenant Coenen was reasonably experienced, with just under 500 hours' flying time and almost 260 hours on Thunderbolts. As a day-fighter pilot, however, he would have been most accustomed to clear-sky operations, so perhaps the violence of the weather he found himself manoeuvring in took him by surprise. He reported later that rough currents in the thick cloud had virtually rolled him over, while vertical rushes had led to disconcerting indications on his pressure-sensing flight instruments. After this his controls had grown sluggish, suggesting a stall, so that as the machine began to turn rapidly he had concluded that he was in a spin.

Shocked by the suddenness of this loss of control, and only too well aware of the high ground at no great remove – although whether it was presently above him or below him he had no clear notion – Second Lieutenant Coenen realised that he had little time in which to attempt a recovery. Realising too, that he was of far more value than any aeroplane, he prepared to abandon; a judicious decision, especially considering that, before the end of the war, the American Government would have taken delivery of nearly 16,000 Thunderbolts alone!

But leaving the rapidly turning machine was not to be so easy, for flight forces held him into his seat. Just as well, then, that he had not delayed! For such forces being in play suggest that, rather than a slow-speed spin, the aircraft was in an increasing-speed spiral dive, a flight condition which required a significantly different recovery technique from that of a spin.

It was his too-hastily streamed parachute that finally extracted him from the cockpit. Only as it billowed back it snagged the tailplane, and although it pulled free almost immediately, a panel was so badly torn that his subsequent descent was not only short but disagreeably unsupported.

'I came down very fast,' he wrote later, 'hitting hard, hurting my back, and coming to rest on my stomach.' In fact, although undetected by the doctors in the immediate aftermath, he had suffered two spinal fractures.

As it happened, his speedy descent had been seen by hikers who were sheltering from the elements in the vicinity of Lee Farm, on the track from Upper Booth to Jacob's Ladder. These stalwarts, appreciating that the pilot had suffered a back injury, commandeered a farm gate for use as a stretcher and carried him back to the farm. After which one of the party was obliged to trek to Edale before coming across a telephone, and being able to summon help.

The hikers were not the only people to have witnessed the parachuting pilot emerge from the clouds, as former postman Mr Alan Chapman, of Barber Booth, testified in 2005. 'It was a Sunday,'

Lee Farm                                                       Mr Roy Cooper: 'a plume of smoke ...'

he recalled, 'and we were going to the Methodist Chapel when we heard this aeroplane coming hell for leather. Then its engine stopped. And moments later we saw the parachute coming down.'

Farmer Mr Roy Cooper, of Highfield Farm, Upper Booth, also saw the crash. 'The plane dived straight out of the clouds into our Cartledge field: I remember the plume of smoke coming up. Then the parachute appeared. Later, those who were on the spot told me that it was twisting rapidly, and seemed to be torn. As for the pilot, they said he was shocked, and in pain, having hurt his back; but that all he seemed to be worried about was that the crash might stop him flying. Of course, whether it did or not, I don't know.'

As his fellow witness, Mr Chapman, had reflected, only a short while before, 'For once such airmen had left the area you never heard of them again. Although it was generally held that this one survived.'

And survive he most certainly did. Nor did his back injury cause his removal from operational flying. Or at least, not immediately. For on 27 September 1943, just five months later, Second Lieutenant Coenen got airborne on his thirteenth operational escort mission, notwithstanding that he suffered severe discomfort whenever pulling tight turns; and tight turns being the basic stock-in-trade of any fighter pilot, that must have meant a very great deal of his airborne time.

Clearly it was a situation that could not last. And it came to an end that very day. For on the return leg of what had been a deep-penetration escort mission to Emden, this inability to manoeuvre to full effect left him out of position at a moment when a bomber element particularly required his protection. Seeing the gap, the opportunist Focke-Wulf 190s streamed in. But fortunately for Second Lieutenant Coenen's future peace of mind the ensuing melee allowed him to down one of them. On top of which, in rejoining the now-scattered escorts, he shot down a second as it was in the very act of stalking one of his fellow Thunderbolt pilots, so forestalling any conceivable plaint that he had endangered either his charges or his section. An exit, then, carried out with style.

But an exit just the same, for a post-landing medical examination finally revealed the seriousness of his spinal condition; in view of which he was summarily grounded and sent back to the United States. But all credit to him, for he bore home with him an Air Medal, and the two clusters that, effectively, denoted a triple award of that worthy decoration.

All those months before, the accident investigation into the Edale crash had returned findings that the violent weather was entirely to blame. Just the same, it had recommended that Second Lieutenant Coenen would have been better served had he been issued with a copy of a written flight-forecast rather than the 'conversational' met update he had received at Speke; although quite how either a forecast or a written 'actual' summary would have helped is difficult to see, when Second Lieutenant Coenen had so recently transited the area. Although conceivably the investigators expected him to pre-empt certain RAF pilots of the next generation who purported to believe that the most efficacious use for their instrument-rating cards was to be propped, talisman-like, against the canopy whenever bad weather was in the offing ...

As for the P-47 Second Lieutenant Coenen had abandoned, it had plunged into a moorland shoulder far above the Lee Farm path, on the southern slope of Horsehill Tor. The aircraft was found to have impacted at high speed which, bearing in mind the low altitude from which Second Lieutenant

Coenen fell free, makes it clear that it had indeed gone out of control in a dynamic, rather than a stalled, condition.

In early 2006 a moderate pool of debris, spitefully grey as a result of the conflagration, still remained; a pile sombre enough in weather such as obtained on that April day in 1943. But given a clear day, the panoramic scene sixty-three years on borrowed colour from the succession of brightly hued paragliders that wheeled so busily only feet above the peat-ringed scar.

The impact site, Horsehill Tor, facing the Vale of Edale

## De Havilland DH82A Tiger Moth Mk.2 T6464, south-west of Chew Reservoir, Blindstones Moss

SE 03350 01592 505m
No.24 Elementary Flying Training School, RAF Sealand (Queensferry, near Chester),
No. 51 Group, Flying Training Command
12 April 1945

Pilot: killed:
Sergeant Michael Augustine O'Connell, Royal New Zealand Air Force

The de Havilland Tiger Moth DH82A, with a pedigree built upon the well-deserved reputation of the Moth trainers which preceded it, went on to establish an even more illustrious reputation in its own right. Unashamedly a machine of the early 1930s and as unsophisticated as they come, it nevertheless proved a first-class trainer when used by Commonwealth-wide Elementary Service Flying Training Schools throughout the Second World War.

The job of such Elementary Flying Training Schools was twofold. Initially they served as an assessment facility whose aim was to determine whether or not a pupil had the aptitude to become a Service pilot. Their second task, following on from the first, was to teach basic flying skills to the successful aspirants.

The Tiger Moth, notwithstanding that it was always docile, was never a sinecure. Besides which, although it was a sturdily built machine, its instrumentation was little less than rudimentary. Therefore, with pupils being the valuable commodity they were, strict rules were laid down regarding flying in cloud, the relevant unit flying order specifying that they should not do so, but should, instead, expeditiously turn back on encountering either bad visibility or cloud. This was an order which every instructor and pupil pilot periodically signed as having 'read and understood'. Among them Sergeant Michael O'Connell, of the Royal New Zealand Air Force.

Sergeant O'Connell, stationed at RAF Sealand, near Chester, had completed one hour and forty minutes of a cross-country detail when he crashed and died near Chew Reservoir, forty-six miles from his base. Some sources say 'on the final cross-country of the course'. But if he was indeed a pupil pilot, and not a staff member, he had amassed a surprising number of flying hours, 345 in total, with over 120 on Tiger Moths. He also claimed a considerable number of hours spent on instruments: 51 in the air, and 38 on the Link Trainer, the flight simulator of the day. Further, although he was a sergeant when the crash occurred, his promotion to flight sergeant had already been promulgated by the time his headstone was commissioned. [Although where Commonwealth casualties were concerned, ranks were habitually advanced in order to entitle relatives to the increased pension; on RAF graves any discrepancy was most often due to the promotion not having been promulgated at the time of death.]

Setting aside any doubt regarding Sergeant O'Connell's status, his detail when he crashed was a solo day cross-country in the course of which he ran into a concentration of cloud. He did not turn back, however, but pressed on; only to become disorientated, to lose control, and to find himself unable to either recover or abandon before hitting the ground.

The court of inquiry did not mince matters. Unit Flying Orders laid down that pilots were not to continue flight in cloud; consequently the court found that Sergeant O'Connell had disobeyed orders by doing so, that he had then lost control when forced to rely solely upon his flight instruments – basic as they were – and crashed, destroying his machine and killing himself. Both the Air Officer Commanding and the Air Officer Commanding-in-Chief concurred with the finding, emphasizing thereby that even the Tiger Moth could, and would, bite if the safety rules were flouted.

Tiger Moth cockpit. Only rudimentary blind-flying instrumentation ... Photograph by courtesy of the Shuttleworth Trust

In 2006 a fair scattering of debris still remained, and although this lay in a singularly broken piece of ground, the assurance that surface indications existed even then should be enough to persuade future searchers to persist; like several other high-Peakland crash sites this one favours concealing, rather than revealing, itself.

Right: Tiger Moth T6464 in 2006, looking towards Chew Reservoir

## De Havilland Tiger Moth, Black Lane, Tankersley, south of Barnsley

SK 35105 99501 141m
RAF Elementary Flying Training School machine
1939-45

In the 1980s, when researcher Mr John Ownsworth visited the area, locals remembered a Tiger Moth setting down in this field to the east of Black Lane, although whether or not it was damaged was unclear. During canvassing visits in both 2005 and 2006, however, enquiries bore no fruit whatsoever. Nor was any specific Tiger Moth indicated during archival searches. Another site then, for posterity.

From Black Lane, the site of the Tiger Moth setdown. The M1 lies at the horizon

## De Havilland Tiger Moth, Spring Head Farm, Upper Cumberworth, near Hepworth

SE 17932 07099 372m touchdown, on the brow
SE 17937 07139 377m terminal site, the drystone wall
Flying Training Command
1940-41

Occupant: solo, unidentified pilot, uninjured

In the early wartime years a Tiger Moth, presumably lost or short of fuel, made a forced-landing approach to a field high on the ridge just across the road from Spring Head Farm, Upper Cumberworth. Mr Phillip Tinker, still resident there in late 2005, was able to describe what happened. 'The pilot must have seen how the field flattened towards the top of the ridge,' he explained, 'only misjudged the gradient lower down. So, at the last moment, although he throttled up and lifted his nose, the slope out-climbed him. The Tiger Moth ran on and into the drystone wall and although the propeller splintered, it carved a great gap before the engine stopped. The pilot, however, wasn't hurt, so

Mr Phillip Tinker indicates where the Tiger Moth touched down

The wall which stopped the Tiger Moth; the approach over Spring Head Farm

Harry Needham, the local ARP warden, took him off and fed him tea until the RAF came for him. As for the aeroplane, that wasn't much use, and it was soon pulled down to the road and taken off by Queen Mary trailer.' Mr Tinker paused. 'Strangely, in the late 1990s a glider came down in the identical spot. It had been flying from Hull to Great Hucklow, and chose to put down there. Again, nobody was hurt.'

Mr Tinker maintained that the repair in the wall, necessitated after the Tiger Moth's propeller had chewed its way through, was still evident, but not even this memento of the crash was to be discerned by a townie's gaze.

As with the Tankersley incident above, archive sources failed to provide a match, although future research might be aided by Mr Tinker's assertion that the aircraft was in camouflage drab rather than Flying Training Command yellow.

## Unidentified RAF trainer, Bassingthorpe Farm, Greasbrough

SK 41764 94329 56m
c.1946

Mr Alan Wood at the terminal site

In December 2005 Mr Alan Wood, of Bassingthorpe Farm, Greasbrough, indicated the spot where this trainer came to rest. 'It was in about 1946, the year before we actually took over here,' he explained. 'It was obviously in difficulties but in putting down it hit one rise, ploughed across the next, and finished up where I'm standing; in what was then a duck pond, but which we later filled in.'

Mr Wood knew no more details, and by November 2006 nothing more had been discovered, notwithstanding that the incident proved to be common knowledge in the local area. Being post-war, it will have been reported in the press, so more diligent research might well bear fruit.

## Trainer, Elementary Flying Training School type, Bella Vista Farm, Penistone

SE 22770 01874 339m
Flying Training Command
1939-45

Occupant(s) unidentified, uninjured

An Elementary Flying Training School machine – either a Tiger Moth or a Magister – made a forced landing in a field below Bella Vista Farm, Penistone. After touching down it struck and penetrated a drystone wall, suffering damage which necessitated its recovery by road some days later. At the time the location was 'the third field below the farm', but the field pattern having changed by 2006, the reference given here relates to the upper part of the undivided field bordering the public road. No further details have become available and nobody could be found who knew anything more than hearsay.

The near end of the set-down field, Bella Vista Farm

### Trainer, Elementary Flying Training School type, Moor House Farm, Long Lane, near Stocksbridge

SK 24862 97971 312m
1939-45

Occupant(s): unidentified, uninjured

The Long Lane set-down field

During the Second World War the pilot of a light training aircraft, lost and short of fuel, put his aircraft down on a field to the north of Long Lane, Whitwell Moor, sensibly choosing this pasture, close to Moor House Farm. The aircraft remained on the ground for some time, but once it was refuelled, the incumbent of the farm, Mr Nelson Kay, helped turn it around; after which it took off again.

An enthusiast source holds that the aircraft was manhandled out to the road to take off, but with no roadside gate, and with a wide pasture as the alternative to the narrow, wall-bordered Long Lane, this hardly seems tenable; particularly as most trainers had little more than a tail skid to aid low-speed directional control (as the author recalls only too well, having totally lost directional control after touchdown on the 'fifties runway at Kuala Lumpur, upon which his Tiger did a swift, and spectacularly precise, 360 degree turn before simply running on; leaving the tower, the fire section, and him, wondering if anything had really happened).

To date, records have revealed nothing more of this Long Lane incident, which probably amounted to no more than a successful precautionary landing; nor did local enquiries up to mid-2006 advance research. The incident is recorded here, therefore, mainly because the field is in such close proximity to the heathery up-slope of Whitwell Moor, the crash site of Anson N9912.

### Avro Tutor K3308, Mill Cottages, Edale

SK 13500 85183 252m
Station Flight, RAF Duxford (Cambridgeshire), No.12 Group, Fighter Command
7 May 1940

Pilot: survived a mishandled precautionary landing:
Sergeant I. Hutchinson, RAF Volunteer Reserve

The Avro Tutor was the basic trainer for the RAF throughout the early nineteen-thirties. A massive machine for such a role – the engine alone weighed over 500 pounds – it was sturdily built and comfortably forgiving; arguably, even too forgiving for a trainer. Yet it had its limits when it came to kindliness of disposition, as Sergeant Hutchinson, of RAF Duxford, was to discover on 7 May 1940, when he became lost and ran short of fuel while ferrying Tutor K3308 to No.11 Maintenance Unit's Aircraft Storage facility at Kirkbride, near Dumfries.

The summary of the RAF's accident investigation, the Form 1180, recorded in telegraphese what Sergeant Hutchinson had testified to: 'Landed in the only available space which was too small. Even with terrific sideslipping he could not get into field, ran aircraft deliberately into trees of river bank.'

The aircraft was so badly damaged that it was initially assessed as a total write-off and fit only for scrap, although a later reassessment showed many components to be suitable for re-use.

Noting that Sergeant Hutchinson had just 220 hours' total experience and only two hours' solo on the Tutor, the investigation attributed the underlying causes of the accident to lack of experience and lack of care in mapreading. Consequently a lenient view was taken; the recommendation being that Sergeant Hutchinson should be dealt with summarily – which meant a Dutch-uncle homily from his flight commander – and given further instruction in mapreading and navigation.

Viewing the incident from the remove of some sixty-five years, it is evident that Sergeant Hutchinson showed good sense in choosing to put down where he did, across the river from Edale Mill. Those upper slopes which were not cloud-covered were clearly too steep to alight on, but the fields bordering the river, where buildings clustered – representing succour and communications – must have seemed flat enough. Yet when he embarked upon his approach he found that even the chosen field was falling away beneath him no matter how steeply he descended. Accordingly, particularly with his forward vision obstructed by the Tutor's bulky cowling assembly, and notwithstanding his 'terrific sideslipping', he was quite unable to put his wheels on the ground in order to employ the Tutor's highly-efficient wheelbrakes. Thereafter, and almost certainly in the hasty process of going round again (putting on full power and climbing away to position for a second attempt), he flew into – rather than deliberately aimed at – the trees lining the river bank. And just as well he did so, for between the trees and the mill the river runs through an unexpectedly-deep gorge, and had the trees not been there to act as a safety net the resulting drop would have been catastrophic.

The approach, towards Edale Mill; the fringe of trees still hides the river gorge

The location for this minor incident was recorded only as 'Edale, Derbyshire'; but in 2005 it was ascertained that local road-mender Mr Arthur Deaken, who had lived at Edale Mill at the time, had been wont to describe the incident to both family and acquaintances. Sadly, Mr Deaken, who had spent thirty years tending the road through the Dale, had been fatally injured upon it not that long before. However, his daughter, Brenda, still lived in Barber Booth, and was able to verify what her father had told them.

## Unidentified 1914-18 aircraft, Air Shaft, Woodhead Tunnel

SK 14720 01750 (area of)

Mr Steve Marsden, a local resident, provenly knowledgeable about other sites, was told of this by his grandfather, a well-known local butcher and reputable local source. On the strength of this account researcher Mr John Ownsworth, of Penistone, scoured the area in 1979, but found nothing. As might have been expected, nothing was evident in early 2006 either, nor have records been found which throw any light on the incident. Another one for posterity.

The air-shaft area

## Unidentified aircraft, Longdendale Valley

c.1935

In June 2006 researcher Mr Arnold Willerton, of Hyde, supplied a copy of a photograph from *The Longdendale Valley*, by Mrs Margaret Buxton-Doyle, of Denton. It was a photograph taken by Mrs Buxton's father, Mr Harry Buxton (1908-83), of a wrecked aircraft which came down in the valley, probably, the caption suggested, in the nineteen-thirties. There was some speculation regarding the

possibility of its being the DH9 which was burnt out at Lower Mudd Farm, Mottram, in 1919 [see this volume], but the wreckage is far too whole to make that likely. As it is, the photograph is reproduced here, by courtesy of Mrs Buxton, in the hope that more information may be forthcoming.

Left: unidentified aircraft in the Longdendale Valley, courtesy of Mrs Margaret Buxton-Doyle, vice her father, Mr Harry Buxton (1908–83), formerly of the Glossop Chronicle

## De Havilland Vampire T.11 XE854, Occupation Road, Rawmarsh, Parkgate, Rotherham

SK 43356 95747 37m

Fleet Air Arm, No.1 Advanced Flying Training School, RAF Linton-on-Ouse (York), No.23 Group, Flying Training Command
9 March 1959

Pilot: pupil pilot, killed:
Midshipman Ian Ferguson Wilson, Fleet Air Arm

At 1047 hours on 9 March 1959, Midshipman Ian Ferguson Wilson, a pupil pilot being trained for the Fleet Air Arm at RAF Linton-on-Ouse, took off in a Vampire T.11 ('Tee eleven') to practise circuit flying at Linton's relief airfield, Full Sutton. Having carried out a number of the landings and take-offs the duty entailed, Midshipman Wilson cleared the Full Sutton circuit and declared his intention of changing to Linton's frequency. He failed to check in with Linton, however, and when a standard, 'Airborne forty minutes' advisory was transmitted to him by the tower, there was no response. In fact, at 1120 hours Midshipman Wilson had crashed his Vampire some thirty miles from Linton, after low flying near his home on the outskirts of Rotherham. Midshipman Wilson had been killed as the machine exploded, but providentially nobody on the ground had been hurt; and although there had been some disruption at a nearby colliery as the aircraft severed power cables, there had been little damage to property.

The incident was covered in typically journalistic fashion by the *Rotherham Star*, particularly as Midshipman Wilson came from a local family and had been a pupil at Rotherham Grammar School. The coroner's investigation on 28 March 1959, however, was rather more pertinent. Quizzing Midshipman Wilson's uncle, Mr James Ferguson, of Rotherham, about his nephew, the coroner observed, 'When he was killed he had been flying ... more or less over his home.' He then asked, 'Do you know if he had done this on any previous occasions?' Mr Ferguson replied ingenuously – and damningly –, 'Oh yes! Several times recently, but in a piston-engined plane. This was the first time in a jet.'

The coroner also heard evidence from Full Sutton's Duty Air Traffic Controller, and from Midshipman Wilson's squadron commander. On being told that the pupil pilot had been briefed to 'do five circuits, then five rollers, then return,' the coroner asked, 'Would these exercises take him over Rotherham?' 'No,' the air traffic control officer replied unequivocally, 'that would take him about 20 miles outside his flying area. He would have known that.' The squadron commander was equally blunt: 'It was an act of indiscipline.'

Describing the crash itself, Mr Raymond Wilkinson, of Rotherham, told the coroner, 'As [the plane] passed over the church it seemed to be losing height ... just above roof level. It made a quick turn away from the houses, and disappeared from sight in cloud. [On diving out of cloud again] there were green flashes as it broke through the power cables, then there was a loud explosion.'

The RAF board of inquiry would have had no need to deliberate over-long; Midshipman Wilson had been illegally low-flying and had been seen leaving his assigned area to do so. After that, witness evidence, professionally interpreted, told the story: Midshipman Wilson had begun a 'hairpin' turn-back for a second run over his home, but on unexpectedly encountering cloud while in a steeply banked climbing turn at very low level, had become disorientated and lost control, his aircraft spiralling into the ground. Case closed.

Before either hearing there had been, very properly, laudatory letters to the bereaved family from a Service responsibly and humanly responding to the fatality of one of its charges. But the morning after the crash had seen the usual press headlines extolling the young pilot's bravery in sacrificing himself to save others, with householders adjacent to the crash site joining in the plaudits. The coroner, however,

The cross marks the impact crater – and the memorial – of the Vampire; the arrow, the approach route. The houses were built later

having ascertained the facts, was in the same mind as the RAF board of inquiry. 'This young man', he declared, '... went off on this jaunt over his home, got into difficulties, and crashed his aircraft through lack of experience to get out of those difficulties.'

In 2006 Mr Alan Smith, of Rawmarsh, described the scene on the evening of the crash. 'The Vampire had dived into the hillside and disintegrated, so that bits were spread back from the crater, over the rail line, and up the far side. I picked up an instrument from the cockpit; there seemed nothing any bigger left. It was gruesome, too ...' He reflected for a while. 'A memorial was built later, rather like a well, but it's years since I saw it, and it was overgrown even then.'

January 2006; *sic transit* ... The overgrown memorial enclosure, looking back along the approach, over the shallow valley, and the power cables

2006, the memorial plaque cleaned of soil and vegetation

18 September 1959; Mrs. T. Fieldhouse, the donator of the memorial plot. The central plinth marks the impact crater and is set over the interred ashes, *Rotherham Star*

And a memorial there was. Except that the slope on which the Vampire impacted had been withheld from the planners by its owner (for reasons unassociated with the crash) and had grown derelict. Indeed in January 2006 it took three traverses of the slope before the monument was detected, having become completely concealed, for all its size, by a thicket; rather in the way of a jungle-swallowed temple. Most unusually, both a machete and sweeping brush were available (the writer had been clearing ivy) and a path was cut into the brambles. It was then discovered that the memorial, raised by the family, took the form of an octagonal enclosure two or three yards across, enclosed by a brick wall some three feet high. A decorative wrought-iron gate opened onto a centrally-located plinth beyond which, set beneath the raised back wall, was a wooden bench. There was also a double stone erected by other members of the family, but it was necessary to brush some four inches of accumulated vegetation from the plinth itself before a metal plaque was revealed, and a dedication could be read.

It transpired that the plot had been donated to the family by the owners of the slope, Mr and Mrs T. Fieldhouse of Parkgate; the memorial, centred over the impact crater, being opened on 18 September 1959, when Midshipman Wilson's ashes were deposited beneath the plinth.

An intriguing insight into the selection of Britain's Service aircrews emerges from this wastefully tragic crash. For both Midshipman Wilson's family and a pupil-pilot colleague vouched for Midshipman Wilson's regular practice of flying over his home; an illegal act under both military and civil law. Further, his mother, speaking of her son's keenness to fly, told reporters that, while at school, he had been awarded, and successfully completed, an RAF-sponsored, Air Training Corps flying scholarship; so gaining his Private Pilot's Licence. Yet Mrs Wilson also revealed that, when her son subsequently presented himself for formal aircrew selection, the RAF ruled him unsuitable for *any* aircrew post. It can be deduced, therefore, that the RAF selection board had recognised that, although provenly capable of physically flying an aircraft, the candidate also harboured less satisfactory traits. The irony being that when the Royal Navy subsequently accepted him as a pilot trainee, the RAF had to do the training. Training during which Midshipman Wilson consistently displayed the lack of self-discipline that had, almost undoubtedly, been at the root of the RAF's apprehension; which eventually killed him; endangered the public; and caused the destruction of the aircraft entrusted to his care.

## Vickers Armstrongs Wellington Mk.1C R1011, Birchen Bank Moss, Bleaklow

SK 10544 98580 486m

No.28 Operational Training Unit, RAF Wymeswold (north-east of Loughborough), No.93
Group, Bomber Command

30 January 1943

Crew: three killed, two injured:

Flight Lieutenant Anthony Winter Lane, Operational Training Unit staff pilot, killed

Pilot Officer Grisdale, navigator, injured

Pilot Officer Charles Douglas Brown, bomb aimer, killed

Sergeant Raymond Gerard Rouse, OTU staff wireless operator/air gunner, killed

Sergeant Miller, wireless operator/air gunner, injured

Although the Wellington was withdrawn from bomber operations in October 1943 it was well suited to the needs of the Operational Training Units (OTUs) whose function was to meld the various aircrew specialities into first-line bomber crews. During the course those trainee crew members not essential to the task in hand would be replaced by specialist OTU instructors who would 'screen', or oversee, the crew member carrying out the relevant exercise; indeed, at times, when a shortfall had occurred, OTU staff would actually fill key roles. As happened on 29 January 1943, when the final night cross-country flights of the course were dispatched from No.28 Operational Training Unit, at RAF Wymeswold, near Loughborough. Among the stream that night was Wellington R1011, captained for the occasion by OTU staff-pilot Flight Lieutenant Anthony Lane.

The round-trip routing of this final trip of the course, designed to introduce the trainee crew members to the sortie lengths they would face when they raided deep into Germany, had taken them to the north of Scotland. At about 0145 hours, however, having been airborne for some six hours and twenty minutes, Flight Lieutenant Lane and his part-pupil, part-OTU-staff crew were just an estimated twenty minutes from base. With the task so nearly completed, it seems that they were desirous of finishing in style: as close as possible to ETA, and exactly on their planned track. For notwithstanding the heavy cloud through which they were flying, and which had prevented them from positively determining their position for some time, the decision was taken to descend and obtain a visual fix.

When it came to making this always-weighty decision Flight Lieutenant Lane, with very nearly fifteen hundred flying hours, had vastly more experience to draw upon than most Service pilots of his day. Further, if he was relatively new to the Wellington, with just sixty-six hours on the type, he was not short of navigational assistance, for in addition to the trainee navigator, who had already proved his capability over the last six hours, he was carrying among his somewhat truncated crew another OTU instructor, Sergeant Raymond Rouse, an experienced wireless operator/air gunner.

Although Sergeant Rouse was a qualified gunnery leader, his function on this flight was to tone up the wireless-operating performance of Sergeant Miller, the trainee wireless operator/air gunner. Patently this task had been satisfactorily accomplished, for when the decision was made to begin the descent Sergeant Rouse took station behind his OTU pilot-colleague the better to assist with the lookout.

Flight Lieutenant Lane was well served then; yet despite all his experience, despite the services of two communications specialists on his crew who might have furnished a confirmatory W/T fix (wireless telegraphy – morse code), and despite the availability of a whole array of external get-you-home aids, just before six and a half hours into the sortie he eased back the throttles, and lowered the nose of the aircraft into a blind descent through cloud …

What happened then is succinctly stated on the official accident report: 'Screen pilot tried to pinpoint himself when off track at the end of a cross-country flight. Struck high ground at 1,700 feet in low cloud and rain.'

All very dry and unemotional. But then the court of inquiry was recording an occurrence that had become only too wearyingly commonplace. As the Air Officer Commanding's curt recommendation makes clear. 'N.F.A', he penned. No further action.

After all, what more preventative action was there left to take? For descending through cloud without having obtained a positive fix had already killed only too many crews; destroyed only too many aeroplanes. Yet there were so many alternative courses of action; and an abundance of flying instructions against the practice, the latter all listed in the *Air Navigation Manual* of the day, the *AP1234*, which, having spelled them out then thundered, 'Above all do not descend below cloud **unless absolutely sure there is no high ground nearby.**' The emboldening being the 1941 original.

For even as he pushed the report aside the Air Officer Commanding would have been only too well aware that, just thirty minutes after R1011 fell into the blind-descent trap, so Wellington R1538, another aircraft of the same stream, but almost thirty-five miles adrift, and half an hour over estimate, had done the same at Cellarhead, near Stoke. Again, 'N.F.A.' [see *Peakland Air Crashes: The South*, page 129.]

The reports completed, it would have been time for the senior officer to allow his thoughts to turn to the rest of that night's stream. To wonder, for example, how many of those who had landed back at Wymeswold uneventfully – and were now operations-ready – had taken similar chances. Only got away with it – on this occasion.

As for Flight Lieutenant Lane and his crew, they had hardly been twelve miles off track after what had clearly been a productive exercise; until that fateful decision had been made. As it was, rather than being safely homed to the Wymeswold overhead, their aircraft had been descended blindly through the cloud-hagged night sky. Only instead of approaching low-elevation Wymeswold, it had still been over the remote, high-moorland waste of Bleaklow's Birchen Bank Moss, which it had struck, killing the three men gathered in the nose and injuring those two still at their stations amidships.

In Memory Of Sergeant Raymond Rouse, Flying Officer Lane, And Pilot Officer Brown, Who Tragically Lost Their Lives, When Their Aircraft A Vickers Armstrong Wellington No R1011 Crashed Into The Ground At This Site On 30th January 1943.

The memorial plaque: still intact in September 2006

The crash site of Wellington Mk.1C R1011, looking north

This is a crash site that seems set to retain its air of remoteness, shielded as it is by moorland contours from the unceasing turmoil of the A628 trunk road running just three quarters of a mile to the north. A remoteness made stark by the scant debris pooled about a monumental plaque; but, at that, the most tasteful of such monuments. And, until September 2006, at least, left gratifyingly unmolested.

## Vickers Armstrongs Wellington Mk.1C DV810, Broomhead Moor, south-west of Stocksbridge

SK 23505 95465 377m impact site
SK 23488 95413 375m terminal site
No.21 Operational Training Unit, RAF Edgehill (north-west of Banbury), No.91 Group, Bomber Command
9 December 1942

Crew: seven on board, four injured:
Flying Officer Stanley Baker, OTU staff pilot
Sergeant Anthony St Clair Turner, Royal Australian Air Force, trainee pilot, injured
Flight Sergeant Donald Norman Dawson, navigator, injured
Flight Sergeant Walter Samuel Sinclair, bomb aimer
Sergeant Morgan, staff wireless operator
Sergeant Alan Gordon Allwright, trainee wireless operator, injured
Sergeant R.D. Weeks, air gunner, injured

The Wellington bomber, though swiftly outmoded by the heavier machines which later entered service, not only stayed the course but served with distinction throughout the Second World War. Always dependable, it also built up a reputation for being able to contain damage that would have crippled any other type; a reputation that relied almost entirely upon the singular 'geodetic' framework developed by Barnes Wallis.

But that there were limits to even this ruggedness was to be shown on the night of 9 December 1942, when, together with five other Wellington crews, Staff-Pilot Flying Officer Stanley Baker and his trainee crew got airborne from RAF Edgehill (north-west of Banbury), at that time a satellite of RAF Moreton-in-Marsh where No.21 Operational Training Unit (OTU) had its headquarters.

Like many of his fellow instructors Flying Officer Baker was 'resting' between operational tours, and probably flying more often than he had ever done on his squadron. For the OTUs were always hard pressed to provide sufficient crews to fill the gaps left in the ranks of the operational units, whether by war or natural wastage. Indeed the urgency had been illustrated that very night when, No.21 OTU having submitted that deteriorating weather conditions would probably preclude landings back at Edgehill, the controlling No.91 Group had ruled, reasonably enough, that diversions were quite in order; once the exercises had been completed.

Flying Officer Baker's main task would have been to hover over the shoulder of Sergeant Anthony Turner, the trainee pilot – most Wellingtons having just the one pilot's seat – but as aircraft captain he would have held a watching brief over every member of the crew, and in particular over the navigator, upon whom so much depended.

Throughout the flight the navigator would have been busy at his lamplit table, poring over that esoteric mystery so beloved of the breed, the Air Plot; his divinations supplemented whenever possible by visual fixes from pilot, bomb-aimer or gunner, and when allowed, by bearings and fixes from the wireless operator. And 'when allowed', because on some exercises wireless silence would be imposed, as on operations. But this was clearly not one of those occasions, because Sergeant Morgan, an OTU instructor, would have been specifically exercising the trainee wireless operator in his craft.

Indeed it was Sergeant Morgan who had the first intimation that all was not as it should be, reporting that they were picking up the hazard signals from a balloon barrage, for such warnings could only mean that they had drifted westwards from their supposed position and were now overflying some sensitive complex.

In this extremity Flying Officer Baker, a pilot with nearly a thousand flying hours, would have liaised with the qualified-but-inexperienced navigator, comparing notes, and seeking to determine just how far astray an unseasonable easterly wind might have taken them. Eventually, however, forced to realise that they were, in fact, quite lost, he then exercised his command authority, exchanging seats with the trainee pilot preparatory to taking remedial action.

It is not clear why, especially with two wireless operators on board, radio assistance was not forthcoming, but this seems to have been the case. Nor does the short-range HF 'Darky' organisation appear to have been called into play from the pilot's seat; for although essentially a get-you-home service it could also furnish a rough – yet, in such an instance, a perfectly adequate – position. But radio-aids aside, there were other self-sufficiency lost-procedures that fitted the bill, and it was upon one of these that Flying Officer Baker decided.

In the Midland area, over which they were most likely to have drifted, England is of the order of one hundred and forty miles wide. At the Wellington's cruising airspeed, which might be taken as 173 mph (150 knots), some fifty minutes' flying time; or rather more, allowing for the healthy easterly wind they would evidently have to head into. Accordingly, Flying Officer Baker set an easterly heading, away from the central spine of high ground and towards the Fenlands, the Wolds, and the North Sea; for once safely over a flat area he could then afford to nose down, break cloud, re-establish their position, and then decide either to check the base weather, or to call it a night, and divert. A workmanlike plan; except that he decided upon just twenty minutes as being enough to see them over terrain reasonably suited to making a blind descent.

Only, what if he had taken the worst-case scenario, and for lack of any better navigational information assumed the hazard signals to be coming from Liverpool's balloon barrage, to the westernmost extremity of the Midlands? And far from being hindsight, this is what many aviators might have done. Then, allowing for even just a twenty-mile-an-hour headwind, this would have given him a speed over the ground of as little as 153 mph (133 knots). Which meant that twenty minutes would only have taken him fifty miles eastwards (ironically, into the Stocksbridge area!). So might it not have been politic to head eastwards for a significantly longer time, in order to afford himself an absolute margin of safety?

True to his plan, however, exactly twenty minutes after setting course, Flying Officer Baker reduced power and committed himself and his crew to a blind descent, any undue concern being allayed, no doubt, by the reflection that at least the altimeter, set with respect to the relatively low-lying RAF Edgehill, might be of some help, the Eastern Fenlands being low-lying themselves.

It would have been a reasonably tense descent in any circumstances, even for a crew positively certain of their position, with all eyes turned outwards and downwards. But with 1,200 feet on the altimeter it was Flying Officer Baker himself who first saw what he took to be yet another layer of cloud beneath him. Aided by a brief inspection with the landing lamp he decided that it was indeed cloud, then switched off the light again. After which, according to a statement attributed to him, 'Almost immediately there was a bang and my port engine was on fire.'

He then closed the throttles fully, hastily warned the crew of an impending crash; and held off until the aircraft finally struck again.

It was providential that the terrain, though high-standing – it stood, in fact, at 1,200 feet above sea level – was relatively level, for the aircraft slithered to a halt on its belly. Just the same, four of the crew were injured, and the instant all aboard had scrambled clear the machine erupted in flames. Worried that the fuel tanks might explode, Flying Officer Baker shepherded his shaken charges yet further clear, all seven being well distanced when, just moments later, the anticipated explosion actually occurred.

In the next hour or so, as the crew began to settle and take stock, the predominance of heather probably persuaded them that they were not in the Fenlands. Only it was not until locals reached them, drawn by the conflagration, that they discovered themselves to have come down, in truth, on a Peakland moor just south-west of Stocksbridge, and some thirty-five miles short of any suggestion of reasonably low-lying ground.

The subsequent court of inquiry, with their deliberations into the cause of the crash completed, attributed most blame to the navigator; a puzzling finding, since, for some time before the final descent all navigational decisions had been arrogated by Flying Officer Baker, the aircraft's captain. As for Flying Officer Baker, he certainly suffered no lasting ill effects, but went on to have a most illustrious war, finishing up as the Wing Commander leader of No.635 (Pathfinder) Squadron, with a well-earned double Distinguished Service Order, and an equally well-earned double Distinguished Flying Cross.

Speaking in 2006, Mr Alwyn Haigh, of West Nab Farm, remembered the crash with guilty relish. 'I was still at school, and when we got to the Wellington, probably the next day, we found that although the front of it had burnt out the rear part was pretty well intact. So, of course, we made a beeline for the tail turret. Only when we started playing with the guns they let fly over the moors.' He grinned. 'At which we legged it away. Not that there were any guards, not on the moor. And like the Stirling crash at Margery Hill, the wreckage stayed there until it was dragged off.'

Researchers in the 1980s, it is held, were able to establish the point of the initial touchdown, but such evidence as they based this upon seems to have vanished since. In

2005, armour plating and a molten mass at the gully secondary site; removed to the main site by 2006

The main terminal site in 2005; by 2006 the two terminal sites had been combined

Mr Alwyn Haigh. He fired off the guns, then scooted

mid-2006, however, a reasonable amount of debris still existed at the point where the aircraft finished its terminal slide and burnt out. Just the same, this is yet another of those sites where heather abounds, and where it is quite possible to be within feet of the debris before it actually reveals itself.

### Vickers Armstrongs Wellington Mk.3 X3348, Kinder East, south-west of the 590m trig column

SK 12803 87554 590m
No.427 Squadron, Royal Canadian Air Force, RAF Croft (south of Darlington), No.6 Group, Bomber Command
26 January 1943

Crew: six, all injured:
Pilot Officer Carl A. Taylor, RCAF, pilot (American citizen)
Sergeant G.T. Southwood, RCAF, supernumerary (second) pilot, on operational experience
Pilot Officer D. Martin, navigator, RCAF
Pilot Officer Donald. R. Mortimer, RCAF, bomb aimer: sprained ankles
Sergeant A.P. Deane, RCAF, wireless operator
Sergeant W. Lumsden, air gunner

By November 1942, when No.427 Squadron of the Royal Canadian Air Force (RCAF) formed at RAF Croft, just south of Darlington, and received its Wellingtons, the type had already been diverted to night, rather than day, bombing. Further, its performance and bomb load were beginning to show palely in comparison to those of the four-engined Halifaxes and Lancasters being introduced into service; in fact, No.427 itself would re-equip with Halifaxes in May 1943. In the interim six months, however, the squadron used its Bristol Hercules-engined Wellington Mk.3s to great effect, not least on 26 January 1943, when nine of its aircraft, Wellington X3348 among them, attacked the U-boat pens in German-occupied Lorient, on the west coast of France.

It was a marathon trip to Lorient, on the far side of the Brittany Peninsula, and even on coasting-in once more over Dorset's Lyme Bay, the raiders were still faced with another 300-mile flight back to their County Durham base; a flight affording time and distance to spare in which to wander off course and either fall behind or race ahead of estimates, with only a forecast wind many hours old to help in calculating their progress. But the basis of crew co-operation is to have faith in one another's expertise, and in Wellington X3348 the navigator's station, where Pilot Officer Martin hunched over his lamplit plotting chart, became the natural depository for that faith.

In this case the navigator was assisted by the bomb-aimer reporting any airfield pundit-beacons opportunely spotted from the nose; pundits being lights flashing a two-letter airfield identifier in morse. Except that one of these, glimpsed through cloud, proved contentious; possibly because of cloud intervening, but equally likely because a pundit's overly slow coding often has to be watched through at least one full cycle before it is possible to determine which are dots, and which dashes. In this case, when the perverse identifier was finally agreed upon, it showed them to be considerably further along track than Pilot Officer Martin had previously reckoned them to be. Nevertheless, accepting the doubtful offering of this so-critical visual fix – and doing so a shade too easily, it is hazarded – he calculated a new heading for RAF Croft; and just a little later assured his pilot that it was now safe to descend through cloud on that heading.

But pilots (being sensitive souls), get 'feelings' sometimes, and evidently such a one overcame the captain of X3348, Pilot Officer Carl Taylor, an American serving with the RCAF, for when well into the descent he suddenly decided to put on power and regain some height. The same discomfort, it seems, had also made him edge slightly eastwards from the new heading; although it is possible that when the navigator passed the adjusted heading, the supernumerary pilot, standing between him and the captain, and on board to gain operational experience, inadvertently set the wrong figure against the compass lubber line. Not an unknown mistake to make, particularly when tired, stressed, and when working in the poor cockpit-lighting of a night-wrapped bomber. Indeed the passage from the contemporary Air Navigation Manual for the RAF, quoted much earlier, is relevant once again:

'The Navigator must keep a wary eye on the … Pilot, who, for various reasons, may not be steering the requisite Course. It is advisable to look repeatedly over the Pilot's shoulder at the Course being steered.' [1940 *AP1234, Vol. 2*, p.300]

Although this sort of overseeing might well have risked denting the aforementioned perfect faith.

Whatever the truth about the heading passed and steered, it is a matter of record that after six hours and forty minutes of flight, and by the grace of God with some height regained, and therefore with some 2,000 feet now showing on the altimeter, the aircraft abruptly lost flying speed as it unaccountably made contact, then bellied its way across the ground, eventually coming to a halt, battered, but on an even keel, and without catching fire.

In 2006, Mrs Milly Heardman, of Edale, then 92, was able to describe the way the wreck had appeared. 'As you approached it looked quite whole, as if it could fly away at any moment. The wings were spread out, and there didn't seem anything wrong with it; but when you got close, you realised that the whole of the bottom was smashed.'

In the aftermath of the touchdown, the shocked crew had scrambled free, found that none of them had any serious injuries, and discovered that they were on high moorland, rather than on the low-lying pastures they might have expected in the vicinity of Croft. They also realised that the moor was exposed, that rain was falling steadily from the overcast, and that the night was chill. At which they re-entered the largely intact, if somewhat tattered, fuselage, and settled down to wait out the remaining hours of darkness.

But as time dragged on the desire to inform the squadron that they were not, in fact, 'missing', proved more powerful than their patience, and three of them set out to seek help, carrying with them a torch and the aircraft's Very signal pistol with a supply of cartridge flares.

The going was rough, over trackless, gully-rifted heather bog, but at a critical moment they had a remarkable stroke of luck. For initially attracted by a sound from far below, they saw, piercing the pitch-dark opaqueness of a blacked-out land, a red glare, moving horizontally, and snuffed out even as they watched. Afterwards they would reason that it was the briefly opened firebox of a train passing along the Vale of Edale on the Sheffield-Manchester line. But for the time being it was enough to know that there really was life of some sort down there in the gloom. Reinvigorated, they stumbled onward, resorting to firing off flares when uncertain of the footing, to eventually find succour on the outskirts of Edale; at which juncture they would discover that they had been just twelve miles east of track, but a full sixty-five miles short of Croft.

The subsequent court of inquiry worried away at both errors earlier postulated: that the pilot may have ignored the navigator's heading, and that the supernumerary pilot may have mis-set it. But in the event the final submission was that 'bad pilotage' had caused the loss of the aircraft; a submission with which higher authority simply concurred. After all, pragmatically viewed, the aim of the operation had been fulfilled, Lorient had been bombed, and all the other aircraft had returned safely, albeit diverting to airfields other than their base with fuel states running low.

And nothing was said about the causative misidentification of the pundit beacon: crew loyalty triumphing, one suspects!

Popular as the Kinder plateau itself has become, it can, when the cloud is down, impart an awesome sense of isolation; the same applies, perhaps in even greater measure, to the bleak, and often waterlogged crash site of Wellington X3348. Despite which, in early 2006, very little debris remained.

The impact site in 2006, looking towards the 590m trig column; visibility characteristically limited

Wellington X3348 debris pool, 2006

## Vickers Armstrongs Wellington TMk.10 MF627, Rod Moor, Ughill

SK 26396 89270 351m
No.6 Air Navigation School, RAF Lichfield, No.21 Group, Flying Training Command
22 October 1952

Crew: three, two injured:
Sergeant Reginald A. Keith, pilot
Pilot Officer David E. Ward, navigator under training, injured
Pilot Officer Brian Thirkell, navigator under training, slightly injured

During its fifteen years of RAF service the Wellington earned its reputation for ruggedness many times over. Indeed an avowal from wartime Vickers-Weybridge worker, Mrs Stella Crofts, freshly illumined that; recalling her detachments to operational stations, she asserted, 'You wouldn't believe the state they came back in! And with such great gaps that you couldn't credit how they got them home. Only we were never allowed to start work until they'd cleaned them up inside. They were in such a terrible state. But it was so strong, that old Wellington of ours!'

That Wellington MF627, at least, was agreeably strong, was a view undoubtedly subscribed to by Sergeant Reginald Keith and his two trainee-navigator charges after they crashed in the course of a post-war night-navigational exercise from No.6 Air Navigation School on 22 October 1952.

The indestructible Wellington, courtesy of Mrs Stella Crofts

Mrs Stella Crofts, former Wellington airframe worker at Weybridge, showing how fabric was secured to the geodetic

Wellington MF627 on Rod Moor, courtesy of the *Derbyshire Times*

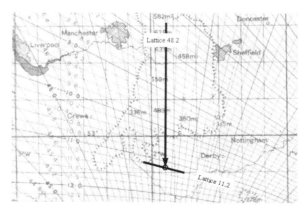

A Gee lattice chart. The known map reference of any airfield (or position) lies on the intersection of two lattice lines: in this example, numbered 48.2 and 11.2. These two figures are fed into the Gee set. The aircraft is then flown down the 48.2 lattice line, the intersection with the 11.2 lattice line putting it overhead

Once Sergeant Keith got airborne from RAF Lichfield, his task was to fly a route under the direction of the two trainees as they took turn and turn about at navigating, although as aircraft captain he was totally responsible for the safe positioning of the aircraft, and for the conduct of the flight.

Cloud was covering most high ground to the north, but the flight, carried out at medium levels, progressed as detailed for some two and a quarter hours. At length, with the body of the exercise completed, Sergeant Keith called for the operating trainee – at that stage Pilot Officer Ward – to get them back to base by setting up for a Gee homing and let-down.

Gee (Ground Electronic Equipment), the RAF's TR1335, was a radar system devised by Mr R.J. Dippy in 1937 for obtaining fixes (accurate to 25 feet) and for homing in bad weather. To obtain a fix, radar-derived signals were plotted on a lattice chart. [How fondly the author remembers, as an RAF Apprentice air-radio-fitter enjoying air-experience in an Anson, long predating computer games by dropping two of Gee's blips into their electronic boxes, having the lattice-plot indicate Bridgewater's looping river; then looking out to actually see the River Parrett's singular serpentine bend!]

For a homing, two co-ordinates of an airfield were dialled into the Gee set, after which the lattice line passing through that airfield could be followed, the overhead being indicated when an intersecting lattice line was reached.

For use as a let-down aid in cloud, heights were calculated against ranges, so that, for instance, when about five minutes from the airfield a descent would be commenced at some 120 knots while losing 250 feet a minute until the ground was seen.

It was a procedure that took only some fifteen seconds to set up. Unfortunately, by that stage of the Wellington's flight, Pilot Officer Ward, having been hunched, head down, toiling over his chart, began suffering from a debilitating airsickness; and possibly because of this, set in the wrong co-ordinates. Which meant that as Sergeant Keith followed the southerly headings fed to him, commencing a gradual descent through cloud as the ranges were ticked off, he was some fifty-two miles north of where he had been told he was; and still over high terrain. So that, although both he and the off-watch trainee-navigator saw the loom of rising ground at the same moment, all Sergeant Keith had time to do was pull up the nose before the aircraft struck.

Having smashed through a section of drystone wall, MF627 slewed about before coming to rest pointing downslope with its fuselage battered and its tail detached; but thanks to the ruggedness of its construction, with the integrity of the forward crew area still intact. There was no fire, and, it transpired, no major injuries, although Pilot Officer Ward would later require hospital treatment …

Once they had settled somewhat, and discussed their situation, Sergeant Keith left Pilot Officer Thirkell to care for his course colleague and found his way to Corker Walls Farm, where he encountered Farmer Harry White. Some time earlier, Mr White and his son, Teddy, had heard shouts, and alert to the possibility of poachers, had chased towards the sound, but foiled by the mist, had eventually returned to their tasks. Accordingly, when Sergeant Keith materialised, Mr Harry White phlegmatically left off sawing wood and drove him to the nearest telephone.

The subsequent RAF investigation held the pilot to blame in that he had not exercised sufficient control, having placed too much faith in the information passed him by the inexperienced navigator. Pilot Officer Ward, for his part, almost certainly because of his evident proneness to airsickness, and not because of his unfortunate mistake, was removed from flying duties.

Farmer Peter Bramall, of Hall Broom Farm, a lad in 1952, remembered the crash well. 'It was very foggy,' he recalled in 2005, 'and it seemed the pilot had pulled up at the last moment, for the plane left two great grooves. It smashed through some iron railings belonging to the Water Board, then through a drystone wall before finishing up on the bank [hillside]. Only hours after the crash, the RAF set up a camp, then stayed for a considerable time, doing what they had to do. They cleared the wreckage, and had the wall rebuilt, although weather has brought some of it down again. But at the start they wouldn't let anyone near the place, not even Dad.'

2005; Farmer Mr Peter Bramall, and the fire-axe from Wellington MF627

The crash site in 2005, looking southerly, upslope, from the impact point and along the line of flight. Inset, the gratifying proof of the site … (re-interred)

However, security was clearly not as tight as it might have been, for Mr Bramall displayed the Wellington's fire-axe which had since passed its days honourably chopping up firewood for the farm.

For his part, Farmer Harry White, at nearby Corker Hill Farm, was reported by the local newspaper as having been 'amazed' to find an aircraft about his ears, leaving him open to ribbing for years to come. For as his son, the aforementioned Mr Teddy White, maintained in 2005, 'Everyone knew that nothing in his life ever amazed Dad. He just wasn't that sort.'

In 2005 the crash site showed not a trace of the incident, and had long been stripped of most residual remains by enthusiasts. However, after several visits a final search did locate debris enough to prove the site. But with that re-interred, the slope remained as it must always have been – bar for those few days after the crash when the salvage crews moved in – a coarse, tufted-grass hill-pasture, wind-ruffled for the most part and populated by the most markedly uninquisitive sheep.

## Vickers Armstrongs Wellington Mk.1C W5719, west-Upper Tor, Kinder

SK 11061 87550 567m
No.150 Squadron, RAF Snaith (west of Goole), No.1 Group, Bomber Command
31 July 1941

Crew: five killed, one injured:
Killed:
Sergeant Percival Harold Charles Parrott, pilot
Sergeant Joseph Arthur Haswell, supernumerary (second) pilot, on operational experience
Sergeant Jack Douglas Evelle, observer (navigator), Canadian
Sergeant Frederick Kenneth Webber, wireless operator/air gunner
Sergeant Dennis Aloysius Monk, air gunner

Injured:
Sergeant Earl Tilley, air gunner, tail turret

In the early days of the Second World War the twin-engined medium-range bombers carried on what would later be seen as a merely embryo offensive against Germany; the Whitleys by night, and the Hampdens, Blenheims and Wellingtons by day. But in mid-July 1941 they were the only striking force the country had that was capable of carrying the fight to the enemy, accordingly, despite all the shortcomings the outbreak of 'the shooting war' had revealed, it was left to them to persevere in the task. But it was not wasted effort, for their crews were learning the lessons, gaining the experience, and in truth, sowing the seeds which would spring up, mature, and ultimately be reaped as a vastly more destructive harvest in the campaigns yet to come.

Among the shortcomings revealed was the near-impossibility of accurately navigating at night over a hostile, blacked-out continent, with no effective radio aids to assist, and no bomb-aiming gear effective enough to make the raid count in the event of actually reaching the target. There was also the ever-increasing effectiveness of the enemy's air-defences. Not forgetting a weather pattern that would as often as not baulk the raiders in locating the target, and then treat them even more harshly when they sought to return to their airfields in the low-lying, mist-prone eastern areas of the United Kingdom.

Again, in the early days in particular, it was held to be of paramount importance to bring the bomb load back if there was no reasonable certainty of hitting the designated target; anything to avoid the charge that the RAF had bombed a non-military locale. But this humanitarian precept had long gone by the board when, on the night of 31 July 1941, Sergeant Pilot Percival Harold Parrot and his crew, together with seven other Wellington crews from RAF Snaith, were briefed to raid Cologne.

The weather on the outbound leg over the North Sea was cloudy, but beyond the enemy coast thunderstorms developed which eventually proved so difficult to circumvent that, in the end, Sergeant Parrott made the decision to abort the operation and turn for home, opting at the same time against jettisoning his bomb load into the sea: humanitarian precepts aside, bombs were expensive!

Having made the turnabout from an arbitrary position, and with thick cloud blotting out both the ground features and the stars, the navigator returned to his air plot, but with little to go on beyond dead – deduced – reckoning. Later, however, he felt confident enough to advise the crew that they had re-crossed the coast in the vicinity of The Wash, and had just seventy-five miles to go.

Notwithstanding static interference on the radio, a magnetic course to steer was then obtained from Snaith. At which stage it must have seemed as if Sergeant Parrott could relax a little, for now it became a case of simply holding the given course until the overhead-time calculated by the navigator. Not that Sergeant Parrott could relinquish the controls, for the supernumerary pilot was only aboard to gain experience prior to being tasked for operations with his own crew. Moreover, any relaxation was to be short-lived, for on the estimated arrival time for Snaith the cloud cover was still total, and despite continuing on the course for some time more, nothing was to be seen below.

So it was that, anticipating that they were at least in the vicinity of low-lying Snaith, a descent through cloud was begun. Only with their altimeter still reading 2,000 feet, so persuading them that they still had some 1,700 feet of clear air below them, the aircraft impacted into the 2,000-feet-above-sea-level crags of Upper Tor, on the southern rim of the Kinder massif, and some thirty-seven miles south-west of Snaith.

The bomb load exploded on impact, killing everyone in the forward part of the aircraft. But the impact had also jarred loose the rear turret, which then broke off and bounced down the precipitous slope below the crags, carrying air gunner Sergeant Earl Tilley clear of the explosion. Hard-proven statistics had it that the rear-gunner's station was the most vulnerable in the aircraft on operations; and yet its very vulnerability paid off here.

Having collected himself, Sergeant Tilley, realising that he had suffered only minor injuries, was able to make his way down the two-mile length of Grindsbrook Clough to Grindsbrook Booth (effectively, Edale), where the alarm was raised.

The subsequent investigation would find that, although the pilot had accurately flown the heading passed over the radio, he had made no attempt to re-check the validity of the navigator's estimate for the Snaith overhead before descending blindly through cloud: the corollary being that neither the pilot nor the navigator was ever to realise that the aircraft had actually overflown Snaith and then carried on towards the high ground.

Continuing on the accusative theme, higher authority caustically observed that none of several laid-down lost-procedures had been employed, and that no emergency 'get-'em-home' service had been called upon for help. Accordingly the accident was attributed to an error of judgement.

Regarding the rest of the force sent to raid Cologne that night, five aircraft found the city and bombed through cloud, while two, totally thwarted by the weather, found and bombed targets in Belgium. Of these seven, six returned safely to Snaith, with the seventh crashing having crossed the Channel.

First level area, where the turret might have come to rest

'sheer, unyielding gritstone crags ...'          The impact point

As for Fortune-favoured Sergeant Tilley, he eventually returned to operational flying, and despite being subsequently shot down and held as a prisoner of war for three years, survived the conflict.

Standing at the crash site and surveying the horrid aspect which that cloudy July night so considerately withheld from the hapless crew, the imagination reels. Above, by just a matter of fifty feet, a grough-riven, but virtually level plain; below, steep slopes falling dramatically to silvery Grinds Brook far beneath; but at the point of impact itself, sheer unyielding gritstone crags.

Yet, despite the accessibility of the site from the increasingly popular path along the rim, tangible evidence of the tragedy still existed in September 2006 in the form of a pool of largely molten debris on a burnt patch of earth – the former two pools of many years' standing had, by then, been combined. Additionally the most modest of plaques was still to be seen, affixed to the overshadowing rock in testimony to this, one of the very few operational losses – as opposed to training losses – occasioned by the too-often totally unforgiving Peaklands.

## Wellington Mk.4 Z1327, Farnley Bank, Farnley Tyas, south-east of Huddersfield

SE 16542 13643 164m cottage impact
SE 16627 13355 221m terminal extent of the wreckage spray
No.460 Squadron, Royal Australian Air Force, RAF Breighton (Selby, Yorkshire), No.1 Group, Bomber Command
17 February 1942

Crew: six, all killed:
Sergeant James Henry Ware, RAAF, screen pilot
Sergeant Robert Litchfield Tresidder, RAAF, pilot
Sergeant William Leonard Ashplant, RAF Volunteer Reserve, observer (navigator)
Sergeant Frederick Dutton, RAFVR, screen wireless operator/air gunner
Sergeant Cyril Caradoe Davies, RAFVR, wireless operator
Sergeant Cyril Raymond Dickeson, RAFVR, air gunner

In November 1941 Wellington-equipped No.460 Squadron of the Royal Australian Air Force came into being at RAF Breighton, near Selby, and by February 1942 was nearing operational readiness. It was always to be a multi-national squadron, although predominantly Australian, so that, on 17 February 1942, when Wellington Z1327 crashed, its crew contained both RAAF and RAF personnel.

Sergeant James Ware and the crew of Z1327 had been carrying out a night-navigational exercise that had initially taken them south and south-west to Peterborough, Harwell and Pershore. They had then been required to head eastwards to Sywell, near Northampton, before steering a northerly course for Breighton, the short, easterly leg being designed to keep them clear of the Midland uplands. In any circumstances it would have been a fair test of their capability as a crew, particularly as many would have been trained in uncluttered, brightly-lit Commonwealth lands rather than totally blacked-out England. On this occasion, however, they had to contend with a typical February weather pattern as well, with extensive cloud over all hills, and with snow dramatically reducing visibility; indeed, neighbouring RAF Snaith, another Bomber Command unit, had cancelled its own night-flying programme outright.

The direction-finding facility at the controlling RAF Holme-on-Spalding-Moor, of which RAF Breighton was a satellite, would record that the two wireless operators on board the Wellington had obtained bearings and fixes during the flight. It was evident, however, that the observer – the navigator – Sergeant William Ashplant, had not made adequate use of these, for when the aircraft crashed it was found to be thirty-eight miles to the west of its planned track.

The first indication the residents of Farnley Tyas had of the impending disaster was when they heard an aircraft circling overhead. Speaking in September 2005, Mrs Janet Sykes, of Farnley Bank, recalled the singular experience of her father-in-law, Mr Harry Sykes. 'It seems', Mrs Sykes recounted, 'that having walked Laura, his wife, to her nursing shift up in Farnley Tyas, Harry was returning to Low Common Farm on the field path. He'd been aware of this aircraft circling and getting lower, although a thick mist had confused him about its height and direction. But he'd left Farnley Bank Wood and was approaching the wall where the footpath crosses the Woodsome Road when he heard the engines cut. The next thing he knew was that he was actually in the road, physically unhurt having regained consciousness, but being tended by two policemen. What had happened was that the plane had hit a cottage down the hill, skipped the road, missed him by feet, and exploded in flames behind him, the blast throwing him clean across the wall.'

Mr J.R. Winn, in 2005 resident in Longwood, but a youth of sixteen in 1942, would be quoted in the *Huddersfield Examiner* of 19 February 1979 as remembering his mother exclaiming 'The woods are all on fire!' The article then related that he had run towards Farnley Bank Wood, to find that the

Mr Harry Sykes, blown over a wall, photo courtesy of his daughter-in-law, Mrs Janet Sykes

aircraft had demolished the roof and an eaves wall of a cottage; that it had then crossed the Woodsome Road 'shedding its wings and engines, spreading wreckage in its trail and up to thirty yards up the hillside and spraying the area ahead with burning petrol.' Mr Winn's account also described how the wreckage was eventually taken away by Queen Mary trailers.

The RAF accident-report summary does not mention the cottage, merely recording that the aircraft 'flew into trees on rising ground in poor visibility, killing all on board.' But the fundamental cause of the accident was all too clear: the aircraft had been descended blind through cloud. However, that the crew should have positively established themselves over Northampton's Sywell airfield and then drifted as far as thirty-eight miles to the west in just one hundred northerly miles seems unlikely. Such a gross westerly error would be fully explained, however, if they had mistaken, say, Banbury for Northampton, and turned northwards too early; for additionally this would explain why they were twenty miles short on their planned along-track distance for the Breighton overhead – albeit just a few minutes' flying time – when they chose to spiral down to break cloud.

On board, as all available eyes stared down to make out Breighton's flare path, the atmosphere would have been one of relief to be finishing the long flight mixed with tense anticipation; but certainly not with apprehension, for nobody would have doubted that they were in the vicinity of twenty-four-feet-above-sea-level Breighton. And so they would have persisted in their descent, knowing that the cloud base was very low, but expecting to see the lights at any moment; and more especially as their altimeter reading neared five hundred feet. It was their tragic misfortune, of course, that, having descended too early, and so far to the left of track, they had spiralled below the cloud-shrouded, near-1,000-feet-above-sea-level Castle Hill and were steering into some adjacent high ground when their left wing struck the 537-feet-above-sea-level cottage. The stricken machine then impacted into the slope beyond and burst into flames, the crew almost certainly dying unaware of what had happened. Providentially, both Mr Clifford Hardy, the resident of the cottage, and an elderly lady from next door were unscathed.

At the time, the loss of their six crew members and a Wellington would have been a daunting blow to both the air and ground crews of the newly formed squadron. But this was just the precursor for No.460. For in the course of their early operational flying they were to lose twenty Wellingtons, together with nearly all their crews, in a period of just three months. Indeed, before the cessation of

1995, and Mrs Marjorie Russell, about to fight a three-year planning battle, views the space formerly occupied by No.3 Farnley Bank

In 2005 Mrs Russell indicates the sole remaining portion of what was No.3 Farnley Bank

From the terminal area, looking back towards the cottage

hostilities, with 6,264 operational sorties behind them, the squadron, having re-equipped in the interim with Lancasters, and with a regular establishment of just 200 aircrew, were to suffer 1,018 aircrew deaths (589 Australian) and to lose 188 aircraft.

The loss of this particular aircraft and crew is commemorated in a memorial centre in Australia's Ayers Rock by a 1995 photograph of the 2006 owner, Mrs Marjorie Russell, indicating the truncated cottage end where the necessarily-demolished No.3 Farnley Bank had been.

In 2006, however, although traces of the erstwhile No.3 were still extant in the stonework of the extensively refurbished No.4 Farnley Bank, there was no other surface evidence of the tragedy.

## Armstrong Whitworth Whitley, Emley Moor, south-east of Huddersfield

SE 22898 13890 224m
RAF Bomber Command
*c.*1941

Crew: presently unidentified: uninjured

Enthusiast lists record that in, or about, 1941, a Whitley ran short of fuel and crashed on Emley Moor, long since the site of the region's television mast. Investigations in 2005, however, showed that the machine did not crash, but rather made a successful precautionary landing in a field at Crawshaw Farm. The aircraft remained on the ground for some days, but after a section of drystone wall had been removed, and a swathe had been cut through unripe, but standing corn, it was flown off once more.

In 2005 few remembered many details, but retired builder Mr Ken Matley, of Thorncliff Green, had vivid memories of the event. 'At the time, 1941, I fancy,' he said, 'I'd have been 23, or so, and lived at Cross Roads. At about seven in the morning we heard this aircraft pass low overhead, and realised that it had come down nearby. On the way to work, therefore, I stopped my motorbike to have a look, but I didn't have the time to wait long: being late would've meant risking the sack. I've no idea what type it was, except that it was a bomber. Although it had dropped all its bombs, for there were none on board. The crew were bunched about Major Wright, of Crawshaw Farm – it was his land – and as far as I know, he took them in until the RAF came for them. The plane was there for some days, maybe even a week, with the army guarding it, for it drew lots of people. Then it was refuelled, from cans, I remember, and on the Sunday – therefore there were crowds free to watch – it took off to the north, towards Grange Moor, running through a gap in the wall and a pathway cut through the unripe corn. It seemed to only scrape over the road, which was worrying, for the ground drops very steeply away beyond that.'

No more details of this forced landing have yet come to hand, and whether or not this was, indeed, another of the few bombers to come to earth in the Peakland area in the course of operations, is not known.

Mr Matley's account is certainly borne out by the location, and particularly by the fact that standing corn had to be cut, and a section of drystone wall dismantled, in order to facilitate the take-off. As a type the Whitley was customarily operated from grass airfields, but this area, though flat enough, and spacious enough with the wall opened up, was an unprepared surface, and the corn, had it not been cut, would have created a prohibitive amount of drag. As it was, the take-off – with the aircraft evidently being held down in order to more rapidly gain adequate flying speed – was as successful as the set-down, for all that the take-off run appeared fraught to the apprehensive onlookers.

The site in 2005, as Mr Matley pointed out, had little enough in common with the way it had been in 1941. 'There were only

Mr Ken Matley, in a gap in the drystone wall, points out the take-off path

a few houses then,' he recalled, 'and no trees and bushes. But since then they've taken coal from the place, and even at the time there was a pond and a tip nearby, both of which the pilot missed.' Mr Matley pointed to the two fields in question, separated once again by a drystone wall – somewhat ruinous at this remove of years – but both smooth-ploughed, observing, 'They weren't smooth like that then, but rough.'

Not a crash at all then, but of possible interest to the walker traversing this moorland area. A traverse to be made, perhaps, a little gingerly, in reflective awareness that a previous TV aerial, equally towering, was brought to earth by an asymmetric load of ice ...

## GERMAN AIRCRAFT IN PEAKLAND AIR CRASHES: THE NORTH

In the course of researching the Peakland series of books it became evident that folk were prone to believe that any fallen aircraft had been German. The truth is, however, that the only German aircraft in the Northern area for which crash sites have been positively identified by the author are the V1 Flying Bombs at Howden Moor and Matley; although these are joined here by the V1 which fell at Beighton, Sheffield, omitted during research for the Central book. On the other hand there are several locations – with provenances of varying degrees of reliability – said to have been the crash sites of German aircraft brought down while raiding Manchester, Sheffield and Liverpool. The purpose of this section, then, is to collate what had been determined at such putative sites by November 2006, so recording the findings in anticipation of a posterity in which more archive material, and more accurate detecting devices, might become available.

Certainly, despite the paucity of evidence on the ground, it is evident that various manned-German aircraft did come down in the area, for there are several contemporary reports of German aircrew being picked up. So that on 16 December 1940, the *Sheffield Telegraph and Independent* reported that five German airmen had baled out at Penistone two days before, and two more a few miles away, near Doncaster; also that a raider had crashed in flames on 8 May 1941, with three of the crew being taken prisoner. Similarly, on Saturday 19 April 1941, the *Holmfirth Express* reported that three German airmen had been caught hiding on the previous Wednesday (16 April 1941), having been shot down the night before.

Equally often proffered during research were German bomb craters, invariably explained as bombs intended for Manchester or Sheffield but 'jettisoned'. Which, if true, would be a damning indictment of German aircrews. Perhaps, then, these partisan beliefs should be weighed against post-war bombing analysis which showed that, even by 1944, by which time Allied aerial bombing techniques had been well honed, over half the RAF's bombs still fell in open country; that much earlier, in late 1941, when the *Luftwaffe* bombers were most active over the Midlands, only three out of five RAF bombs

Researcher Mr John Ownsworth, who provided much information on northern sites

A handbell made from downed German-aircraft debris, depicting Churchill, Roosevelt, and Stalin

fell within five miles of their targets; and that as a comparable measure of enemy bombing accuracy, few bomb craters are to be found as far as five miles from the nearest then-blacked-out city, be it Sheffield or Manchester.

It will become evident throughout this section that much guidance was given regarding these sites by Mr John Ownsworth, of Penistone, who was active as a walker and crash-site researcher in the 1970s and 1980s. By 2005, unfortunately, a knee condition precluded him from accompanying the author to the sites.

## German bomber, Bull Clough, Ewden Bridge, Broomhead (probably spurious)

SK 23705 96790 223m
1940-41

In the late 1970s veteran crash-site researcher, Mr John Ownsworth, was told by a friend, Mr Tom Button, that in 1946 he had come across a wrecked aircraft with a swastika on its tail lying in the water in Bull Clough, at the confluence of Upperwood Dike and Ewden Beck; in substantiation of which Mr Button then connected Mr Ownsworth with his walking companion from 1946. At about the same time another, quite independent informant, affirmed that he had attended this Ewden Beck crash as a part-time fireman.

The confluence of Upperwood Dike and Ewden Beck

Another strand of Mr Button's report concerned two German crew members who had walked to Mr Walt Couldwell's Garlic House Farm, to the north of Ewden Beck, 'and given themselves up after their aircraft had crashed nearby'. In August 1978, however, when Mr Ownsworth and his wife, Josie, sought to substantiate these reports, Mr Couldwell and his sons, Lewis and Wilfred, long-term incumbents of the farm, disclaimed all knowledge of either the aircraft or the crew. Subsequently, Mr and Mrs Ownsworth found debris on the confluence but concluded that it had come from Stirling LJ628, at Upper Commons, discarded there, no doubt, by souvenir hunters wearying of their burden: although it is evident that the overgrown lower slopes of Ewden Beck Clough must have been more easily navigable in former times than they had become in mid-2006, when nobody would have chosen the Beckside as a return route from Upper Commons.

Asked about such a crash in early 2006, Mr Alwyn Haigh, of Bradfield, who had visited most local crashes as a schoolboy and had been long-acquainted with many more, was mystified; but he suggested that the crew members concerned, rather than downed Germans, were more likely to have been one of the two pairs who had set out from the RAF Stirling and found succour at, in fact, Ewden Lodge Farm, just a little further north of Mr Couldwell's holding.

This was where the matter rested, until, in July 2006, the author was brought into touch with a gentleman from Deepcar, who proffered an account of wreckage he had cycled to see as a ten-year old in 1957, 'possibly half a mile, but a mile would be too far', from Ewden Bridge, describing 'a wing with a swastika' lying on the bank and a long debris trail thereafter; although being pressed on, the gentleman conceded that the emblem might have been a cross (*Luftwaffe* practice being to display the swastika only on the tailplane). The emblem aside, the description of the wealth of wreckage remaining at that late date made it virtually certain that what the witness had really visited was the Stirling, nearly two and three-quarter miles from the bridge; the distance clearly foreshortened by memory, with the mis-identification furnishing yet another example of the propensity to regard any crashed aircraft as German.

Notwithstanding this, and in a bid to finally try to establish whether the enemy-bomber tale had any substance at all, the author then carried out an exhaustive, and certainly exhausting-and-not-to-be-recommended, four-hour stream-bed trawl of Ewden Beck up to the Stirling site; all to no avail. Indeed, not until just before Gallows Rocher was any debris sighted, and although that was indeed a wing section, in pieces, and badly corroded – and nearly missed, being above the stream bed, and on the bank –, it was clearly from the Stirling, and long vouched-for in that location (at SK 21326 95900 361m).

In the course of this re-visit it was established that Broomhead Estate Keepers David Beaumont and Chris Cunningham, who had been familiar with the Moor for many years, knew nothing of wreckage nearer Ewden Bridge than the wing section; and even beyond it, only of oddments inadvertently bounced into the beck at the crossing point used by the wartime salvage party; nor had either ever heard of a German aircraft crashing anywhere in the vicinity. Perhaps even more pertinently, Mr Lewis Couldwell, in 2006 of Stocksbridge, but who was brought up at Garlic House Farm, just above Ewden Beck, was categorical in his denial that there had ever been a crash in the vicinity of Bull Clough, an area which, despite being strictly private during his childhood, had been surreptitiously-enjoyed free-range to him and his brother. He fondly recalled the distant Stirling wing section, however, and the rain shelter it afforded, back then, to beaters en-route to the northern side of Broomhead Moor.

All this negativity aside, the supposed German bomber site, with a provenance going back 1946 and rooted in otherwise-dependable sources, is recorded here in case something should come to light in the future; even something that might illumine the other apparently-spurious German crash at the so-similar, clough-negotiating Agden Bridge, four and a half miles down Mortimer Road towards Strines. In the interim, Ewden Coppice, from Ewden Bridge to Bull Clough, though for the most part sadly overgrown with bracken and brambles, and with rhododendron hovering, makes a delightful short walk; and the confluence, with ancient drystone remnants to evoke its long-gone pastoral past, an equally delightful picnic site.


### Unidentified German bomber: Agden Bridge, Broomhead (probably spurious)
SK 24293 93794 307m

Although a German bomber crash at this reference has a long provenance in enthusiast lists, nothing could be found to substantiate it in late 2005; nor could either researcher Mr John Ownsworth or local farmer Mr Alwyn Haigh throw any light upon it. A subsequent visit to the Ewden Bridge site in July 2006, found several other knowledgeable locals who were equally mystified at a reference to a crash in the Agden Bridge area. It seems highly likely, therefore, that this is a spurious listing.


### Unidentified aircraft, believed German, south-east of Emlin trig column (spurious)

SK 24201 93294 364m

This site figures on enthusiast lists, but was the result of a misunderstanding by miscreant Mr John Ownsworth who attributed it to Mr Alwyn Haigh, of West Nab Farm, Bradfield, in the seventies. Approached by the author in 2006, however (*after* a 2005 site visit!), Mr Haigh, still resident at Nab Farm, knew nothing of an aircraft on Emlin, and felt that what he had been indicating with outstretched arm to Mr Ownsworth, all those years back, had been the Dragonfly site on Thornseat Delf, just three degrees to the left of the Emlin reference above; a clarification subsequently conceded by Mr Ownsworth. The site, therefore, is recorded to save a walker using the enthusiast list from repeating the labour of what had been, in 2005, an unremitting heather bash.

An enduring piece of walker's lore Mr Haigh did proffer in this context, however, was that in the early post-war years his father had been approached to transport the materials for constructing the Emlin trig point, but had recommended another farmer with a more suitable vehicle.

## German Bomber, Tanyard Beck, Hoylandswaine, west of Barnsley

SE 26068 05939 170m
*Luftwaffe*

In the 1980s several long-term Hoylandswaine residents told researcher Mr John Ownsworth of this incident. By 2006, however, no one could be found who knew anything of it. The impact site was held to be at the junction of the drystone wall and double-wire fence at the bank top to the east of the infant Tanyard Beck. By 2006 the south-easterly field division leading to the junction from beyond the gully had been obliterated, only a stump of wall remaining at the bank top. No aircraft debris was discernible at the reference either in the 1980s or during canvassing and site visits in 2005-6.

2006, the junction of the drystone wall and wire fence above Tanyard Beck

## German Bomber, Penistone Agricultural Showground (probably spurious)

SE 24800 03500
*Luftwaffe*
*c.*1940-42

This is another incident which appears on enthusiast lists; and researcher Mr John Ownsworth's cousin, Mr Graham Wilson, a schoolboy during the early war years, certainly remembered seeing a crashed German aircraft here. The site, however, by 2006 long occupied by a housing estate, was that traditionally used for the Penistone Agricultural Show; the sort of venue commonly used to display downed German aircraft during such wartime fund-raising initiatives as the 'Wings for Victory', 'Save for Victory', and 'Dig for Victory' weeks. Accordingly Mr Wilson conceded that this could well have been the case with the aircraft he recalled.

2006, the former Penistone Showground, and a chance passer-by ...

It might be observed here, that, in the course of researching this Peakland series, many – indeed, very many – serendipitous encounters occurred in which a person, encountered purely by chance, proved to be the one person with first-hand knowledge of the event. Researching this location, however, had a coincidental twist all of its own. Having finally penetrated the blocked-off roads of the heavily built-over location and arrived at the GPS fix supplied by Mr John Ownsworth, random passer-by Mr Roy Taylor was asked to confirm that this was indeed the former Penistone showground site. Mr Taylor did so, but on learning that the enquiry had to do with crashed aircraft, pointed towards the far side of Penistone: 'In that case, you want to speak to my father-in-law, John Ownsworth ...'

## German Bomber, Crook Hill area, Woodlands Valley

SK 18281 86695 315m (area of)
*Luftwaffe*
1940–42

As Mr Maurice Cockerell, of Hayridge Farm, in the Woodlands Valley, was able to verify in 2006, a joint Home Guard and Observation Corps post was maintained on nearby Crook Hill throughout the war; accordingly, when this enemy machine came down just below the prominence, Home Guard

2006, Crook Hill, the impact area

personnel, including a Mr George Hallam, were virtually on the spot.

As Mr Hallam later described it, 'The plane came down on the flat moor on the far side of the hill from Crookhill Farm. The three crew members gave no trouble, but as the post's communications were out they had to be escorted around the hill to the farm, Stephen Elliot's place, which had a telephone. The responsible officer was billeted at the Derwent Hotel in Bamford, and directed that the airmen should be held at the farm until next day when Regular Army personnel could pick them up. So us Home Guard watched the prisoners, two hours on, two hours off, while the Elliot family watched everyone.'

A relatively cursory visual search of the area in June 2006 revealed no sign of the incident, but this, of course, was hardly surprising. However, canvassing area-residents proved equally unrewarding. Farmers Mr Peter Wood of Crookhill Farm, and the aforementioned Mr Maurice Cockerell, together with Birchinlee Keeper Mr Reg Cripps, and former Derwent Water Board official Mr Guy Woodhead, were all conversant with the other local crash sites, but had never heard of this one. Accordingly both the photograph and the reference given are merely locaters to the general area.

It is understood that a diary kept by Dr Mary Andrews, who organised the local Air-Raid Precautions branch, was willed to the care of the museum near the Fairholmes Information Centre. This diary is said to have logged all aircraft passing over the area and might well – should it become generally available – furnish more details on the Crook Hill incident, and indeed on other occurrences in the area. That aside, Farmer Mr Maurice Cockerell, in 2006 a local councillor of fifty years' standing, had fond memories of the visits Dr Andrews made to his school. 'She was very popular; she had a short haircut, and always dressed as a man, and when she came to train us in air-raid precautions there was always water splashing about.'

It might be noted that from April 1941, the Observer Corps, mentioned above, was re-styled the Royal Observer Corps, its proud span of service being destined to extend from 1925 until 1995.


## Heinkel He.111, near Lady Cross, Langsett Moor

SK 14811 99586 461m
*Luftwaffe*
Possibly 17 November 1940

Area of the Heinkel He.111 impact site, looking towards Lady Cross

A Heinkel He.111 ['One eleven'] is widely believed to have come down on the Langsett Moors close to Lady Cross. Other accounts describe the same location, but in terms of the raider having come down in 'the moors behind the Dog and Partridge public house'; the pub being at the bottom of Bordhill on the southern side of the A628. This was the version proffered to researcher Mr John Ownsworth by Mr Stephen Marsden, whose father, a butcher at Thurlstone, remembered from 1940 that the aircraft had been trailing smoke from one of its engines prior to crashing. Another witness vouching for the smoking engine specifically held that the crash occurred on 17 November 1940 and that the machine had been coming from the direction of Manchester at very low level.

Mr Ownsworth and some associates carried out metal-detector searches in the area in 1987 but found no evidence of the crash. Nor was anything to be found in 2006. The site, in unbroken heather, is not all that far from a minor footpath branching away from the main ridge path.

## Heinkel He.111, Ashway Gap, above Dovestone Reservoir (probably spurious)

SE 04000 04480 460m (general area reference)
*Luftwaffe*
16 April 1941

A German bomber is listed as having come down in this vicinity on 16 April 1941. No more certain location was available, however, and nothing was known of the aircraft by those approached in the area between 2004 and 2006. The general feeling is that this is a spurious report, although the specific dating lends some credibility. As with similar, rather nebulous reports, it is included here for a posterity in which archival or other evidence may be found.

## Junkers Ju.88-A5 (B3+DC), Dean Head Hill, north-west of Black Hill

SE 06602 05737 516m
*Luftwaffe Kampfgeschwader 54*, Lille, France
15 April 1941

Crew: three survived, initially attempted to evade capture

On the night of 15 April 1941, Junkers Ju.88 (B3+DC) of No.54 '*Totenkopf*' (Death's Head) *Kampfgeschwader* (bomber group), based at Lille, in France, was shot down by an anti-aircraft battery at Almonbury, Huddersfield, and crashed at Dean Head Hill, on Wessenden Head Moor, to the north-west of Black Hill. The aircraft 'fell within a mile of the Isle of Skye Inn', which stood at the junction of the A635 and Wessenden Head Road (at SE 07709 07239), but has long been demolished. Later, three German aircrew were discovered hiding in the area and initially taken to the Inn.

The crash site, as given above, is within yards of the footpath (still partially staked in 2006) running north-west from Black Hill to meet the A635. It was searched by enthusiast groups in the seventies, but whether any debris was found is not known. Certainly nothing was to be seen in September 2006.

At that time, welcome additional input was supplied by aviation author Mr David W. Earl. Having noted that the above information conforms, in the main, with a feature article in the *Huddersfield Daily Examiner* dated 12 May 1979, he advised that an 'After the Battle' publication, *The Blitz: Then and Now*, holds that the Ju.88 bearing the registration B3+DC actually crashed at Rughouse Farm, Holcombe Burnell, in Devon; which means that a caveat has to be added regarding the specific Ju.88 involved in the Dean Head Hill crash.

The area of the crash site at Dean Head Hill, looking westerly

## Junkers Ju.88, Low Tor, Howden Edge (inconclusive)

SK 20196 92209 466m (area of)
*Luftwaffe*
*c.*1941

Enthusiast sources hold that a Junkers Ju.88 came down 'near the shooting cabin situated to the north of Low Tor', on Howden Edge, and that German ammunition was found at the reference given above. The latter proves to be a marshy patch in Bents Clough, to the north of Low Tor, and high above Abbey Brook; but reference to a shooting cabin in this vicinity mystifies.

In 2006 nobody could be found who could verify this report; nor

The reputed Junkers Ju.88 site, north of Low Tor

did archival sources reveal anything to give the entry more substance. Perhaps it can best serve, then, as a lure to entice walkers up from the Strines Bridge car park to Howden Edge, for though the marsh might be found devoid of interest, the additional labour of taking just some scores more convex-terrain-foiling paces towards Berristers Tor affords a spectacular view over Abbey Brook.

## Junkers Ju.88, Tooleyshaw Moss, south-west of Black Hill

SE 06692 03800 493m
*Luftwaffe*
*c.*1941

This crash site, long attributed to a Junkers Ju.88, is to the south-west of Black Hill, on Tooleyshaw Moss, and only yards from the paved Pennine Way. In the 1980s, Mr Kevin Wynn, of Knottingley, introducing researcher Mr John Ownsworth to the site, remembered wreckage being scattered there. He also remembered, however, that several groups had busied themselves at the site during the seventies. Mr Ownsworth found nothing on that occasion, nor was there any surface evidence in 2006. This does seem to be a site, however, which promises more than most.

The Tooleyshaw Moss Ju.88 site, looking towards the Holme Moss TV mast

## Junkers Ju.88 of KG106

Luftwaffe
3 July 1942

This aircraft was recorded by *Dark Peak Aircraft Wrecks* author Mr Ron Collier, who might have expanded upon it had ill-health not intervened; he also named crew members Bergman and Majer, but gave no other details, and no location. It is entered here because, as Mr Collier was specific about the date, the unit, and the names of two crew members, it is possible that more information might be forthcoming in the future. Its inclusion also furnishes the present author with an opportunity to further acknowledge the debt owed to Mr Collier by all walkers who have puzzled over metal fragments chanced upon in their traverses of the Peaklands.

Author and researcher
Mr Ron Collier

## FZG76 V1 (*Vergeltungswaffe* 1) *Fieseler* Fi103 Flying Bomb, Cut Gate, Howden Moor, north-west of Margery Hill

SK 18586 96522 527m
*Luftwaffe*: launched by Heinkel He.111s of KG53
24 December 1944

V1 (Vergeltungswaffe 1) Fieseler Fi103. Some 9,000 were ramp-launched; others, like those recorded in this volume, were carried by Heinkel He.111s. Courtesy of Crown Copyright

The German *Fern Ziel Geraet* (Long-Range Target Apparatus), their *Vergeltungswaffe 1* (Reprisal Weapon Number One), was a normally-ramp-launched pilotless flying bomb with a range of some 150 miles. It was powered by a singularly-sounding pulse-jet engine which, at a preset range, cut out, the cessation of the sound indicating to the initiated below that an explosion was imminent.

The main V1 campaign started on 12 June 1944, and was sustained at high intensity, mainly against London and Antwerp, for eighty days. As early as 9 July 1944, however, as the Allied armies overran the launching sites in France, the Germans began to employ V1s launched from Heinkel He.111 ('One-eleven') bombers of *Kampfgeschwader* (bomber group) No.53, initially operating from Venlo, in Holland. This meant that the V1s could strike targets in the Midlands; the Heinkel hosts, with the V1s carried under a wing-root, approaching the East Coast below the radar screen then briefly pulling up to 1,500 feet for the launch. This evasion measure failed, however, and fighter interceptions were so successful that the Germans were unable to maintain the offensive.

A Heinkel He.111 loaded with its V1 Flying Bomb: 865 were air-launched in this fashion. Photo by courtesy of Crown Copyright

Just the same, a raid dispatched on Christmas Eve 1944 gave chilling notice of what the future might hold, with thirty-one V1s falling – one as far inland as Kelsall, near Chester – causing many casualties, and severe damage to property. During this wave of 'cruise-missile' attacks, the V1 featured here came down on remote moorland to the north-west of Margery Hill summit, on Howden Moor.

The V1 crater on Howden Moor in 2006

The peat would have muted the explosion caused by the weapon's one-ton load of amatol high-explosive; nevertheless the crater was very evident in 2006, albeit shallow and waterlogged, and fragments of the bomb could still be found.

## FZG76 V1 (*Vergeltungswaffe* 1) *Fieseler* Fi103  Flying Bomb, Westwood Farm, Matley

SJ 97550 95290 166m
*Luftwaffe*: launched by Heinkel He.111s of KG53
24 December 1944

One of the V1 Flying Bombs of Christmas Eve 1944, air-launched against the Midland cities, landed at Matley, near Hyde, Tameside. Striking a clump of trees, it exploded, demolishing the adjacent Westwood Farm and killing two of the occupants: Master Gordon Foulkes, the sixteen-year-old son of the house, and his grandmother, Mrs Elizabeth Greenwood, who was on a Christmas visit. Farmer Mr Edwin Foulkes (erstwhile Royal Flying Corps) and his wife were injured but his daughter, Betty, then aged thirteen, was physically unscathed and all three survived the blast.

Westwood Farm, Matley. Built in 1693. Photograph by courtesy of Mrs McKeown, née Foulkes

Westwood Farm, Matley. Destroyed, but also looted, in 1944. Photograph by courtesy of Mrs McKeown, née Foulkes

Mrs Betty McKeown (née Foulkes) and her husband, in 2005

The trauma for the survivors, however, was to be life-long. As Betty, by 2005 long since become Mrs Betty McKeown, testified, 'Dad was never the same again. Gordon was gone, and Grandma. So was the house. Then six cattle had been killed. And while dad was in hospital', her lips stiffened, 'the property was looted!' Nor did her severity lessen as she continued, 'Dad was left with a facial scar. Nevertheless, he lived to a ripe old age – until he got this cough, and I called in the doctor, who gave him an injection.'

Except that their family doctor was the infamous mass murderer Dr Harold Shipman, and Mr Foulkes was dead before the doctor got back to his car.

Another casualty of this V1, all those years before, had been the New Inn, across the road, which lost all its roof tiles. By 2006, the Inn, unlike the farmhouse, had long since been repaired. However, stepped back only slightly from the Inn was a post-war terrace which had itself been truncated, the end dwelling having been purposefully demolished, its last incumbents having been Moors Murderers Ian Brady and Myra Hindley. Some triangle; encompassing within so few yards Brady and Hindley, Shipman, and Herr Hitler!

The impact site is to the right of the building

The post-war terrace, truncated at the diagonal cross

Mr Arnold Willerton, of Hyde. The V1 impacted in trees to the left. The now-ornamental phone kiosk stands on the site of the farmhouse

## And two V1s, (one problematical) more properly in *The Central Area*:

### FZG76 V1 (*Vergeltungswaffe* 1) *Fieseler* Fi103  Flying Bomb, Cow Lane, Beighton, Sheffield

SK 44494 81407 47m (area of)
*Luftwaffe*: launched by Heinkel He.111s of KG53
24 December 1944

Among the fifty or so V1s known to have been air-launched against the Midland cities on Christmas Eve 1944 was one which came down in a field off Cow Lane, Beighton, in the south-eastern area of Sheffield. No casualties resulted, although blast damage was reported at both Halfway and Killamarsh. By 2006 Cow Lane had become the Rother Valley Way, the map reference given being at the 'boundary of Halfway', a refining location in early reports. The area, however, had been totally transformed by the spread of industrial units, so that no more certain location could be arrived at in the time available before publication.

The approximate site of the Beighton V1

## FZG76 V1 (*Vergeltungswaffe* 1) *Fieseler* Fi103 Flying Bomb, Meadow Farm, Ringinglow (problematic)

**SK 30630 84901** 185m
*Luftwaffe*: launched by Heinkel He.111s of KG53
*c.*1944

In mid-2006 retired farmer Mr Derek Sanderson, described how, in 1960, at Meadow Farm, near Ringinglow, his plough unearthed what enthusiasts at the time told him was the flap assembly from the B-17 which crashed in Endcliffe Park (SK 32857 85899, see *The Central Area* p25) some 1.5 miles away. In about 1980 he gave the item to Mr David Sier, of Sheffield, and by 2006, when it passed into the possession of Mr John Ownsworth, of Penistone, it had come to be regarded as one of the gyroscopic assemblies of a V1 Flying Bomb. Having inspected a photograph of the mechanism, author Mr Peter J.C. Smith (*Flying Bombs over the Pennines*, 1988, see bibliography), thought it unlikely that it was a V1 gyro; a view seemingly supported by photographs in a handbook on German guided missiles (see bibliography) supplied by the RAF Museum. As a result, the present author investigated the possibility that it might have been part of the then-secret Norden bombsight, just conceivably jettisoned once it was realised that the Endcliffe Park B-17 was irretrievably out of control; however, reference to a technical drawing supplied by the RAF Museum (*Bombardier's Information File*, see bibliography), effectively ruled that out. Certainly, aviation author Mr David W. Earl was unable to match manufacturing numbers on the item with any American parts, while a search by the Boeing Company proved similarly negative; on the other hand, canvassing the area revealed nobody who remembered a Flying Bomb falling nearer than Beighton, eight miles further east; nor did normally-dependable archive sources record such an event.

Notwithstanding the above, many V1 components are known to have undergone significant development during the 34,000 [choose your source] production run of 1944-5: metal wings giving place to wooden ones, for example. Accordingly, should the gyroscope assembly, against all the odds, indeed prove to be that of a Flying Bomb then the case could certainly be made that this was all that has come to light of a V1 which suffered a malfunction and exploded in mid-air, fragmenting so thoroughly that those pieces of metal which were too light to bury themselves on impact, passed unnoticed by the police and ARP engaged in logging the fall of enemy bombs; conceivably one of those many Flying Bombs hit by, but in this instance not immediately exploded by, the increasingly effective coastal defences. It is to be hoped that a more satisfying identification will emerge in the future.

Gyroscope and gearing, reputed to be from a V1, ploughed up by Farmer Derek Sanderson in 1960, photo by courtesy of Mr John Ownsworth

2006: the spot where the gyroscope assembly fell.

## An example of a Royal Air Force crash-report summary, Form 1180

Any RAF aircraft accident generated a plethora of paperwork. Once a finding was reached a summary of the investigation was produced. Often hard to decipher, the summaries are notoriously lax when it comes to recording the location of the incident. In 2006 the repository for the many summaries still extant was the RAF Museum, Hendon; while Squadron Operational Record Books and many full accident reports were held by the Public Records Office, Kew. It is stressed that when such documents are missing it is not due to some dastardly cover-up, but to the benign, periodical pruning of archival material which was deemed, at the time, of no further interest, and without which even the National Archives would soon have become choked. Further, as observed elsewhere in the text, investigations were carried out by junior RAF officers reporting to their seniors, so that no latitude existed, besides which it was in the common interest to both determine, and to disseminate throughout the RAF, the cause of any air accident.

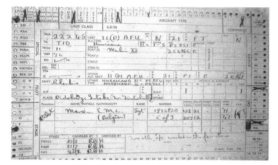 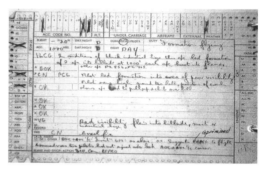

Hurricane pz-851, Tintwistle Kharr

## Crash-site Perspex Sculpture

It may be that the urge to collect souvenirs from crashed aircraft entered the human psyche when a fisherman retrieved some waxed feathers after Icarus disobeyed family flying orders and flew too near the sun. Certainly it flourished during the Second World War, when so many sons of Icarus fell within the Peaklands, and indeed after it, judging from post-war pleas made for the return of souvenirs by crash investigators seeking causes for effects.

2006. Mrs Beryl Rush (née Mellor) of Youlgreave. Inset: her perspex ring [Mark, this one must be included, please, Pat]

Most debris filched, then as now, finished up in dustbins, but in researching this series it became evident that Perspex from turrets and cockpit canopies was fashioned into artefacts, into cigarette boxes, pendants, and most frequently, rings. Former exponents of the art described how fragments would be pierced through with pokers heated in domestic coal fires, then filed into shape, and sometimes polished. An isolated variation was the use of aluminium tubing, but Perspex was the material of choice.

The first instance encountered was that of a Halifax flight engineer who made Perspex rings for his mother and sister from the crashed Wellington at Conksbury, but several more were to follow, most related by former-schoolboy creators who then sold – or bartered – their products to local lasses. The only example encountered to be fashioned from an actual Peaklands crash, however, was both retrieved and crafted by then-schoolgirl Beryl Mellor, of Friden. In 2006, Beryl, long since Mrs Beryl Rush, of Youlgreave, smiled as she displayed her creation. 'It was all the rage then, to make rings,' she said. 'I'm sure I didn't use a poker, but I remember sitting with newspaper on my knees, filing away for hours.'

### 'Darky' and associated emergency-homing facilities

Throughout the Peakland series various emergency 'get-you-home' systems are mentioned, and 'Darky' in particular. This was a quintessentially British facility which made a strength out of the limited, twenty-five mile range of the airborne R/T (voice) radio installations of the day, the Transmitter Receiver TR1196s and TR9s carried by bombers and fighters respectively. The facility was operated at RAF stations, but also at certain Royal Observation Corps posts, button 'D' being the emergency channel on which a lost aircraft could transmit blind for 'Darky'. Any listening post hearing the call would respond with its position, thus furnishing the aircrew with a location accurate to twenty-five miles, often enough to enable them to plot a course for base. Alternatively, especially if the aircraft needed to land quickly, the ground station could pass it the course to the nearest airfield. This would be followed up by a phone call to the next ground station in that direction, who, when it heard the aircraft call, would take over and refine the lead-in.

Among non-radio aids were 'Occults', aerial lighthouses radiating a white, periodically-shaded (or occluded) light flashing a single identifying letter, and visible at 30 miles, which could direct their beams towards the nearest airfield.

'Granite' was supplementary to both facilities, the station sending off red flares to show its position, or alternatively to warn of high ground.

The Royal Observer Corps was able to make the proud claim that over 7,000 Allied aircraft were saved by use of such systems, with 1,800 other damaged machines being guided to safe landings.

### The 'Queen Mary' Trailer, the Fordson Tractor; and their precursor

**The 'Queen Mary' trailer:** throughout the series reference is made to crashed aircraft being towed from the site by 'Queen Mary' trailer. These low-loader trailers were built by Tasker's of Andover in response to a 1938 Air Ministry requirement for a recovery vehicle which could carry a complete fighter aircraft. Within ten days Tasker's submitted not only a design, but a prototype vehicle. Their

contract bid was successful, and over 4,000 of their trailers, the largest available, were built. Regarding handling them, *The Reluctant Erk* (see bibliography) has a new airman-driver declaring, 'Anybody that tells you he's backed an articulator round a corner's a liar. He just happened to get one that was going round there anyhow.'

**The Fordson tractor:** another vehicle mentioned in the series is the Fordson tractor which farmers used to help retrieve crashed aircraft. Reference is almost invariably made to the vehicle being a prized possession, and the only one in the area, bringing it home that at the time the term horsepower on most British farms meant just that.

**The Fordson's 1944 contemporary:** Jess, with Mr Alan Waller of Blaze Farm, Wildboarclough, courtesy of Harold and Florence Waller.

# DO GHOSTLY AVIATORS HAUNT
# PEAKLAND'S MOORS?

It would seem that all desolate places stir up a certain disquiet in the human psyche. Perhaps then, the media's otherwise unaccountable readiness to dally with specious accounts of spectral aircraft crashing in the Peaklands is attributable to some deep-seated visceral unease. More easily discounted are the vaporous utterances on Ghostly Planes that appear on the web, for these immediately disbar themselves by their unashamed *Sunday Sport* content and their so-evident lack of serious research.

Yet major search operations have indeed been mounted in the Peaklands for aircraft reported to have crashed, of which no trace was ever found; not only that, but the alerts have been initiated by concerned, level-headed persons. So, provided that each of these considerations is researched no further, it might well seem that, if phantasmal aviators do not wing the Peakland skies, then the wicked Big Brother Ministry of Defence must be engaged in some dark, high-moorland conspiracy. Then again, one's natural bent towards the arcane might argue that, in the Peaklands, where so many aircraft have crashed with the loss of a substantial number of lives (albeit nowhere near as many as on the region's roads), it is only reasonable to expect some mystic forces to be operating.

One of the fundamentally unsound web articles purported to focus upon the Broomhead Moor operation of 27 March 1997, mounted after a widely reported moorland explosion. The histrionic spin applied, however, was to imply that the authorities had been mystified to find no wreckage; another step, and we might well have had the authorities being misled by a Ministry cover-up!

Of course, everyone loves a ghost story, not least a sceptical fellwalker-aviator; although it is hazarded that most would find the *divertissement* a little less attractive on an upper moorland with the weather bleakly closing in and the light rather too rapidly fading.

But before getting overly bound up with wondering whether spectral aircraft just might exist, it has to be appreciated that sophisticated terrain-avoidance avionics enable very powerfully-engined jet aircraft to fly very fast and very low across the Peakland moors, by night and day, and in all weather conditions. Only even accepting such intellect-bedazzling technological advances, it seems to be an ineradicable trait of the Freudian id that it insists upon inventing spectres. As the author discovered in the course of flying with several generations of otherwise well-balanced air hostesses who discovered ghosts in nearly every hotel room they were allocated. On occasion, to ease the minds of the poor misguided dears, he would change rooms with them. Of course, it took some time to sink home that in doing so he was exchanging a captain's executive suite, bowl of fruit, and luxurious bathroom – with fluffy towels and bidet – for a basic cell lacking all fripperies.

But what of the barren Peaklands? So many aircraft lost! So many young lives cruelly and untimely extinguished! Can anyone doubt that some unquiet spirits among them might well haunt the moors where they crashed?

Well, setting aside his naivety in exchanging rooms with less-than-truly-susceptible young women, the author certainly can.

For the Peaklands have been peopled since the dawn of time; so that even the eponymous Pecsaetons ('*peek*-seetons') were relative latecomers. But mortality in the United Kingdom runs at some 629,500 a year, the rate in the Peakland moors area being 9.6 in every thousand of its population. From which it follows that if even a proportion of unquiet spirits decided to roam – especially once augmented by the district's erstwhile road users – there would be no vacant spaces on Kinder, and precious few anywhere else. What chance then, amid that ruck, for a paltry few-score of Johnny-come-lately airmen to find elbow room?

So where is the logic in this lurid sentimentalism that conjures up spectral aviators? For bearing in mind that the vast majority of crashes are caused by fallible human beings doing jobs as mundane as maintaining and driving a car, and simply getting it wrong, any lingering spirit-aviators would be far more inclined to hang their heads than to flaunt themselves.

Nor are the ghost-mongers supported by those who were actually on the moor during that 1997 call-out. Accordingly the log of the Buxton Mountain Rescue Team ends its summary of the incident with the wryly derisive note, 'The media speculated that this was a "ghost aircraft" from WW2'. Similarly, Ranger Josef Hergi and his former mentor, Mr John Campion Barrows – 'Campy' – both found the search perfectly logical, but the puerility of the superstitious lobby utterly unfathomable. 'The gamekeeper and his wife who reported the explosion,' Ranger Hergi reasoned, 'and all the others who phoned in, knew it hadn't been thunder, or a quarry detonation, so we had to make certain it hadn't been a crash. There was nothing inexplicable about it, still less a cover-up. Indeed it was thought from the start that it had been a sonic boom: no aircraft were missing. But what could the Ministry of Defence do, when approached, but reiterate that their pilots were forbidden to break the sound barrier over land? You could hardly expect the crew concerned to own up to it!' [Allowing that the crew in question had even been aware of directing a boom towards the ground: given the right in-flight parameters it only takes the tiniest forwards twitch of the stick!]

By 2006 Peakland denizen Mr Peter Jackson had concurrently amassed 36 years as a part-time ranger and 27 years as a mountain rescue team volunteer; additionally, during his full-time police career, his beat had been the Snake and Derwent Valleys; also the Longdendale Valley – the 'haunted valley', as those votaries of the ghost mongers would have it. In March 2006, Ranger Jackson told of sensationalist spin being brazenly manufactured by a TV crew he had taken to a wartime crash site. 'Their presenter,' he recalled, 'made her way into shot through the mist-wreathed wreckage declaiming, "I'm walking through a graveyard – an *aeroplane* graveyard – where for years now many people have reported seeing ghostly …" Which I knew to be blatant fabrication.'

Ranger Jackson paused. Then said feelingly, 'I've walked these moors by day, and by night too, all my life, and I must have come across every phenomenon the imagination could conjure up. But never one that relied upon ghosts for an explanation.' He paused again, before expostulating with more than just a touch of acerbity, 'These people who have to sink to manufacturing sensation! The truth being that the Peakland moors encompass many a truly beautiful mystique; but not a single mystery.'

# DETAILS OF THE AIRCRAFT INTRODUCED IN
## *PEAKLAND AIR CRASHES: THE NORTH*

This section aims to provide the walker with a potted guide to the aircraft types introduced in *Peakland Air Crashes: The North*. Details of those already encountered in *Peakland Air Crashes: The South* and *The Central Area* will be found in those volumes; although supplementary anecdotal material is added to the details previously given of the Lancaster and the V1 Flying Bomb.

It will be appreciated that only representative details are supplied. The same applies to the performance figures given, for these are never immutable. For example, values quoted in Pilot's Notes always incorporate a healthy safety margin, while workaday machines of a given type often differ significantly. Then again, published sources display marked variations, not a few perpetuating values originally enhanced for wartime propaganda purposes. Notwithstanding all of which, the details given here aim to be comprehensive enough to satisfy the passing interest of the walker-reader.

Similarly, it is to cater for this happy non-specialist class of reader that Arabic numbers are employed throughout in designating aircraft marks, the problem of deciphering Roman numerals being left to the enthusiast. For the latter, on the other hand, a note might be usefully added regarding the author's use throughout of 'stick', which, certainly from the fifties, was always the preferred term among pilots; 'pole' was equally acceptable but somewhat informal, 'joystick' almost antediluvially archaic, and 'control column' too pedantic even for Central Flying School: as a working instructor, try 'pattering' control column, rather than stick! So stick it is, even where the aircraft in question had a wheel, or a yoke.

## Avro Avian

The Avro Avian single-engined biplane, designed as a sporting, long-range racer, first flew in 1922. With two tandem seats in an open cockpit it was powered by a 100-horsepower de Havilland Gipsy I in-line engine, had an all-up-weight of 1,600 pounds, a top speed of 100 mph (87 knots), a cruising speed of 90 mph (78 knots), an initial climb rate of 600 feet a minute, a range of 360 miles, and a ceiling of 12,500 feet.

## Boeing B-29 Superfortress: F-13 variant

The B-29 development of the B-17 Flying Fortress first flew on 21 September 1942, and was powered by four 2,200-horsepower Wright Cyclone Eighteen supercharged radial engines driving 16.5-foot, four-bladed, Hamilton propellers. This combination gave the B-29 Superfortress a cruising speed of some 220 mph (191 knots) in the region of 28,000 feet, and a ceiling of 33,600 feet. At a maximum take-off weight of 133,500 pounds, and carrying a bomb load of 6,000 pounds, it had a range of 3,700 miles, although this reduced to 1,000 miles with the maximum bomb load of 20,000 pounds.

The B-29 carried a normal crew complement of ten, the bomber version being furnished with multiple 0.50-inch calibre machine guns in chin, dorsal, ventral and tail turrets, with others in remotely-controlled fuselage barbettes. It also mounted 20 mm calibre cannon.

The F-13 variant was a dedicated photographic machine in which specialists swelled the crew to thirteen.

Although there were profound internal differences it was virtually identical in outward appearance to the B-29 bomber.

## Fairey Barracuda

The Barracuda torpedo bomber first flew in December 1940 and with its retractable undercarriage and Fairey-Youngman flaps was a step up from the naval biplanes it replaced. Deliveries to the Royal Navy did not begin until January 1943, however, and in the interim the need to strengthen certain components for deck landings and the addition of extra equipment meant that the Barracuda was overweight, its design performance suffering accordingly.

The 1,940-horsepower Rolls-Royce Merlin 32 in-line engine gave the weighty 14,250-pounds production machine a cruising speed of 205 mph (178 knots), a ceiling of 21,600 feet, and a range of 1,150 miles. A typical armament fit was two 0.303-inch calibre wing-mounted machine guns, while the ordnance load was a single 1,620-pound torpedo; or bombs, mines, or depth charges to the same weight. The last Barracuda was retired in 1953, after a production run of just over 1,700.

## De Havilland Beaver

The de Havilland of Canada L-20A Beaver first flew in August 1947, and being designed to operate from restricted spaces had good short-field capabilities and a steep climb out. As certificated in 1948, the Beaver could carry a pilot and seven passengers, had a cruising speed of 125 mph (109 knots), a maximum speed of 135 mph (117 knots), a ceiling of 18,000 feet, an initial rate of climb of 1,020 feet a minute, and an extended range of 676 miles. Some 1,700 were built and many were still being operated in 2006.

## Blackburn Botha

Blackburns first flew their new design in December 1938, but after it was delivered to the RAF a year later several Bothas were lost in fatal accidents. The aircraft, normally carrying four crew, had already proved to be underpowered for its envisaged use as a twin-engined reconnaissance torpedo bomber and was accordingly re-allocated to training. Even so the type lingered on as a target tug until 1944, by which time 580 had been built.

The Botha's twin 930-horsepower Bristol Perseus radial engines gave it a cruising speed of 212 mph (184 knots) with a ceiling of 17,500 feet. It had a maximum take-off weight of 18,450 pounds and was armed with a single fixed 0.303-inch calibre machine gun firing forwards, and two others in a dorsal turret. In addition it could carry an internally stowed torpedo, or up to 2,000 pounds weight of depth charges or bombs.

## De Havilland Chipmunk TMk.10

Designed as a replacement for the de Havilland Tiger Moth biplane trainer, the prototype Chipmunk monoplane first flew on 22 May 1946, paving the way for nearly nine hundred which were to be used by RAF training schools, by RAF Reserve units, and by University Air Squadrons. The single-engined Chipmunk had tandem seating for two – but to maintain its balance it had to be flown solo from the front seat – and a fixed, tailwheel-configuration undercarriage. Easy to fly in a casual fashion, it was an extremely demanding machine to fly accurately, while its spin occasionally showed lethal qualities. Just the same a delightful aircraft. [And with a warm, enclosed cockpit, unlike the so-draughty Tiger Moth.]

Powered by a Gipsy Major Mk.8 engine driving a two-bladed, fixed-pitch, metal propeller it had a maximum permitted speed of 199 mph (173 knots), a normal cruising speed of 104 mph (90 knots), and a stalling speed of 52 mph (45 knots). Its maximum permitted weight was 2,100 pounds.

## Airspeed Consul

The Airspeed Consul was the post-war passenger version of the RAF's twin-engined Oxford. It was most often a machine repurchased from the Service by Airspeed then modified to meet civilian standards, the war-role equipment being replaced by passenger seats. Although the Oxford was less docile than its contemporary, the more versatile, and ultimately multi-tasked, Anson, it had nevertheless been tried and tested, and the Consul variant proved a worthy bottom rung for several emergent airlines.

Powered by two 375-horsepower Armstrong Siddeley Cheetah Ten engines the machine had a maximum speed of 190 mph (165 knots), cruised at 163 mph (142 knots), had an initial rate of climb of 1,070 feet a minute, and a ceiling of 23,500 feet. At a maximum all-up weight of 8,250 pounds, and with its complement of six passengers and a crew of two, it had a range of 900 miles.

## Douglas Dakota (DC-3)

The Douglas DC-3, the doyen of air transports, first flew in 1935 and was still flying commercially in 2006. Carrying twenty-one passengers and a crew of three, it was variously known as the 'Mainliner', 'Silverliner', 'Flagship', 'Skyliner' and 'Skyclub', with its 'Douglas Sleeper Transport' version becoming the 'Sky-Sleeper' and 'Flagship Sleeper'. The RAF was to dub it the Dakota.

After the war many airlines gladly seized upon the DC-3. So that in August 1946, the restyled British European Airways finally painted up twenty-one DC-3 'Pionairs' – the modifications for this class had included an airstair door – having operated them in Service drab since their transfer from RAF Transport Command six months before.

Typical performance figures for the DC-3 when powered by two 1,000-horsepower Wright Cyclone radial engines give a maximum speed of 220 mph (191 knots), a cruising speed of 194 mph (169 knots), a stalling speed of 67 mph (58 knots), and a ceiling of 21,900 feet. Maximum take-off weight is 25,200 pounds, and the range 2,125 miles.

## De Havilland DH9 (Aircraft Manufacturing Company – AIRCO)

During the First World War the de Havilland DH9 long-range day bomber of 1917, a modification of the DH4, served in France with the Royal Flying Corps, and after the institution of the new Service on 1 April 1918, with the Royal Air Force. It also served with the effective precursor of Bomber Command, Trenchard's defiantly-styled Independent Force.

Although both the 230-horsepower Siddeley Puma engine and the 240-horsepower BHP engine were variously installed, neither proved all that reliable. Besides which, as the DH9 could only reach 10,000 feet with its full bomb load of 460 pounds, it suffered accordingly from ground fire.

A fuel capacity of 74 gallons gave it a duration of four and a half hours, it had a maximum speed of 111 mph (96 knots) at 10,000 feet, required just 112 yards to lift off, and at a landing speed of 57 mph (50 knots) a 160 yards' run from touchdown. As defensive armament it had a forward-firing 0.303-inch calibre Vickers machine gun, and in the aft cockpit, one, or sometimes two, 0.303-inch calibre Lewis machine guns.

## De Havilland 9A

The de Havilland 9A biplane bomber entered the RAF in June 1918, served in France from August 1918, and remained on strength as the standard day bomber until 1931. Powered by either a 400-horsepower Liberty motor, or a 375-horsepower Rolls-Royce Eagle, with a service ceiling of 16,500 feet, and operated in close formation, it suffered only light losses in France while proving most effective as a bomber. Nearly 900 were built by the end of the First World War and several hundred more followed in the post-war years when the type became the core of the squadrons in Aden, Iraq, India, Egypt and Palestine. The DH9A also served many day-bomber units in the home establishment and from 1925 was widely used by the Auxiliary Air Force and many flying training schools.

The DH9A had a 112-gallon fuel tank which gave it an endurance of five and a quarter hours and it could carry up to 660 pounds of bombs. The service ceiling was 16,500 feet, it had a landing speed of 59 mph (51 knots) and a maximum speed of 126 mph (109 knots) at 10,000 feet; a more typical speed when laden, however, was 114 mph (99 knots). The DH9A was armed with two 0.303-inch calibre machine guns; a forward-firing Vickers and a ring-mounted Lewis in the rear cockpit.

## De Havilland DH85 Leopard Moth

First flown on 27 May 1933, the Leopard Moth was a three-seater, high-winged monoplane with an enclosed cabin accommodating two side-by-side passenger seats behind the pilot. It was powered by a 130-horsepower de Havilland Gipsy-Major four-cylinder in-line air-cooled inverted engine, had an all-up weight of 2,250 pounds and a maximum speed of 138 mph (120 knots). Its initial climb rate was 625 feet a minute, its ceiling 17,300 feet,

and its range 715 miles.

Sales were helped when a Leopard Moth won the 1933 King's Cup air race two weeks after its first flight, and 133 were built.

## De Havilland DH89 Rapide

This de Havilland light-transport biplane was developed from their other successful models during the 1930s, and in RAF service during the Second World War was renamed the Dominie. The RAF used it both in its design role as an eight- to ten-seater communications machine, and as a five- to six-seater navigation and radio trainer.

Many civil Rapides had been impressed into service, notably with the Air Transport Auxiliary, and after the Second World War the type was welcomed by many emergent and re-emergent airlines. So it was that when the Government set about nationalising the independent domestic airlines in 1947, fourteen of these re-emergent pre-war concerns became part of British European Airways, and brought their Dominies with them.

Driven by two 200-horsepower de Havilland Gipsy Queen in-line engines the Rapide could cruise at 132 mph (115 knots) and attain 16,500 feet with a range of 570 miles. In all, 728 of the type had been built when production ended in mid-1946, and in 2006 some were still earning their living giving pleasure flights, notably at Duxford.

## De Havilland DH90 Dragonfly

In 1935, building on the success of their range of multi-engined types exemplified in the 1933 Dragon Rapide biplane, de Havillands brought out a five-seater luxury tourer intended for wealthy customers, building just 66. This machine, the Dragonfly, was one of many civil types to be impressed into RAF service during the Second World War and was employed in the same training and communication roles as the Dragon Rapide – the Dominie to the RAF.

Powered by two 130-horsepower Gipsy Major engines, the Dragonfly cruised at 125 mph (109 knots), had a maximum speed of 145 mph (125 knots), a range of 534 nautical miles, and a ceiling of 18,000 feet.

## Gloster Gamecock

The Gamecock biplane fighter first flew in February 1925. It had a reputation, not unfairly gained, for having flutter problems, and right-hand spins were prohibited; yet for all that it proved a popular machine and was well suited to aerobatics. Powered by a 425-horsepower Bristol Jupiter engine it had a maximum speed of 155 mph (135 knots) at 5,000 feet and 145 mph (126 knots) at 10,000 feet. It could climb to 10,000 feet in just under eight minutes, to 20,000 feet in 20 minutes, and had a service ceiling of 22,000 feet. It was armed with two Vickers 0.303-inch calibre machine guns.

## Gloster Gladiator

The prototype of what would be the RAF's last biplane fighter first flew in September 1934. Although initially developed from the Gloster Gauntlet as a private venture by Gloster's designer, Mr Henry Folland, the single-seater, metal-framed, fabric-covered Gladiator was ordered by the RAF in 1935, over 200 being delivered by the time production stopped in April 1940.

Typically powered by an 840-horsepower Bristol Mercury Nine radial piston engine, it had a maximum speed of 255 mph (222 knots) at 14,500 feet, cruised at 210 mph (182 knots), and could climb to 20,000 feet in nine and a half minutes. It had a service ceiling of over 30,000 feet, a range of 440 miles, and an endurance of two hours. As armament the early Gladiators had four Browning 0.303-inch calibre machine guns.

## Hawker Hind

The Hawker Hind day bomber was conceived in the early phase of the build-up of the RAF in the thirties, and first flew in September 1934, so that by September 1938 a total of 528 had been built. It was a refined version of the Hart, its fully-supercharged, 640-horsepower Rolls-Royce Kestrel engine giving it a maximum speed of 186 mph (162 knots) at 16,400 feet and enabling it to reach 6,500 feet in four minutes. It had a range of 430 miles, a ceiling of 26,400 feet, could carry 500 pounds of bombs, and was armed with two 0.303-inch calibre machine guns; a Lewis to the rear and a forward-facing Vickers.

## Lockheed Hudson

The twin-engined, twin-finned, five-crewed Lockheed Hudson was the military version of the Lockheed 14 Super-Electra airliner, and was ordered for the RAF in June 1938. The initial order for 200 caused outrage among those who believed that buying any but British aeroplanes was heinous. Fortunately, on this occasion, this pernicious lobby was overruled; but how often in the coming years the Service would be saddled with inferior types; saddled in the 1960s, for example, with the British Argosy rather

than the American C-130 Hercules! In the case of the Hudson, however, over 2,000 were eventually received, most delivered under their own power.

Although intended as a navigational trainer the Hudson was pressed into the maritime-reconnaissance and anti-submarine roles, carrying an air-droppable lifeboat while on air-sea rescue duties. It was also used as a bomber, and as a clandestine delivery vehicle for supplies and agents. Finally, once superseded as a first-line aircraft, it served as both trainer and transport.

Converting the airliner into the Hudson meant, among other things, re-engining with Cyclone power plants; providing a bomb bay and a transparent nose to facilitate bomb-aiming; fitting a British Boulton-Paul powered turret – mounted well aft in order not to impede the cabin door; and installing twin, forward-firing machine guns below the nose.

Typically powered by two 1,100-horsepower Wright Cyclone engines, the Hudson had a maximum speed of 246 mph (214 knots) – increasing to 284 mph (247 knots) in later versions – an endurance of six hours, and a range of 2,160 miles. It cruised at 170 mph (148 knots), had an initial rate of climb of 1,200 feet a minute, and a ceiling of 22,000 feet. Carrying between 750 and 1,000 pounds of bombs, it mounted five 0.303-inch calibre machine guns; the two below the nose, a moveable dorsal-fitted gun, and a pair in the rear turret. It could also carry two beam-mounted guns.

## Hawker Hunter TMk.7

The Hunter, the first British-produced transonic fighter, was the RAF's mainstay first-line fighter from 1954, when it began replacing the Meteors and Sabres, until 1963, when it, in turn, was replaced by the missile-armed, fully-supersonic Lighting. But many other air forces would use it for years more, while not a few retired aircraft found eager private owners.

The prototype got airborne on 21 July 1951, and the first production model on 16 May 1953, after which nearly two thousand were built.

As might be expected, there were progressive modifications, but typical data shows the Hunter to be powered by a Rolls-Royce Avon 203 turbojet developing 10,000 pounds of static thrust. This drove it to a maximum speed of 715 mph (621 knots) at sea level, and Mach 0.95 at 36,000 feet. Fully laden, with drop tanks, it weighed 24,600 pounds. It had an initial climb rate of 17,200 feet a minute, took eight minutes to climb to 46,000 feet, and had a ceiling of 51,500 feet. It had a clean combat radius of some 320 miles, and a seemingly niggardly endurance of just 1 hour 18 minutes. [Partially excusing the invariable Hunter re-joining call, so irritating to the transport aircraft they barged in front of, 'Downwind, minimum fuel'.] Underwing drop tanks would give the Hunter a range of 1,840 miles, and standard armament was four 30mm Aden cannon together with underwing pylons for bombs or rockets.

Easy to fly – delightful rather – pilots who later transferred to Lightnings wistfully described the Hunter as 'the last Fun fighter'.

## Avro Lancaster

Background and performance details of the Lancaster are to be found in the southern volume of this series. However, such is the interest in this revered type, of which nearly 8,000 were built, that some anecdotal points which emerged during research for this book are included here.

It is held, for example, that far exceeding the number of Lancasters produced at Avros were the surreptitiously turned out cigarette lighters; an estimated 10,000 of them.

Among the unimpeachable workers, however, was a young draftee who was to become Mrs Connie Ibbetson, of Upper Maythorn Farm, Holmfirth, who, in 2005, recalled, 'I was living in the Horspeth hostel, and did the night shift, working in the pilot's station, which we knew as D2, wiring the electrics into conduits. The panels themselves came complete, but I particularly remember the socket for heating the flying gloves.'

But she remembered too, the senior NCO members of a Lancaster crew who found her name and address pencilled on one of the electrical panels she had fitted, and wrote to 'Our Dear Connie' from the Sergeants' Mess at RAF Elsham Wolds, near Barnetby, Lincolnshire. The navigator – a Canadian, 'married to a grand English girl' – introduced the other crew members as 'eligible (and gay, if I may add) bachelors' and explained that all wanted

signed photographs of Connie and her colleagues.

'Our newly acquired Lanc', the navigator went on, 'had your name and address on it and seeing that the plane has steadfastly brought us back we consider you our "lucky charm".' The flight engineer followed suit: 'we have penetrated deep into the heart of enemy territory & on every occasion the performance of this particular aircraft has been superb … it has always brought us safely back and long may it continue to do so … aircrew are notoriously superstitious & we felt that a great deal of luck is due to your pencilled message.' The rear gunner, in turn, subscribed, 'The rest of the fellows have laid it on thick so I won't add anymore to it, but I am just the rear gunner [sic] and she sure is a good kite, so thanks a million for it'. [RAF air gunners tend view the term 'rear gunner' as an Americanism, but that is what the man himself wrote.] And finally there was the mid-upper gunner, 'All I can say is I hope the kite comes back for a long time.' Gratifyingly, a 2006 check with the Commonwealth War Graves Commission indicated that good fortune continued to attend each of Mrs Ibbetson's correspondents, for none are listed as casualties.

In 2006, Mr Bert Waller, of Hardwick Farm, Todwick, also had a Lancaster tale to tell. 'I've seen a Lancaster do a loop!' He paused, and then elucidated. 'A man from Anston, just down the road, became a pilot and used to beat up the area quite frequently. When he graduated to Lancasters he brought one over. I saw it climb quite high, then begin to dive. But it dived for so long that I thought he was going to fly straight into the ground. But then he pulled up. Yet I couldn't believe it as he continued to pull, until he actually went right over the top! Sadly, some time later, he failed to return from operations.' Again, not the norm; but then a substantial number of Oxfords and Ansons were lost (none in this Peakland series) as a result of pilots carrying out full-blooded aerobatics on these strictly non-aerobatic types.

2005: ex-Avro worker, Mrs Connie Ibbetson

Certified Flying Log Book entry of Sergeant Peter Garrison, flight engineer, showing single-engined flying on a Lancaster at the Lancaster Finishing School

Equally unusual is evidence of a Lancaster being flown on one engine; and with official approval. The source being the officially-certified flying log book of a cousin of the Waller family, Mr Peter Garrison; by 2006, long resident in Canada, but who flew 36 operations as a flight engineer with Nos 625 and 170 Lancaster Squadrons. His first sortie at the Hemswell Lancaster Finishing School in September 1944 was a fifty-minute detail of familiarisation including 'Twin, three, and single-engined' flying; moreover this was with his regular captain-to-be, and not a dedicated instructor! Referring to this terrifying-sounding exercise, all packed into just 50 minutes, the erstwhile flight engineer remarked, 'A real confidence builder, this thing would actually fly on one engine; not very well, but nevertheless it would fly.'

But then the affection and the trust the Lancaster engendered means that such anecdotes as these are legion.

## North American P-51 Mustang

The Mustang first flew in September 1940, the RAF taking deliveries in 1942. The Americans themselves were slow to appreciate their home-constructed product and in consequence they lacked a long-range escort fighter when their European bomber offensive began later that year and they discovered how losses soared when the limited-range fighter escorts had to turn for home. In December 1943, however, when the Rolls-Royce Merlin-engined, long-range-escort Mustangs arrived in Europe, the hard-pressed American bomber crews could finally rely upon fighter support throughout the entire raid.

Several versions of the Mustang were produced, many for the ground-attack role, with some variants employing airbrakes to give an enhanced dive of 450 mph (391 knots).

Typical performance figures may be quoted for the Mustang Three P-51B which was powered by a 1,520-horsepower Packard Rolls-Royce Merlin V-1650-3 liquid-cooled engine driving a three-bladed Curtiss electric constant-speed propeller. This combination gave it a maximum level-flight speed of over 400 mph (348 knots), and a ceiling of over 40,000 feet. It had a range of more than a thousand miles.

As armament the Mustang mounted six or eight 0.5-inch calibre machine guns, or four 20 mm calibre cannon. It could also carry 1,000 pounds of bombs slung underwing.

## North American Sabre (American, F-86)

In the early 1950s the British-designed replacements for the by-then outclassed Meteor and Vampire fighters were suffering many developmental problems, so the appearance early in the Korean War (1950-53) of the Soviet MiGs quite discomfited the Royal Air Force planners.

Accordingly, in fulfilment of a mutual defence agreement, America made over to the RAF 431 Sabre jets, many of which had been both developed and built in Canada. Fortuitously, the RAF was not a total stranger to the swept-wing type, for a few of its pilots had flown with the Americans in Korea, in the process shooting down a number of MiG-15 jets.

The first of the F-86 Sabre series flew in late 1947, but the version the RAF received was a 1950s development with, significantly, in terms of performance, an all-flying tail. Powered by an Allison J47-GE-13 engine developing 5,200 pounds of static thrust, it had a maximum speed of 679 mph (590 knots) at sea level, an initial climb rate of 7,250 feet a minute, and a laden weight of 17,806 pounds.

Most pilots found the Sabre a delight to fly and many expressed disappointment when it was replaced by the Supermarine Swift and by the early marks of the Hawker Hunter. Just the same, by mid-1956 Hunters had completely replaced the RAF's Sabres, both in Germany and in the UK.

## Fairey Swordfish

The single-engined Swordfish torpedo-reconnaissance biplane bomber entered the Fleet Air Arm in mid-1936, so that by the outbreak of the Second World War it must have seemed obsolescent. But with thirteen squadrons Swordfish-equipped it was inevitable that it was pressed into first-line service. And indeed it distinguished itself on several occasions, notably during the Norwegian campaign, and spectacularly when launched against the Italian fleet at Taranto in November 1940. Even as late as 1942 the venerable type was to show its teeth against major units of the German Battle Fleet, but the debacle that ensued forced its redeployment to the anti-submarine warfare role. Just the same, the Swordfish was not withdrawn from operations until May 1945.

Nominally a three-seater, yet for some roles reduced to a two-seater by the necessity of installing extra fuel tanks, the Swordfish, powered by its 750-horsepower Bristol Pegasus Thirty radial engine, had a cruising speed of 120 mph (105 knots), a ceiling of 10,700 feet, and a maximum range of some 1,000 miles. It had a maximum take-off weight of 4,700 pounds and was a surprisingly large machine, standing at over twelve feet when configured as a landplane, and even higher when floats were fitted. Nearly 2,400 Swordfish were built, the typical armament being a single 0.303-inch calibre Vickers machine gun firing through the propeller, and a 0.303-inch calibre Vickers or Lewis in the rear-cockpit mounting. Additionally it could carry a 1,600 pound torpedo, or the same weight of mines, bombs, or depth charges.

## V1 (*Vergeltungswaffe*) Flying Bomb

It is said that of 10,000 V1s launched against England, 7,000 landed on the mainland. Indeed as former WRNS Margaret Herbert, of Derby, recalled in 2006, 'In our operations centre under the Royal Naval College at Greenwich we recorded 3,876 on London alone!'

WRNS Margaret Herbert

Dating air-launched V1 attacks against the Midlands has proved controversial. Mr Peter J.C. Smith, both in his *Flying Bombs over the Pennines*, 1988 (see bibliography); and a work still on the stocks in late 2006, maintains that the mass V1 raid of Christmas Eve 1944 was the only such incursion. Other sources, however, hold that as early as July 1944 some V1s fell in the area. Mr John Ownsworth of Penistone, researching in the nineteen

eighties, was told of V1s falling before Christmas Eve, while the present author was assured by three interviewee groups that 'their' V1 had come certainly come down earlier; not least Mr and Mrs Bill and Jean Hollinrake, of Peak Forest, who, in September 2006, reasserted, 'Definitely not on Christmas Eve, but after the Saturday-night dance a week or so earlier, for that's when we got engaged.'

Complementing this stance, also in September 2006, Mr Trevor Matthews, formerly of Sheffield, reminiscing from Ontario, wrote: '[we heard] what sounded like a very bad two-stroke motor cycle ... and a plane came over us with flame coming out of the back.' Mr Matthews then proffered, 'the raid in question was on Saturday December 23, 1944 ... a date given with certainty as the night of my cousin's 21st ... a big thing back then...and [memorable as] one of the first occasions our family had attended any outside [evening] function since the war began.' A fruitful point then, the possibility of 'trial' air-launches against the Midlands before Christmas Eve 1944, for future researchers to worry out!

(For newer generations it might be politic to reiterate that while the V2 was a rocket, the V1 [these days, too-often termed 'V1 rocket'] was a pilotless pulse-jet aircraft)

## Zenair Zodiac HC601

(see below, Supplement to *The Central Area*) This single-engined, two-seater, low-winged monoplane, an all-metal 'home-build' aeroplane, was designed by Zenith's Chris Heintz and introduced in 1984 as a low-cost primary trainer. The liquid-cooled Rotax 912 engine, burning just four gallons an hour at cruise power, afforded a range of 480 miles, the standard fuel capacity being 16 gallons. The ceiling was 12,000 feet while the initial rate of climb was given as 1,200 feet a minute. With two occupants the maximum speed was 135 mph (117 knots), the cruise 120 mph (104 knots), and the basic stalling speed 44 mph (38 knots). The never-exceed speed was 150 mph (131 knots) and the stress limitations a very generous plus and minus 6.8g (sturdiness itself compared with the Cessna's limit of plus 4.4g and negative 1.6g!) although Zenair did not recommend aerobatics being carried out.

### German bomber, Newhaven, Ashbourne–Buxton Road (possible)
SK 16499 60510 350m
Luftwaffe
1941

In 2006, when Mrs Beryl Rush (née Mellor) of Youlgreave, once of Friden, produced the Perspex ring she had made ('Crash-site Perspex Sculpture', this volume), she described the crash it came from. 'We used to live at Friden,' she said, 'in No.3 Ladysmith Cottages. One night we heard that a German bomber had crashed. So next evening, after Dad and some others had finished work – they were all Home Guard as well – we walked up the road to The Newhaven [Hotel], then towards Buxton, and found all the wreckage in the second field past the Newhaven Garage. We climbed the wall, and I took a piece of windscreen.'

Possible German bomber site, Newhaven

Throughout Mrs Rush's narrative, the author had assumed that she had been talking of Wellington DF611 [*Peakland Air Crashes: The South*, p.145], which, on 10 April 1943, crashed two miles further up the Buxton road from the location indicated (beyond the Jug and Glass pub); benignly accepting that lore would inevitably hold the Wellington to have been German. Mrs Rush, however, raised some cogent arguments to refute both these rather impertinent assumptions.

'We walked to Biggin School daily,' she said, 'three miles each way; but this was hardly a mile off. And it was the Home Guard said it was German. Again, we moved to Friden when I was eleven; and when it happened I was twelve, making it 1941. But we moved to Bakewell in January 1943, so we'd been gone three months by the April, when you say the one crashed near the Jug and Glass.'

Canvassing very long-term residents in the Newhaven area brought no positive confirmation of this as an additional site, although two ladies, one still resident in Friden, had vague recollections of the occurrence, albeit without details. Nor did press searches of the Derby, Ashbourne or Buxton papers further research. Accordingly the incident is recorded here as a possible German bomber crash, serving, at least, as a basis for future enquiry.


### (Supplementary) Vickers Armstrong Wellington Mk.3 Z1566 Sheldon Farm, Grindon
(*Peakland Air Crashes: The South*, p.149)
Sergeant Chappell's full name was Sydney John Chappell.

## Zenair Zodiac HC601 G-YOXI, Hellaby Park Farm, Ravenfield, Rotherham

SK 50350 93598 103m
Privately-owned, 'home-build' kit aircraft
25 August 2006

Occupants, both killed
Mr Brian Leslie Yoxall, owner, and operating pilot
Mr Terence John Whitfield, passenger

At 1630 hours on 25 August 2006, a privately-owned, home-build kit aircraft, Zenair Zodiac HC601 G-YOXI, suffered a catastrophic structural failure while essaying to carry out a low-level pass at Hellaby Park Farm, near Rotherham, crashing and burning, and killing both occupants.

The aircraft was owned by Mr Brian Yoxall, a builder, while the passenger, farmer Mr Terrence Whitfield, had been for many years a civilian ground instructor with No. 300 Squadron of the Air Training Corps at Crowle.

The couple had departed from Mr Whitfield's landing strip at Askern, to the north of Doncaster, with the intention of carrying out a light-hearted aerial inspection of three newly-seeded fields at Hellaby Park Farm, shown on the aeronautical chart as Ravenfield Helipad. Prior to getting airborne they had telephoned for permission for the overflight, and as with helicopter visitors, had been passed a contact frequency and advised of the thirty-foot-high power cables running across the site.

Mr Ray Wharam, the owner of Hellaby Park Farm, a helicopter private pilot, having failed to make radio contact as the Zodiac came into sight, positioned himself the centre of the holding and flashed his signal lamp in acknowledgement as his visitors commenced to orbit the relevant fields. 'It was just a joyride, really,' Mr Wharam said. 'But as I'm no farmer, Terry [Mr Whitfield] had given me some advice on re-grassing, so it formed a nice focus for their flight.'

Mr Wharam had evidently eyed the initial overflight with equanimity. 'They'd carried out three orbits at a good, safe height; at about fifteen hundred feet, I'd say. Only having cleared some way to the south, they then turned back and pushed down the nose, clearly intent on doing a low level pass over where I was standing. [With fellow feeling, one can just picture the occupants' glee as they swept downwards …] They levelled off, but as they closed with me they were so low that I became disturbed, and very aware of the power cables running just behind me, I first flashed my signal lamp in warning, then began waving them off. But clearly they had not forgotten the cables, for at about one hundred metres from them, they began to lift – gently enough, as it seemed to me – and I even saw the white of the belly as the nose came up. Then I was momentarily unsighted as the machine passed directly overhead.' He paused. 'I turned through one-eighty. Only even as I came about it was to see both wings fold upwards! I knew immediately then, that a crash was inevitable.' He shook his head. 'I gunned the vehicle back to the house, grabbed my fire extinguisher, and when Doreen, my wife, asked what the matter was, I shouted, "The aircraft's going to crash; call 999."'

The M18 motorway, engorged with the build up of bank-holiday traffic, was only one hundred yards or so distant from the crash site, consequently there were many additional witnesses. 'This red and white light aircraft had been circling the area,' one man told the local press, 'and then began a steep dive.' Another witness, giving information, sketched an aircraft with wings folded up vertically beside the fuselage, as they might be seen aboard an aircraft carrier: a sketch which was initially viewed with incredulity first by the police, and later by officials of the Air Accidents Investigation Branch (AAIB).

Speaking just days after the accident, Mr Wharam, a more-informed witness, and with official investigations still in train, was circumspect regarding what he had proffered to the AAIB as the prime cause of the failure. As events had unfolded, however, he had evidently had his hands full.

'The aircraft touched the ground,' he said, 'bounced, then struck hard some yards further on, spinning about.' Standing once more at the crash site, he pointed to his original tyre tracks, curving in to within feet of the soiled patch of fragment-strewn earth. 'There were already flames licking up, but for a moment, as I reached the cockpit and looked in, I thought my fire extinguisher could deal with them. But suddenly the whole thing just erupted; and everything began to dissolve in front of me ...'

He took a moment then, to collect himself. 'I drove back to the house and hitched up my water bowser. By the time I got back to the aircraft, however, a policeman had come down from the motorway, and wouldn't let me near.' Again he paused, but then said soberly. 'Not that there was anything to be done.' He reflected. 'The only heartening thing was that every motorist I saw come down the banking had a fire extinguisher: clearly they'd come to help, not simply to rubberneck.'

And what had Mr Wharam been about, leaning over a burning cockpit as he had done? He smiled grimly. 'I've done fire courses. And I know how I'd be criticized. But when it comes to a question of human life ...' And he pragmatically brushed aside all notion that his action had been in any way heroic.

As the AAIB's findings were yet to be published when this volume had to close, no definitive cause can be attributed to the accident. That the aircraft was home-built, of course, is not of significance, because all aircraft have to meet the stringent requirements of the aviation licensing authority. Then again, most test reports encountered on the web reported a pleasing harmony in the controls using the kit-tail supplied. One, however (Pilot Friend), recorded 'a marked degree of instability in pitch [nose-up and down] at all speeds between 96 and 150 mph' [the latter being the Never Exceed Speed: 150 mph (131 knots)].

The stresses imposed upon the structure, certainly, would have to form the main line of inquiry. True, whether easing the nose down into a dive, or checking back to pull out of one, Zodiac pilots are assured that they can safely subject the machine to steadily-applied stresses of nearly seven times its own weight (6.8g, positive or negative); in comparison, the sturdy Jet Provost trainer of the RAF was limited to positive 6g and negative 2.5g. However, that anywhere near the limiting stress could be applied in a dive as innocuous as that described by those who saw G-YOXI crash seems highly unlikely.

Then again, all fliers are aware that too-spirited an evolution brings into play dangerous aerodynamic forces, that at high speed any too-hasty control input – be it a snatch back or a check forwards –, or even hitting a patch of rough air, can significantly increase the stress loadings. Much more likely then, that the easy-to-slide-through 150 mph limit was inadvertently, but grossly, exceeded in the exhilarating dive from 1,500 feet; further, that the excess had not sufficiently bled off during the period of level flight, so leading to disproportionate force being generated by a pull-out stick force that felt, and from the outside, looked, normal.

Alongside such a scenario the investigators will also have sought to determine whether pre-flight damage might have weakened the thin-metal structure noted in other web-located reports.

The wreckage of Zodiac G-YOXI

The crash site of G-YOXI

There is no indication, as this is written, whether any memorial will be raised at the site, but the hard-packed ground has left nothing to be seen; beyond this it is remote from any public footpath, and on strictly private land.

This tragedy, occurring just before submission date for this final volume, forms a saddening coda to the series, which was, until then, relatively well distanced by comforting Time from the last Peakland accident considered; accordingly, instead of a paean to flight safety the whole must be accepted more in the nature of a continuum dirge reflecting the timelessness of Captain Lamplugh's remarks, fully rendered in the introduction, *'the air, to an even greater extent than the sea, is terribly unforgiving* [and] *carelessness, neglect or overconfidence are paid for more quickly and more dearly than in other forms of transport'*. Long before this is in print, the air accident investigators will have discovered whether carelessness, neglect, or overconfidence lay at the roots of this accident; the findings assuaging no human hurt thereby, but, it is to be hoped, advancing, albeit in some small measure, the yet-faltering cause of flight safety.

### Supplementary information to *The Central Area*

p47 Cessna G-BFSR, Thorpe Salvin. The CAA report clarifies that at 400 feet the instructor (holder of a Private Pilot's Licence, with 274 hours' experience, and 180 on type) closed the throttle to simulate an engine failure only to see the individual propeller blades appear. He assumed control, applied full throttle, then, when the engine did not pick up, closed it again, to re-open it more slowly; equally without success. A forced landing ensued.

p80 Meteor VW267, which crashed at Todwick, was, in fact, a Mk.4, and had no ejection seat.

p163 Heinkel He.111, Burbage area.
In September 2006, Mrs Kate Brown, a long-term Burbage resident, told Mr Peter Rolland, of the Buxton Local History Society, that a crew member from a German aircraft which came down near Burbage was initially buried in Burbage Cemetery with full military honours, but was transferred after the war. Supplementing this, Mr Eddie Wrigley, of Ollerton, formerly of Burbage, told the present author that when his uncle, a former Home Guard who had escorted two German aircrew to nearby RAF Harpur Hill, showed him the grave, he was surprised to see an iron cross rather than a swastika. And certainly, one extant grave marker, still, regrettably, not identified by publication date, was a cast-iron cross, bearing nothing but, *'Pro Patria'*. [To refresh the memory, Horace's Odes maintain, *Dulce et decorum est pro patria mori* (Literally: It is sweet and fitting to die for the fatherland); a sentiment 1914-18 poet Wilfred Owen denounced as 'the old lie'.] In the Burbage case the anonymity brings it to mind that during the years  when the aircrew from Junkers Ju.88 6213 (*Peakland Air Crashes: The South*, p57) lay in Leek Cemetery (before post-war transfer to Cannock) their graves bore no identification.

For the record, the 1961 document, *'The transfer of German War Dead from Derbyshire Cemeteries to the German War Cemetery at Cannock Chase'* (D2425/9/6, Derbyshire Record Office, Matlock), shows no airmen, only army dead from 1918; although this includes two soldiers from Burbage.

In passing, the above-mentioned Mr Wrigley also furnished an intriguing insight into an early-fifties confrontation when, as an RAF ground wireless operator (W/T: morse; using Z and Q signals), he tried to keep track of RAF (Lincoln) bombers. Having re-trained as a Russian/Polish operator at Cheadle, and been posted to Germany to monitor Soviet W/T stations, he discovered that, as the Russians knew exactly where the RAF's aircraft were, it was much easier to keep track of them by eavesdropping than had ever been the case at the RAF Bawtry headquarters.

p165 Europa G-KWIP, Bradley. Witness Mr Jonathon Tye, the owner of the Lee Rhododendron Gardens, whose aviation expertise was of such assistance to the inquiry, was formerly the RAF's Vulcan Bomber display pilot.

## Corrections to *The Central Area*

**p.3** *line 4 up from bottom,* Meteor Mk.8, Todwick to become: **Mk.4**

p.14 *para 5, start of line 3*: delete first occurrence of 'not only'

p.49-50, refers to DH10s being assembled and flown off from Ringway in 1918. Author Mr Peter Clowes has kindly advised that Ringway was not opened until 1938, that the aerodrome concerned would have been Alexandra Park

p.78 *Caption, Far left* to read: **Right**

p.80 *Heading,* Meteor Mk.8 to become **Mk.4**

*second line, add* **Mk.4,** *to read*: **Meteor Mk.4 VW267 ...**

*line six, insert* **colon,** and add clause to read: **abandon: the Mk.4 having no ejection seat.**

p.95 *omitted caption should read*: **Oxford LX745, looking north, towards Cats Tor**

p.102 *top photo,* the white cross indicates where the undercarriage fell

p.153 *third line down,* read: **all three members of its trainee crew**

p.153 reverse the captions

p.157 *para two,* after enemy bombing accuracy, amend to read; **few bombs are recorded as having come down in the open moorlands, most having fallen much closer to a then-blacked-out city, be it Sheffield or Manchester.**

p.161 *caption,* capital **M** for **Margaret**

p162 *four lines up from bottom,* for Stoke, to read: **Stokes**

p166 *third line down,* Bureau to read: **Branch**

p.171 *caption* should continue: **at the touchdown point**

p.190 *top caption,* should continue: **direction of RAF Ashbourne**

p.30 *para 2, line 13,* insert 'the': **aircraft and the pilot**

p.30 *caption* should read: **2006**

**Copyright holders authorising the use of their photographs in this volume**
Bramley, Phil, *Derbyshire Times*, Chesterfield
Buxton-Doyle, Margaret, *The Longdendale Valley*
Duggins, Ron, Matlock
Editor, *Glossop Chronicle*
Editor, *Sheffield Morning Telegraph*
Gordon, Bruce, Mosquito Trust, Hatfield
Guess, Barry, BAE Systems, Farnborough
Gunn, Michael A, intellectual property, Rolls-Royce, aircraft
Haigh, Richard, manager, intellectual properties, Rolls Royce; aircraft
Hunt, Nicola, intellectual property rights copyright unit, MOD; most aircraft
Jackson, Peter, Peak Park Ranger, Glossop
Lintern, Shaun, *Your Leek Paper*
Miller, Gordon, formerly Area Ranger for Kinder, including Edale, Castleford, and Hayfield
Nokes, Judy, licensing, HMSO/Crown Copyright/MOD; most aircraft
Parker, Stanley, Woolley Flats Blenheim, vice Mr Entwistle
Royal Air Force Museum; aircraft
Seal, Carol, photographic section, *Derby Evening Telegraph*
Skinner, Nigel, *Tameside Reporter*, Stalybridge
Steiner, Ralph, Mosquito Museum, Hatfield, aircraft
Temple, Julian, archivist, Vickers, Brooklands Museum, Weybridge; aircraft


**Authors and Websites**

Barrass, Malcolm, air historian, *Air of Authority* website (www.rafweb.org)
Collier, Ron; with Wilkinson, Roni, *Dark Peak Aircraft Wreck* series
Earl, David W., *Hell on High Ground* series
Kedward, Brian, *Angry Skies across the Vale*
*Air Britain* authors


**Technical and Professional assistance**

Allen, Nicky, Spondon photographic
Barker, Anita, Spondon photographic
Baker, Julie, Air Historical Branch, MOD
Bruce, Becky, Spondon photographic
Buie, Jim, secretary, Manchester Fleet Air Arm Association
Burch, Simon, *Derby Evening Telegraph*.
Byron, Jack, ex-No.149 Squadron air gunner (26 Ops)
Campbell, Maureen, Civil Aviation Authority Accident research
Carr, Clare, Assistant Curator, RAF Museum, Cosford
Cunningham, Dot, Spondon photographic
Day, Graham, Air Historical Branch, MOD
Derby Local Studies and Main Libraries, Staff
Dickinson, Susan, Air Historical Branch, MOD
Elliot, Peter, Senior Keeper, and all staff, RAF Museum
Gamble, Carol, Commonwealth War Graves Commission
Gatfield, Tom, ex-No.49 Squadron, navigator, Lancasters
Griffiths, Ann, Spondon photographic
Goddard, Margaret, Polish Archives, MOD Northolt
Stebbing, Paul, Derbyshire Records Office, Matlock

Holloway, Julie, Spondon photographic
Keohane, Jan, archivist, Fleet Air Arm Museum
Kroll, Barbara, Polish Archives, MOD Northolt
Lawrence, Hayley, Spondon photographic
Leith, Gordon, Curator, RAF Museum
McGrath, Peter, of Sheffield, ex-Wellington Wop/AG (40 Ops)
McKinnon, Jo, Spondon photographic
Public Records Office, Kew, Staff
Shantonas, Jaimie, MOD map library, Feltham
Somay, Julie, Commonwealth War Graves Commission
Sparks, Angie, Spondon photographic
Stainthorpe, Peter, Commonwealth War Graves Commission
Towns, Sam, Spondon photographic
Tameside Local Studies Library, The Staff, Stalybridge
Wakefield, Julie, Spondon photographic
Wilson, Barbara, Commonwealth War Graves Commission (German graves)
Withers, Jackie, Commonwealth War Graves Commission


### Bamford and Derwent area

Cockerell, Maurice, Hayridge Farm, Woodlands
Cripps, Reg, Birchinlee House
Stannish, Jeremy, Strines Inn
Wood, Peter and Janet, Crookhill Farm
Woodhead, Gary and Christine, Derwent


### Broomhead Moor

Beaumont David, Bolsterstone, Estate keeper
Clancy, Margaret, Garlic House Farm
Couldwell, Lewis and Jean, Stocksbridge
Cunningham, Chris, Deepcar, Estate keeper
Haigh, Alwyn, West Nab Farm


### Buxton Area

Brown, Kate, Burbage resident (German grave)
Flower, Ellen, Old House Farm, Newhaven
McPhie, David, Buxton Bookstore
Raper, Ian, Bakewell
Roland, Peter, Buxton Local History
Rush, Eric and Beryl, Youlgreave
Swindle, Derek and Kath, Newhaven Farm
White, Richard, Tansley
Wrigley, Eddie, Ollerton, formerly Burbage


### Edale area

Atkin, Robert Allen, Lady Booth Farm
Baker, James, Chapel-en-le-Frith
Barrows, John Campion, 'Campy', Peak Park Ranger, Fairholmes

Bricklebank, Jack, Eyam
Carrington, James, Ivy House
Chapman, Alan and Jean, Barber Booth
Cooper, Roy, and son, Peter, Highfield Farm, Upper Booth
Critchlow, Andrew, Shaw Wood Farm
Dakin, Billy, Hillside Farm
Deaken, Brenda, Barber Booth
Heardman, Milly, Edale
Heygi, Josef, Park Ranger, Fairholmes and Edale, Sheffield
Low, Arthur, gamekeeper
Mount, David and Sarah, Lee Farm
Neaves, Roger, geologist, Edale
Nields, John, Whitmore Lea Farm
Shaw, Alen, Hope (Chartech)
Thornley, Jim, Hollobrook Farm, Edale
Townsend, Ron, Intake, Sheffield
Watson, James, Tunbridge Wells (Heyford information)
Worsley, Frank and Helen, Digleach Farm, Chapel-en-le-Frith


## Glossop area

Atkinson, Louise, Tameside Art and Events Team
Boucher, Mrs, Mottram
Bower, John, Carr House Farm
Bradbury, James, Kinder Intake, Greenfield
Brown, Graham, local historian, Stalybridge
Brown, Lee and Judy, Cross Cliffe
Brown Mike, Glossop Heritage Centre
Cooper, Barry and Dorothy, Crossgate Farm, Tintwistle
Cooper, Wright, Townhead Farm, Tintwistle
Eckersley, Terry and Brenda, Greenfield
Evans, Christian, Paper Mill, Crowden
Fletcher, Mrs, Landslow Farm
Gregory, Colin, Home Farm, Woolley Bridge
Gregory, David and Geoffrey, Home Farm, Woolley Bridge
Hallam, Dale, Arnfield Farm
Heginbottom, Joyce, Glossop
Holden, Jack, Glossop
Johnson, Bill, local historian, Mottram
McCarthy, Dennis, Lynn, and Dominic, Wrigley Fold Farm
McKeown, Betty and Joseph, Westwood Farm Cottage, Matley, Hyde
O'Malley, Terry, Whaley Bridge
Schofield, Peter and Josephine, The Mudd, Mottram
Shaw, Phillip, Glossop
Sherratt George; and Tim, PhD, Glossop
Sidebottom, Eric, Gorsey Brow, Broadbottom
Slack, Derek, Glossop
Smith, Dr John, historian, Glossop
Summerscale, Ellis, Farmer
Thomas, David, Glossop
Timperley, Ben and Beryl, Warhill Farm, Mottram

## Holmfirth area

Batton, Louie, Nabbclose Farm, Cartworth Moor
Bellamy, Trevor and Kathleen, Corn Loft House, Holmfirth
Bishop, Stephen, Upper Maythorn Farm, Holmfirth
Bradbury, Gerald and Mary, Darfield, Barnsley
Brook, Frank and Violet, New Mill, Holmfirth
Denton, Kenneth, Broad View, Holme
Gill, John, Lanehead Farm, Holme
Grange, Theresa, Cartworth Moor
Ibbetson, Connie, Upper Maythorn Farm, Holmfirth
Noble, Derek, Higham, Barnsley
Tinker, Phillip, Spring Head Farm, Upper Cumberworth
Yates, David, part-time ranger

## Huddersfield area

Brook, Kathleen, Gatefoot Lane, Shepley
Butterfield, Andrew and Sandra, Hermit House Farm, Gawber
Carey, Martin and Rachel, Hunter's Nab, Farnley Tyas
Glenhill, Catherine, The Poplars, Kirkburton
Matley, Ken, Kirkburton
Milnes, Graham, Marsden
Mossley, Chris, Gate Foot Barn, Shepley
Parkin, May, Barnsley
Roslyn, Janet, Cawthorne, Barnsley
Russell, Marjorie, Farnley Tyas
Sykes, Colin and Janet, Hunter's Nab, Farnley Tyas
Thompson, Christine, Thorncliff Green, Kirkburton
Townend, Lawrence, Lane End Farm, Shelley
Wilson, Catherine, Gatefoot Lane, Shepley
Winn, J.R., Longwood, near Farnley Tyas

## Oldham area

Jones, Patricia, Grasscroft, Oldham
Lord, Stuart, Roegate Farm, Oldham
Taylor, Walter and Jean, Button Hole, near Oldham

## Rotherham area

Anderson, Geoff and Nancy, Wath Upon Dearne
Bradbury, Gerald and Mary, Darfield, Barnsley
Chappell, Clive G., Wath Upon Dearne
Darby, Alison, Sheffield Local Studies
Dixon, Faye, Hightown, Castleford
Hobson, Maurice, Rawmarsh
Morrison, Mary, Occupation Road, Rawmarsh
Oldroyd, Albert, Cawthorne
Pearson, Geoffrey, Peacock Lodge Farm, Wentworth
Plowright, Rex and Dot, Hooton Robert
Plowright, Roy, Weston Super Mare, formerly Hooton Robert

Smith, Alan, Rawmarsh
Spedding, Carl, Home Farm, Firbeck, Worksop
Thompson, Sheila, Wath Upon Dearne
Walker, Jeff, The Farm, Ulley, Sheffield
Ward, Alan and Margaret, Wath Upon Dearne
Wharam, Ray and Doreen, Hellaby Park Farm, Ravenfield
Wheelhouse, John, Holly Farm, Hooton Roberts
Wilson, Stephen, Droylsden, Manchester
Wood, Alan, Bassingthorpe Farm, Greasbrough
Wydell, Ruth, Primary School, Wath Upon Dearne

## Sheffield area

Matthews, Trevor and Carol, Ontario, formerly of Sheffield
Sanderson, Derek and Bettina, formerly Meadow Farm, Ringinglow
Sier, David, formerly Sheffield Museum

## Standedge Moor area

Birse, Bob, Uppermill
Casseli (née Hooley), Joyce, formerly of Marsden
Jackson, Richard, Eileen, and Graham, Marshlea, Diggle
Paul and Natalie, Diggle Edge Farm, Diglea
Taylor, Brian, Diglea Farm
Taylor, Jack, Diglea (in grateful memory …)

## Penistone area

Ashby, Roy, Wakefield
Hinchcliffe, Adam, Penistone
Hinchliffe, Rodney, Sett Stones Farm, Victoria
Illingworth, John, Hoylandswaine
Jackson, Alan, Penistone
Marsden, Ian, Hoylandswaine
Middleton, Robert, Barnside Cote Farm, Stocksbridge
Miller, Judith Elizabeth, Foulsham, Dereham
Norton, Angela, Penistone
Ogley, Geoffrey and Catherine, Conisbrough, Doncaster
Pears, Nicholas, Bella Vista Farm, Penistone
Steers, Sylvia, Stocksbridge
Wainright, George and Sheila, Upper House Farm, Barmford

Air Ministry (1937) *Royal Air Force Pocket Book, AP1081.* London: HMSO

Air Ministry (1941) *Air Navigation Volume 1, AP1234.* London: HMSO

Air Ministry (1943) *Elementary Flying Training, AP1979A.* London: HMSO

Air Ministry (1948) *The Rise and Fall of the German Air Force (1931 to 1945).* London: HMSO

Air Ministry (1954) *Flying, Volumes 1 and 2, AP129.* (Sixth edition). London: HMSO

Air Ministry (1960) *Flying Instructor's Handbook,* AP3225D. London: HMSO

Air Ministry (1960) *Pilot's Notes Vampire T.11.* London: HMSO

Bairnsfather, Bruce (1916–1918) *Fragments from France.* London: *The Bystander*

Baring, Maurice (1920) *RFC HQ 1914–1918.* London: Bell and Sons

Barrass, Malcolm (2005) *Air of Authority* (www.rafweb.org), (RAF organisation)

Bennett, D.C.T. (1936) *The Complete Air Navigator.* London: Pitman

Boase, Wendy (1979) *The Sky's The Limit: Women Pioneers.* London: Osprey

Buxton-Doyle, Margaret (2003) *The Longdendale Valley.* Stroud: Tempus Publications

Collier, Ron; Wilkinson, Roni (1979/1982) *Dark Peak Aircraft Wrecks 1 and 2.* Barnsley: Pen & Sword

Director of Flying Training RAF (1955–1970 various) *Air Clues.* London: MOD

Fellowes, P.F.M. (1942) *Britain's Wonderful Air Force.* London: Odhams

Freidheim, E.; Taylor, S.W. (1944) *Fighters Up.* London: Nicholson Watson

Hammerton, J. (1943) *ABC of the RAF.* London: Amalgamated Press

Heimann, Jim (2002) *I come from California.* Holmfirth: locally published

HMSO (1944) *Target: Germany.* London: Air Ministry

HMSO (1942–1943) *Aircraft Recognition.* London: Sampson Clark

HMSO (1937) *RAF Pocket Handbook, 1937.* London: Air Ministry

Jane, Fred T. (1919) *Jane's All the World's Aircraft.* London: Jane's Publishing Co.

Kedward, Brian (1996) *Angry Skies across the Vale.* Cheltenham: Self-published

Lamplugh, A.G. (1931) *Accidents in Civil Aviation.* Royal Aeronautical Paper,
    Institution of Aeronautical Engineers, 29 October 1931, London

Macadam, John (*c.*1942) *The Reluctant Erk.* London: Jarrolds Publishers Ltd

Monday, David (1994) *Hamlyn Concise Guide to British Aircraft of World War II.* London: Hamlyn

Morris, Alan (1968) *First of the Many, Independent Force.* London: Jarrolds

Ogilvy, David (1977) *Bleriot to Spitfire.* (Shuttleworth) Shrewsbury: Airlife

Ollis, Ray (1957) *101 Nights.* London: Cassell & Company Ltd

Phelps, Anthony (1944) *I couldn't care less.* (Air Transport Auxiliary) Leicester: Harborough

Royal Flying Corps Communiqués: research in Imperial War Museum.
    (But see volumes by Donovan: London, 1969; and Grub Street: London, 1998)

Saville-Sneath, R.A. (1945) *Aircraft of the United States, Volume One.* London: Penguin

Smith, Peter J.C. (1988) *Flying Bombs over the Pennines.* Manchester: Neil Richardson

Stewart, Oliver (1941) *The Royal Air Force in Pictures.* London: Country Life

Thetford, Owen (1958) *Aircraft of the Royal Air Force 1918-58.* London: Putnam

Tudor, L. Thomas (1930) *The High Peak to Sherwood.* London: Robert Scott

United States War Department (1945) *Bombardier's Information File.* vice RAF Hendon

United States War Department (1946) *Handbook on Guided Missiles of Germany and Japan.*
    vice RAF Hendon

Winchester, Clarence (1938) *Wonders of World Aviation, Vols 1 and 2.* London: Waverley

# ADDENDUM

## Armstrong Whitworth Whitley Mk.5, Z9289, Pogmoor, Barnsley

SE 33135  066580 142m
No.102 Squadron, RAF Dalton (south of Thirsk, Yorkshire), No.4 Group, Bomber Command
6 January 1942

Occupants: five, two killed, one injured, two uninjured:
Sergeant Alexander Hollingworth, Royal Australian Air Force, pilot, killed
Sergeant John Toker Clough. Hazeldine, RAF, second pilot, parachuted successfully
Sergeant E.A. Brain, Royal Canadian Air Force, observer, parachuted successfully
Flight Sergeant Alexander Gibson Buchanan, RCAF, wireless operator/air gunner, killed
Sergeant Leonard Jackson, RAF, air gunner (rear), parachuted, injuring ankle

At 0424 hours on 6 January 1942, Whitley Z9289 got airborne from RAF Dalton, near Thirsk, Yorkshire, as part of a Whitley force tasked to raid dock installations and shipping at Cherbourg. Encountering total cloud cover over the target, the captain, Sergeant Alexander Hollingworth, an Australian attached to No.102 Squadron, decided to abort the sortie. While still over the target, however, the starboard power plant malfunctioned in a manner which precluded the propeller being feathered to reduce the drag, so that the aircraft, a type with poor enough performance even with both engines giving full power, was unable to maintain

**Impact site** ✗

Mrs Kitty Moss, witness

altitude. Despite this, having crossed the Channel, rather than setting down at the first available airfield, Sergeant Hollingworth elected to hold a course for RAF Dalton, still some 240 miles distant – for the Whitley, at best, over a hour and forty minutes flying time away! The aircraft continued to lose height even though, twelve miles short of Sheffield, the still safely-armed bombs were jettisoned onto moorland. But then, at 1005 hours, to the south-west of Barnsley at a reportedly very low level, the heavily put-upon starboard engine caught fire as the windmilling propeller began to overspeed. The vastly increased drag this runaway condition caused, together with the associated raising of the critical handling speed, effectively rendered the aircraft uncontrollable; accordingly Sergeant Hollingworth hurriedly ordered an evacuation. Three crew members baled out successfully, although Sergeant Jackson injured an ankle on landing, all three coming down close together in the Broadway area. Flight Sergeant Buchanan, jumping altogether too low was killed when he struck the railway lines, barely a quarter of a mile further on. Sergeant Hollingworth himself had no time to jump as the aircraft dived into, and exploded in, Phase Quarry, just yards beyond the railway, and closer still to Cresswell Street, Pogmoor.

In October 2006 researcher Mr John Ownsworth was able to supply details from the full, thirty-five page accident report, while Mr and Mrs Trevor and Carol Stockdale, of Cresswell Street, verified the impact area and affirmed that, the quarry-pit notwithstanding, debris was widespread. At the same time another Cresswell Street resident, Mrs Kitty Moss (née Goodyear), at a hale 90 years, readily recalled the crash itself. 'I was scrubbing my front step,' she said, 'when I saw this bomber coming down. It was almost vertical, and it was trailing fire and smoke, and I saw a parachute towards Broadway. I knew my mother was in, so I ran down, and round the corner, to her place.' She pointed across the street. 'At the time,' she explained, 'There were two terraces, separated by a gap where the garages are now, both long gone. The end house was where mum's was. The plane crashed where the playing field is now, and although no houses were damaged, a wing landed in the gap. Then the police arrived, and the RAF lads, who very soon took the wreckage away.' She smiled. 'Mum always used to say, "He were a good man that pilot, for if he'd flown down with his wings level he'd have destroyed the terraces on each side! As it was, by coming down vertically, he missed them both."'

The RAF court of inquiry, understandably, was censorious of Sergeant Hollingworth's judgment in pressing on rather than putting down at the first of the many available airfields he had overflown. The technical malfunction, it found, had been caused by the failure of a component crucial to propeller-pitch control.

By 2006 the tragedy, one of the very few in this series which occurred in the course of an actual Bomber Command operation, was commemorated by a tasteful plaque on the wall of a British-Legion-owned bungalow not that many yards from the filled-in-quarry impact point.